MW00592619

AGS®

American Guidance Service, Inc.
Circle Pines, Minnesota 55014-1796
1-800-328-2560

Consultants

Daniel A. McFarland
Science Department Chair
Durant High School
Plant City, FL

Dr. Helen Parke
Director, Center for Science,
 Mathematics, and Technology
East Carolina University
Greenville, NC

Photo Credits: p. 15—Guy Bumgarner/Tony Stone Images; p. 16—Jon Riley/Tony Stone Images; p. 21—Rosemary Weller/Tony Stone Images; p. 23—Ron Kimball/Ron Kimball Studios; p. 25 top—Stephen Dalton/Photo Researchers, Inc.; p. 25 Mid—Gary Meszaros/Visuals Unlimited; p. 25 bottom—Suzanne L. Collins & Joseph T. Collins/Photo Researchers, Inc.; pp. 30–31—Darrell Gulin/Tony Stone Images; pp. 32, 55 Right —Art Wolfe/Tony Stone Images; pp. 36, 56—Will Troyer/Visuals Unlimited; p. 39 bottom—M. Abbey/Photo Researchers, Inc.; p. 39 top—Ray Elliot/Tony Stone Images; p. 40—Hank Morgan/Photo Researchers, Inc.; pp. 44–45—Jeff Lepore/Photo Researchers, Inc.; p. 46—David R. Frazier Photolibrary/Photo Researchers, Inc.; p. 47 left—S. Maslowski/Visuals Unlimited; pp. 47 Cent, 117—Breck P. Kent/Animals Animals; p. 47 Right—Joe McDonald/Animals Animals; p. 50—Darren Bennett/Animals Animals; p. 54—J.M. Labat Jacana/Photo Researchers, Inc.; pp. 55 left, 200—Stuart Westmorland/Tony Stone Images; p. 57—Andrew Martinez/Photo Researchers, Inc.; p. 59 top—Bob Cranston/Animals Animals; p. 59 bottom—A. Rider/Photo Researchers, Inc.; p. 60—Scott Smith/Animals Animals; p. 61—James H. Robinson/Animals Animals; pp. 66–67—Val Corbett/Tony Stone Images; p. 69—Biophoto Associates/Science Source/Photo Researchers, Inc.; p. 70—Alan & Linda Detrick/Photo Researchers, Inc.; pp. 72, 73, 77—Saxon Holt/Saxon Holt Photography; pp. 82–83, 98, 134—Michael P. Gadomski/Photo Researchers, Inc.; p. 84 left—Biophoto Associates/Photo Researchers, Inc.; p. 84 Cent—Eric V. Grave/Photo Researchers, Inc.; p. 84 Right—CNRI/Science Photo Library/Photo Researchers, Inc.; p. 85—Ed Resthke/Peter Arnold, Inc.; p. 86—Hugh Spencer/Photo Researchers, Inc.; pp. 89, 107 top—Lawrence Naylor/Photo Researchers, Inc.; p. 90—Andrew Syred/Science Photo Library/Photo Researchers, Inc.; p. 91—Oliver Meckers/Photo Researchers/ Inc.; pp. 96 bottom, 107 Bot—Astrid & Hanns-Frieder Michler/Science Photo Library/Photo Researchers, Inc.; p. 96 top—Jewel Craig/Photo Researchers, Inc.; p. 97—E. R. Degginger/Photo Researchers, Inc.; p. 99—Phil Dotson/Photo Researchers, Inc.; p. 103—Ken Eward/Science Source/Photo Researchers, Inc.; p. 104—Brock May/Photo Researchers, Inc.; pp. 108–109—J & B Photographers/Animals Animals; p. 123—Chris Priest/Science Photo Library/Photo Researchers, Inc.; p. 131—Kjell B. Sandved/Visuals Unlimited; pp. 132–133—Jack Dykinga/Tony Stone Images; p. 135—Stephen J. Krasemann/Photo Researchers, Inc.; p. 136—Jerome Wexler/Photo Researchers, Inc.; p. 138—Dr. Kari Lounatmaa/Science Photo Library/Photo Researchers, Inc.; pp. 142, 143—John D. Cunningham/Visuals Unlimited; p. 145—Ken M. Highfill/Photo Researchers, Inc.; pp. 152–153—Simon Bruty/AllSport USA; p. 156—Meckes/Ottowa/Science Photo Library/Photo Researchers, Inc.; p. 158—Jeff Greenberg/Science Photo Library/Photo Researchers, Inc.; p. 162—National Cancer Institute/Science Photo Library/Photo Researchers, Inc.; pp. 188–189—Petit Format/Nestle/Science Source/Photo Researchers, Inc.; p. 192—Bill Bachmann/PhotoEdit; p. 201—Bonnie Sue/Photo Researchers, Inc.; pp. 214–215—Myrleen Ferguson/PhotoEdit; p. 216—Archive Photos/Archive Photos; p. 219—Robert Brenner/PhotoEdit; p. 221 left—Felicia Martinez/PhotoEdit; p. 221 bottom right—Steven Needham/Envision; p. 221 top right—Richard Hutchings/PhotoEdit; pp. 232–233—Will Hart/PhotoEdit; p. 240—David M. Phillips/Visuals Unlimited; p. 246 left—Eastcott/Momatiuk/Photo Researchers, Inc.; pp. 246 Right, 330 Right—Tim Davis/Photo Researchers, Inc.; p. 250 left—Dr. Tony Brian/Science Photo Library/Photo Researchers, Inc.; p. 250 Right—Stan Flegler/Visuals Unlimited; p. 255—Ray Woolfe/Photo Researchers, Inc.; pp. 260–261—Pat & Tom Leeson/Photo Researchers, Inc.; p. 266 top—Michael Townsend/Tony Stone Images; p. 266 bottom—Tom Bean/Tony Stone Images; p. 275—James Darell/Tony Stone Images; pp. 288–289—Liaison Agency/Liaison Agency; p. 290—Rob & Ann Simpson/Visuals Unlimited; p. 293—David Newman/Visuals Unlimited; p. 294—Cabisco/Visuals Unlimited; p. 297—Benelux Press B. V./Photo Researchers, Inc.; p. 299—Bernd Heinrich/Bernd Heinrich; pp. 310–311—Tom Bean/Corbis; p. 312—Daniel J. Cox/Liaison Agency; pp. 315 left, 315 Right—Tom & Pat Leeson/Tom & Pat Leeson; p. 318—A. J. Copley/Visuals Unlimited; p. 322—Tom McHugh/Photo Researchers, Inc.; p. 330 left—Rob Simpson/Visuals Unlimited; pp. 334, 335—John Reader/Science Photo Library/Photo Researchers, Inc.

Illustration Credits: pp. 154, 167, 169, 170, 175, 176, 177, 178, 204, 205, 208—David Mottet; all other illustrations—John Edwards Illustration.

Contents

How to Use This Book: A Study Guide

What is biology? Biology is the study of life. It is sometimes called life science. Many medicines we use were discovered by people who study biology. Doctors have gained knowledge about disease by knowing how body systems work. The foods we eat, the way we stay healthy, and the way we look at nature are all affected by this science.

As you read the chapters and lessons of this book, you will also learn many ways that biology is important to the way we live.

How to Study

- Plan a regular time to study.

- Choose a quiet desk or table where you will not be distracted. Find a spot that has good lighting.

- Gather all the books, pencils, and paper you need to complete your assignments.

- Decide on a goal. For example: "I will finish reading and taking notes on Chapter 1, Lesson 1, by 8:00."

- Take a five- to ten-minute break every hour to keep alert.

- If you start to feel sleepy, take a short break and get some fresh air.

Before Beginning Each Chapter

■ Read the chapter title and the opening paragraph.

■ Study the photograph. What does the photo tell you about the chapter?

■ Study the Goals for Learning. They describe what you will learn in the chapter.

■ Look at "Organizing Your Thoughts." The diagram is another way to see information that is in the chapter.

■ Look at the headings of the lessons and paragraphs to help you locate main ideas.

■ Read the chapter summaries to help you identify key issues.

■ Look at the chapter review. The questions cover the most important points from the reading.

Each chapter covers a different biology topic.

Before Beginning Each Lesson

Read the lesson title. It is in the form of a question that the lesson will answer. For example:

| Lesson | 1 | What Is the Basic Unit of Life? |

The pages that follow will answer the question "What is the basic unit of life?" The objectives also describe the knowledge you will gain from the lesson.

Look over the entire lesson, noting . . .

- lesson objectives
- pictures
- captions
- tables
- charts
- figures
- bold words
- text organization
- questions in the margins
- vocabulary definitions in the margins
- self-check questions

Self-Check

1. What are cells?
2. What are three functions of cells?
3. What are tissues made of?
4. What are organs made of?
5. Name four kinds of organs.

Also note these features . . .

- *Did You Know?*—Interesting facts related to the topic being studied.
- *Investigations*—Hands-on activities to try in class
- *Science in Your Life*—Relates science to your everyday life
- *Science Words*—A handy list of science-related words that acts as a vocabulary study aid

As You Read the Lesson

■ Read the major headings. The paragraphs that follow are about each heading.

■ Answering the questions in the lesson will help you determine if you know the lesson's key ideas. If you cannot, reread the lesson to look for the answers. If you are still unsure, ask for help.

Using the Bold Words

Bold Type

Words seen for the first time will appear in bold type

Glossary

Words listed in this column are also found in the glossary

Knowing the meaning of all the boxed words in the left margin will help you understand what you read.

These words appear in **bold type** the first time they appear in the text and are defined in the paragraph.

These tiny structures are called **organelles.**

All of the words in the left column are also defined in the **glossary**.

Organelle—A tiny structure inside a cell (p. 17)

Plants are made up of cells that contain organelles.

Taking Notes in Class

Some students prefer taking notes on index cards.

Others jot down key ideas in a spiral notebook.

As you read, you will be learning many new facts and ideas. Your notes will be useful and will help you remember when preparing for class discussions and studying for tests.

- Always write the main ideas and supporting details.

- Use an outline format to help save time.

- Keep your notes brief. You may want to set up some abbreviations to speed up your note-taking. For example: *with = w/ and = + dollars = $*

- Use the same method all the time. Then when you study for a test, you will know where to find the information you need to review.

Here are some tips for taking notes during class discussion:

- Use your own words.

- Do not try to write everything the teacher says.

- Write down important information only.

- Don't be concerned about writing in complete sentences. Use phrases.

- Be brief.

- Rewrite your notes to fill in possible gaps as soon as you can after class.

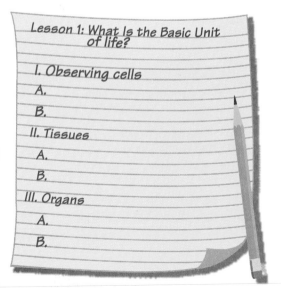

Lesson 1: What Is the Basic Unit of life?

I. Observing cells
   A.
   B.
II. Tissues
   A.
   B.
III. Organs
   A.
   B.

Using an Outline

You may want to outline the section using the subheads as your main points. An outline will help you remember the major points of the section. An example of an outline is shown at left. Your teacher may have you use the Student Study Guide for this book.

Getting Ready to Take a Test

The Summaries and Reviews can help you get ready to take tests.

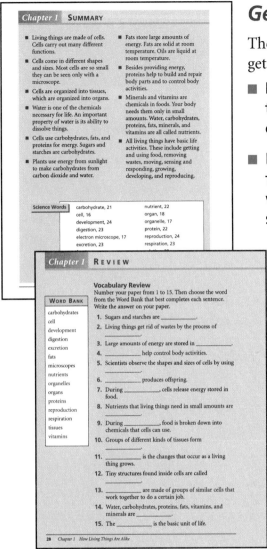

- Read the summaries from your text to make sure you understand the chapter's main ideas.

- Make up a sample test of items you think may be on the test. You may want to do this with a classmate and share your questions.

  - Review your notes and test yourself on words and key ideas.

  - Practice writing about some of the main ideas from the chapter.

  - Fill in the blanks under Vocabulary Review.

  - Complete the sentences under Concept Review.

  - Write what you think about the questions under Critical Thinking.

  - The questions in the reviews look like those in state and national tests you may take.

Use the Test Taking Tip

- Read the Test Taking Tip with each Chapter Review of the text.

| Test Taking Tip | When looking for information in a paragraph, read through the entire paragraph first. Then study it one sentence at a time. |

Chapter

1

How Living Things Are Alike

What do you, the flowers and woodchuck in the picture, and the bacteria in a pond have in common? All of these things are living. Living things are alike in several ways. They all are made of the same basic unit. Living things all contain the same basic chemicals. They use these chemicals to stay alive. Living things are also alike in how they stay alive. They all carry out similar basic life activities. Using food, moving, growing, and reproducing are among those activities.

ORGANIZE YOUR THOUGHTS

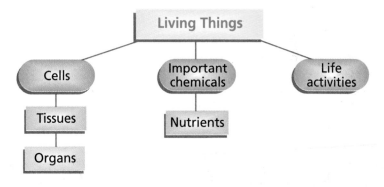

Goals for Learning

▶ To explain what a cell is and describe the organization of cells in living things

▶ To identify chemicals that are important for life and explain how living things use these chemicals

▶ To describe some basic life activities

All living things are made of **cells**. A cell is the basic unit of life. It is the smallest thing that can be called "alive." Most living things that you have seen are made of many cells. Depending on their size, plants and animals are made of thousands, millions, billions, or even trillions of cells. Cells are found in all parts of an animal: in blood, bone, skin, nerves, and muscle. Cells also are found in all parts of a plant: in roots, stems, leaves, and flowers.

Cells carry out many functions, or jobs. Some cells are specialized to do specific functions. Some of the functions of the specialized cells in your body are listed below.

- Skin cells: cover and protect
- Muscle cells: allow for movement
- Bone cells: support and protect
- Nerve cells: send and receive messages
- Blood cells: transport materials and fight diseases

Some living things, such as bacteria, are made of only one cell. That one cell performs all of the necessary life functions.

Observing Cells

Cells come in different sizes. However, most cells are so small that they are invisible to the naked eye. They can be seen only with a **microscope**. A microscope is an instrument that scientists use to magnify small things, or make them appear larger. Some microscopes are similar to a magnifying glass. You may have used a magnifying glass to look at tiny insects. Without the magnifying glass, an insect might look like just a black dot. With the magnifying glass, you can see the insect's tiny structures, such as legs and eyes. The

The technician uses this microscope to enlarge blood cells to identify disease.

Did You Know?

There are about 200 different types of cells in the human body.

same thing happens when scientists use a microscope to look at things. Tiny structures that were not visible before can be seen through the microscope.

When you look at cells through a microscope, the different shapes of the cells become visible. Cells may be shaped like rectangles, squares, triangles, or circles. Cells may be long, short, wide, or narrow.

Electron microscope

An instrument that uses a beam of tiny particles called electrons to magnify things.

Organelle

A tiny structure inside a cell.

Magnifying glasses and most microscopes use beams of light to magnify objects. However, they can magnify an object only so much. Then the image of the object gets blurry. Scientists use special microscopes, called electron microscopes, to magnify objects even more. **Electron microscopes** use beams of tiny particles instead of light. When a cell is viewed under an electron microscope, tiny structures inside the cell can be seen very clearly. These tiny structures are called **organelles**. They perform specific functions in the cell. The picture shows organelles in a plant cell.

Plants are made of cells that contain organelles.

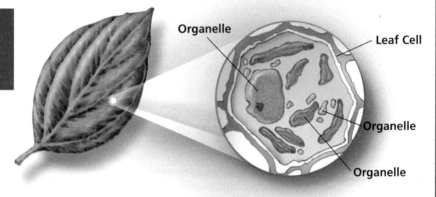

Organelle · Leaf Cell · Organelle · Organelle

Tissue

A group of cells that are similar and work together.

When you eat meat, what kind of tissue are you eating?

Tissues

Groups of cells that are similar and act together to do a certain job are called a **tissue**. For example, muscle cells are joined together to make muscle tissues. These tissues include leg muscles, arm muscles, stomach muscles, and heart muscles. The cells in muscle tissues work together to make the body move. Other examples of tissues in animals are nerve tissue, bone tissue, and skin tissue.

Plants also have different kinds of cells, such as root cells, stem cells, and leaf cells. Similar cells are organized together into tissues. Different tissues carry out different functions necessary for plant growth. These functions include covering the plant and moving water and other substances in the plant.

Organs

Organ

A group of different tissues that work together.

Different kinds of tissues join together to form an **organ**. Organs are the main working parts of animals and plants. Organs do special jobs. Your heart is an organ. It pumps blood through your body. Your lungs are organs. They allow you to breathe. Other organs in your body include your stomach, liver, kidneys, and eyes.

You can see in the picture that the main organs of plants are roots, leaves, and stems. Roots take in water from the soil. Leaves make food for the plant. Stems support the plant and carry water and food to different parts of the plant.

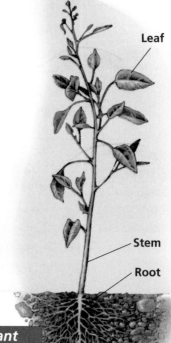

Leaf

Stem

Root

The main organs of a plant are roots, stems, and leaves.

Self-Check

1. What are cells?
2. What are three functions of cells?
3. What are tissues made of?
4. What are organs made of?
5. Name four organs.

INVESTIGATION

Comparing Cells

Materials

✓ prepared slides of animal, plant, and bacterial cells

✓ light microscope

✓ pencil

✓ paper

Purpose

To observe differences and similarities among different types of cells

Procedure

1. *Safety Alert: Handle glass microscope slides with care. Dispose of broken glass properly.* Choose one of the prepared slides. On a sheet of paper, record the type of cells you selected. Look at the slide without using the microscope. What can you see?

2. Place the slide on the stage of the microscope. Refer to the instructions for the microscope you are using. Focus and adjust the microscope so that you can see the cells on the slide clearly. Look at the slide under different levels of magnification. How does what you see now differ from what you saw without the microscope?

3. Observe one of the cells on the slide. What is its shape? Do you see any organelles inside the cell? If so, what do they look like? Make a drawing of the cell on your paper.

4. Repeat the procedure, observing at least one type of animal cell, one type of plant cell, and one type of bacterial cell.

Questions

1. What were some similarities between the plant cells and the animal cells? What were some differences?

2. How did the plant cells and animal cells differ from the bacterial cells?

Solution

A mixture in which the particles are evenly mixed.

id You Know?

Humans can survive up to several weeks with no food. However, they can survive only a few days without water.

Besides having cells, living things are alike because they have similar chemicals. Living things use these chemicals to stay alive. Water is one of the chemicals all living things use.

Importance of Water

Life cannot exist without water. It is the most plentiful chemical in living things. Water is found in each of the approximately 100 trillion cells in the adult human body.

Water is a useful chemical. Have you ever put sugar in a cup of tea? When you put sugar in tea, you stir the liquid until the sugar disappears. The sugar dissolves in the liquid. As the sugar dissolves, it breaks apart into tiny pieces that you can no longer see. The water in the tea is the chemical that does the dissolving. Special properties of water allow it to break things apart into tiny particles. When the water, sugar, and tea particles become equally mixed, they form a **solution**.

The ability to dissolve other chemicals is one of the most important properties of water for life. Cells are so small that the materials that go in and out of them must be very tiny. When a material dissolves into tiny pieces, it can move more easily from cell to cell.

Have you ever accidentally bitten your tongue so hard that it bled? Blood tastes salty. Your body fluids and the liquid in your cells are not pure water. They are a solution of many things, including salts. One example of a salt is sodium chloride. Another name for sodium chloride is table salt. The liquid found in living things is a solution of salts, water, and other chemicals.

Other important chemicals found in living things are carbohydrates, fats, and proteins. Each of these common chemicals has a job to do in the body of a living thing.

Carbohydrates

Carbohydrates are sugars and starches. Cane sugar is a carbohydrate that is used to sweeten drinks and cakes. Many fruits and vegetables, such as oranges and tomatoes, contain sugar too. Starches are found in foods such as bread, cereal, pasta, rice, and potatoes. Plants use the energy from sunlight to make carbohydrates from carbon dioxide and water. Carbon dioxide is a gas found in air. Animals get energy from the carbohydrates that plants make.

Energy is needed to carry on life activities. Energy comes from fuel. You can think of carbohydrates as fuel chemicals. Carbohydrates in your body work like gasoline in a car. Gasoline from the fuel tank gets to the engine, where it is broken down and energy is released. This released energy runs the engine. When carbohydrates are broken down in your body, energy is released. This energy powers your body. The same thing happens in other animals. Plants and other living things use carbohydrates for energy too.

Fats

Fats also can be thought of as fuel chemicals. Fats store large amounts of energy that are released when they are broken down. Of all the chemicals important for life, fats contain the most energy. They are found in foods such as beef, butter, cheese, and peanut butter. Fats are related to oils. Fats are solid at room temperature. Oils, such as corn oil used for frying foods, are liquid at room temperature.

Foods contain water, carbohydrates, fats, and other chemicals important for life.

Which foods have you had today that are good sources of carbohydrates? Which ones are good sources of protein?

Mineral
A chemical found in foods that is needed by living things in small amounts.

Nutrient
Any chemical found in foods that is needed by living things.

Protein
A chemical used by living things to build and repair body parts and regulate body activities.

Vitamin
A chemical found in foods that is needed by living things in small amounts.

Proteins

Proteins are another kind of chemical important for life. Meats, such as beef, chicken, and fish, contain large amounts of proteins. Beans, nuts, eggs, and cheese also contain large amounts of proteins.

Like carbohydrates and fats, proteins provide energy for living things. But they have other important functions too. Proteins help to repair damaged cells and build new ones. Hair, muscles, and skin are made mostly of proteins. Proteins also help control body activities such as heart rate and the breaking down of food in the body.

Importance of Nutrients

Keeping your body working properly is not a simple job. You must get a regular supply of carbohydrates, proteins, and fats from the foods you eat. Each kind of food provides different chemicals your body needs. Therefore, it is important to eat a variety of foods every day.

In addition to water, carbohydrates, proteins, and fats, your body also needs **minerals** and **vitamins**. Your body needs these chemicals in small amounts only. Different foods contain different kinds of minerals and vitamins. The chemicals that are needed for life and that come from foods are called **nutrients**. To be healthy, living things need to take in the right amounts of nutrients every day.

Self-Check

1. What is one of the most important properties of water for life?
2. How does your body use carbohydrates and fats?
3. What do proteins do in your body?
4. What are vitamins and minerals?
5. How can you get all the nutrients you need?

Objectives

After reading this lesson, you should be able to

▶ identify some basic life activities.

▶ compare how plants and animals get food, move, and respond.

▶ explain the difference between growth and development.

Digestion
The process by which living things break down food.

Excretion
The process by which living things get rid of wastes.

Respiration
The process by which living things release energy from food.

Most living things carry on the same kinds of activities. These activities allow living things to stay alive. Some examples of basic life activities are described below.

Getting Food

A familiar example of a life activity is getting food. Animals get food by eating plants or other animals. Plants make their own food. They use the energy from sunlight to make carbohydrates from carbon dioxide and water.

Using Food and Removing Wastes

Digestion is a life activity that breaks down food into chemicals that cells can use. Respiration is another basic life activity. During **respiration**, cells release the energy that is stored in the chemicals. Oxygen is used to release the stored energy. Cells use the energy to do work. Respiration also produces wastes. **Excretion** is the process that removes wastes from living things.

Movement

Movement is another activity that is common to living things. Plants do not move from one place to another, but they still move. Plants have roots that hold them in place, but their parts bend and move. For example, leaves may move to face sunlight. As shown in the picture, animal movement is easier to see. Most animals move freely from place to place.

The movements of most animals are obvious.

Besides outward movement, there is constant movement inside living things. The insides of plants and animals are always changing. Liquids are flowing, food is being digested, and materials are moving into and out of cells.

Sensing and Responding

Living things sense and respond. Animals and plants have tissues and organs that pick up, or sense, signals from their surroundings. These signals include light, sound, chemicals, and touch. Plants and animals change something, or respond, based on the kinds of signals they pick up. For example, some moths fly around lights at night. Fish swim to the top of a tank for food. Dogs respond to the sound of a human voice. Many flowers open in the morning light and close as the sun goes down.

What are five ways that you sense things?

Growth

Growing is part of being alive. You were once a baby, but you have grown into a larger person. You are still growing. You will continue to grow until you reach your adult size. Most living things go through a similar pattern of growth.

Development

The changes that occur as a living thing grows.

Development

Many living things develop as they grow. **Development** means becoming different, or changing, over time. Tadpoles hatch from eggs and develop by stages into frogs or toads. Notice in the photos on the next page that tadpoles look more like fish than like frogs. Unlike frogs, tadpoles have a tail and no legs. Tadpoles also have no mouth when they first hatch. As a tadpole develops, a mouth forms and changes in shape. The legs form, and the tail is absorbed into the body.

Reproduction

The process by which living things produce offspring.

Reproduction

Living things produce offspring, or children, through the basic life activity of **reproduction**. Some living things reproduce by themselves. For example, bacteria reproduce by dividing in two. For other living things, such as humans, reproduction requires two parents. The offspring of all living things resemble their parent or parents.

As tadpoles develop, they grow legs and lose their tail.

Self-Check

1. List three basic activities of living things.
2. How do animals and plants get food?
3. What is the difference in the way animals and plants move?
4. Contrast growth and development.
5. What does "sensing and responding" mean?

Identifying life activities

Living things around you carry out basic life activities all the time. Animals move around a lot of the time. A flowering plant being pollinated by a bee is involved in reproduction. Even when living things seem to be just sitting there not doing anything, they are carrying out basic life activities. A plant is constantly making food with energy from the sun using carbon dioxide and water. The cells of a dog resting in the shade are carrying out respiration. If the dog just finished a meal, it is also carrying out the basic life activity of digestion.

Can you recognize basic life activities? Take pictures of living things around you or look for photographs in magazines. Nature magazines may be easiest to use. Try to find at least one example of each basic life actitivy. Some examples like those above may not be seen directly in the photographs. Cut out the photos and arrange them as a collage on a large sheet of paper. Then number the images. On a separate sheet of paper, list the basic life activities that you can identify in each picture. Most pictures will show more than one basic life activity.

- Living things are made of cells. Cells carry out many different functions.

- Cells come in different shapes and sizes. Most cells are so small they can be seen only with a microscope.

- Cells are organized into tissues, which are organized into organs.

- Water is one of the chemicals necessary for life. An important property of water is its ability to dissolve things.

- Cells use carbohydrates, fats, and proteins for energy. Sugars and starches are carbohydrates.

- Plants use energy from sunlight to make carbohydrates from carbon dioxide and water.

- Fats store large amounts of energy. Fats are solid at room temperature. Oils are liquid at room temperature.

- Besides providing energy, proteins help to build and repair body parts and to control body activities.

- Minerals and vitamins are chemicals in foods. Your body needs them only in small amounts. Water, carbohydrates, proteins, fats, minerals, and vitamins are all called nutrients.

- All living things have basic life activities. These include getting and using food, removing wastes, moving, sensing and responding, growing, developing, and reproducing.

Science Words			
carbohydrate, 21		nutrient, 22	
cell, 16		organ, 18	
development, 24		organelle, 17	
digestion, 23		protein, 22	
electron microscope, 17		reproduction, 24	
excretion, 23		respiration, 23	
fat, 21		solution, 20	
microscope, 16		tissue, 17	
mineral, 22		vitamin, 22	

Vocabulary Review

Number your paper from 1 to 15. Then choose the word from the Word Bank that best completes each sentence. Write the answer on your paper.

WORD BANK

carbohydrates

cell

development

digestion

excretion

fats

microscopes

nutrients

organelles

organs

proteins

reproduction

respiration

tissues

vitamins

1. Sugars and starches are _____.

2. Living things get rid of wastes by the process of _____.

3. Large amounts of energy are stored in _____.

4. _____ help control body activities.

5. Scientists observe the shapes and sizes of cells by using _____.

6. _____ produces offspring.

7. During _____, cells release energy stored in food.

8. Nutrients that living things need in small amounts are _____.

9. During _____, food is broken down into chemicals that cells can use.

10. Groups of different kinds of tissues form _____.

11. _____ is the changes that occur as a living thing grows.

12. Tiny structures found inside cells are called _____.

13. _____ are made of groups of similar cells that work together to do a certain job.

14. Water, carbohydrates, proteins, fats, vitamins, and minerals are _____.

15. The _____ is the basic unit of life.

Concept Review

Number your paper from 1 to 4. Then choose the answer that best completes each sentence. Write the letter of the answer on your paper.

1. All living things are made of _____.

   a. only one cell **b.** one or more cells   **c.** many cells

2. The most plentiful chemical in living things is _____.

   a. water   **b.** fat   **c.** minerals

3. Plants make _____ using carbon dioxide, water, and energy from the sun.

   a. minerals   **b.** vitamins   **c.** carbohydrates

4. Reproduction, digestion, movement, and growth are examples of _____.

   a. nutrition   **b.** basic life activities   **c.** development

Critical Thinking

Write the answer to the following question.

What basic life activities are described in the following paragraph?

A kitten sees a ball of yarn and pounces on it. It was just a few weeks ago that the kitten was not even able to walk. When it was born, the kitten was tiny. Its eyes were continually closed, and it could barely crawl. Now, suddenly, the kitten stops and sniffs the air. Its mother has returned from hunting for food. The kitten walks over to its mother and begins to nurse, drinking milk.

Test Taking Tip | When looking for information in a paragraph, read through the entire paragraph first. Then study it one sentence at a time.

Chapter 2

Organizing Living Things

Look at all the things around you. Everything in the world can be grouped as living or nonliving. Examples of living things are the trees, grass, and bighorn sheep in the picture. Examples of nonliving things are clouds, rocks, and air. Living and nonliving things have many differences. Only living things are made of cells. Only living things carry out all basic life activities, such as growing and using food. But living things are not all alike. Living things are organized into groups based on their similarities and differences.

ORGANIZE YOUR THOUGHTS

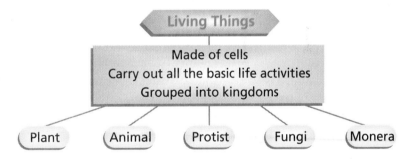

Living Things

Made of cells
Carry out all the basic life activities
Grouped into kingdoms

Plant · Animal · Protist · Fungi · Monera

Goals for Learning

▶ To identify the differences between living and nonliving things

▶ To explain how the living world is divided into five kingdoms

▶ To describe the similarities and differences between living things in different kingdoms

What Is the Difference Between Living and Nonliving Things?

Property

A quality that describes an object.

How do you tell the difference between living and nonliving things? You observe their properties. A **property** is a quality that describes an object. A property of a rock is its hardness. A property of a person is eye color. Properties can describe how an object looks or feels. Properties can also describe how an object behaves. All things have different properties.

Properties of Nonliving Things

Like living things, nonliving things have properties that you can see and feel. The color of a rock or mineral is one of its properties. The property of hardness also helps to identify a rock or mineral. For example, some rocks, such as chalk, are so soft you can write with them. Others are hard enough to cut steel. Did you know that diamond is the hardest mineral of all? It is used in cutting tools because of that property.

The properties that nonliving things do not have are as important as the properties they do have. Unlike living things, nonliving things do not carry out life activities. They do not move by themselves. They do not develop and reproduce. Nonliving things are not made of cells. Recall that a cell is the basic structure of all living things.

A nonliving thing may seem to carry out one life activity. But it will not carry out all of them. For example, sugar crystals in rock candy can grow. But they do not move, need food, or react to their environment.

Mountains, rocks, snow, and water are all nonliving things.

Properties of Living Things

Like nonliving things, living things have properties you can see and feel. But living things carry out basic life activities. They move, grow, and reproduce. They use food and remove wastes. They sense and react to their environment. Another word for a living thing is an **organism**.

Can you identify a nonliving thing that seems to carry out one of the basic life activities?

What is an organism? An organism is a complete, individual living thing. It can carry out all the basic life activities. Large living things such as an elephant or a redwood tree are organisms. But so are some tiny living things that have only one cell. The bacteria that cause sore throats are organisms. Bacteria are the simplest single cells that carry out all basic life activities.

The *organ* in *organism* comes from a Latin word that means "tool." Just as a tool does a certain job, an organ does a certain job in a living thing. Organs are organized tissues and cells that carry out basic life activities. Your organs include your heart and your kidneys. Simple organisms, such as bacteria, do not have organs. They carry out life activities in cells.

Self-Check

1. Into what two groups are most things in the world divided?
2. What are three examples of nonliving things?
3. What are three examples of living things?
4. List some properties of living things.
5. What is an organism?

INVESTIGATION

Classifying Things

Materials

✓ 5 pictures from a magazine or book (numbered 1–5)

Purpose

To classify things as living or nonliving

Procedure

1. Copy the data table below on a sheet of paper. Leave blank columns beneath the headings. Different pictures will have different numbers of objects. You may need more than one line to list the properties of an object.

Data Table 1

Picture 1	
Object	**Properties**

2. Look at the first picture. In your table, list all of the objects that you see in the picture. Leave several blank lines between objects to list properties.

3. List the properties of each object. For example, is it a solid, liquid, or gas? What is its shape and color? Do you know if it moves, grows, reproduces, senses things, and reacts? Does it get food and remove wastes?

4. Make a new table for each of the other four pictures. Label them Data Table 2 through Data Table 5. List the objects in the pictures and their properties.

5. Copy the data table below on a sheet of paper. Review the properties you recorded for each object. Use the properties to decide if the object is living or nonliving. Write the name of each object in the correct column.

Data Table 6

Picture	Nonliving Things	Living Things
1		
2		
3		
4		
5		

Questions

1. List three living things that you observed in the pictures.

2. List three nonliving things that you observed in the pictures.

3. Did any of the nonliving things carry out a basic life activity, such as growing? Give an example. Then explain why you decided that it was a nonliving thing.

4. Did any of the pictures show *only* living things? List the living things in the picture.

Explore Further

Copy Data Table 6 again. Look around you and classify everything you see as living or nonliving. Write the name of each object in the correct column.

Biology
The study of living things.

Kingdom
One of the five groups into which living things are classified.

Living things are more like one another than they are like nonliving things. For example, living things all carry out the basic life activities. However, living things can be very different from one another. A cat is different from a dog. A bird and a tree are even more different from each other.

Scientists divide the world of living things into five groups, or **kingdoms**. Organisms are grouped according to how they are alike and how they are different. This makes them easier to study. The study of living things is called **biology**. Most of the living things you know are either in the plant kingdom or the animal kingdom. There are three other kingdoms that you may not know very well.

The Plant Kingdom

Most plants are easy to recognize. Examples of plants are trees, grasses, ferns, and mosses. Plants don't move from place to place like animals. They don't need to do so. Plants make their own food, using sunlight and other substances around them. All plants have many cells. These cells are organized into tissues. Many plants also have organs.

The Animal Kingdom

Animals have many different sizes and shapes. You probably recognize dogs, turtles, and fish as animals. Corals, sponges, and insects are animals too.

Animals gets their food by eating plants or by eating other animals that eat plants.

Animals cannot make their own food. They get their food from other living things. They eat plants, or they eat other animals that eat plants. Most animals move around to capture or gather their food. Moving also helps them to find shelter, escape danger, and find mates. All animals have many cells. These cells form tissues in all animals except the sponge. In most animals, the tissues form organs.

The Protist Kingdom

At one time, biologists divided the living world into only two kingdoms, plant and animal. Then the microscope was invented. When biologists used the microscope, they discovered tiny organisms. They called them **microorganisms** because biologists could see these organisms only under a microscope. These organisms did not fit into either the plant or the animal kingdom. Biologists placed them in a separate kingdom. They called the organisms **protists**.

Most protists have only one cell. A few have many cells. Some protists make their own food. Others absorb food from other sources. **Algae** are plant-like protists. **Protozoans** are animal-like protists. Some protozoans have properties of plants and animals. All protists can carry out the basic life activities.

Algae live in lakes, streams, rivers, ponds, and oceans. ᵛ have probably seen the algae that grow as a green ⸱ a pond. The green scum is thousands of tiny al⸍ plants, algae can make their own food. Algᵃ the organisms that live in waters around larger algae are called seaweeds. Somᵛ become as long as a football field⸍ oxygen that other organisms ⸱ classified algae as plants. ᴬᵛ plants and have more ⸱

Protozoans live iⁿ Most protozᵒ⸍ cause disease⸍ humans and ot⸍ and stomach painⸯ

Algae
Protists that make their own food and usually live in water.

Microorganism
An organism that is too small to be seen without a microscope.

Protist
An organism that usually is one-celled and has plant-like or animal-like properties.

Protozoan
A protist that has animal-like qualities.

Parasiᵗ⸍
An organisᵗ⸍ absorbs foodⸯ living organisᵐ harms it.

Pseudopod
Part of some one-celled organisms that sticks out like a foot to move the cell along.

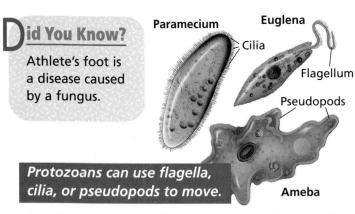

Protozoans can use flagella, cilia, or pseudopods to move.

Paramecium
Euglena
Cilia
Flagellum
Pseudopods
Ameba

Protozoans behave like animals by getting food and moving. Different kinds of protozoans have different methods of moving. Amebas push out a part of their cell. This part is called a **pseudopod**. It looks like a foot and pulls the ameba along.

Some protozoans have tails, or **flagella**, that move them back and forth. Others use **cilia** to move. Cilia are tiny hair-like structures that beat like boat paddles.

Euglenas are protozoans that behave like both plants and animals. Like plants, they make their own food when sunlight is present. Like animals, they can absorb food from the environment. They absorb food when sunlight is not present.

The Fungi Kingdom

You are probably more familiar with organisms in the fourth kingdom, **fungi** (plural of *fungus*). Mushrooms and the mold that grows on bread are fungi. Most fungi have many cells. At one time, fungi were classified as plants. Like plants, fungi do not move around by themselves. But unlike plants, fungi do not make their own food. They absorb food from other organisms.

Because of the way fungi get food, they are important to other organisms. Fungi release special chemicals on dead plant and animal matter. The chemicals break down, or **decompose**, the matter. The fungi then absorb the decomposed material. But some of the decomposed matter also gets into the soil. Other organisms, such as plants, can then use it.

Some fungi are **parasites**. They absorb food from a living organism. Some fungi harm plants. For example, Dutch elm disease kills elm trees. Other fungi harm animals. A fungus causes ringworm, a human skin disease.

Cilia
Hair-like structures that help some one-celled organisms move.

Decompose
To break down or decay matter into simpler substances.

Flagella
Whip-like tails that help some one-celled organisms move. Singular is flagellum.

Fungus
organism that ally has many nd decomposes l for its food.

n that from a n and

Fungi decompose dead plant and animal material.

The Monera Kingdom

The last of the kingdoms contains **monerans**. *Monera* means "alone." This kingdom has only one kind of organism, which is bacteria. Monerans are one-celled organisms. Like animals, some can move and get food. Like plants, some stay put and make their own food. You may wonder why bacteria are not placed in the protist kingdom. The cells of bacteria are different from the cells of all other organisms. Bacteria do not have organelles in their cells. Organelles are tiny structures in cells that do certain jobs. The cells of all other organisms have organelles.

Some bacteria cause disease. For example, bacteria cause strep throat. Most bacteria, though, are harmless. Many are even helpful. Like fungi, bacteria help to decompose the remains of plants and animals. People also use bacteria to make foods such as cheese and yogurt.

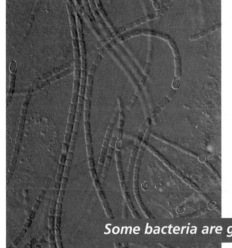
Some bacteria are green like plants and make their own food.

Self-Check

1. Name the five kingdoms of living things.
2. List two differences between plants and animals.
3. How are protists similar to plants and animals?
4. What is an important function of fungi?
5 Why are bacteria placed in a kingdom by themselves?

SCIENCE IN YOUR LIFE

Bacteria: Helpful and harmful

Bacteria live everywhere. They are in the ocean, on top of mountains, in polar ice, on your hands, and even inside you. You cannot go anywhere without coming in contact with bacteria.

Most bacteria are helpful. Bacteria in soil break down plant and animal material and release nutrients. They also take in gases from the air, such as nitrogen. They change nitrogen into a form that plants and animals can use. Bacteria in your intestines make vitamin K. This vitamin helps your blood clot when you are cut.

Bacteria can also be harmful. Many bacteria cause diseases in people. Bacteria cause diseases such as tuberculosis, tetanus, and cholera. Food that is contaminated by certain kinds of bacteria can cause illness.

Microbiologists are scientists who work with bacteria and other microorganisms. Some microbiologists help to identify bacteria that cause disease. They grow the bacteria on special plates. Each cell multiplies until it forms millions of bacteria cells, called a colony. It is impossible to see a single bacterium without a microscope. But it is easy to see colonies of bacteria.

There are ways to get rid of most harmful bacteria. Antibiotics are drugs that kill bacteria in people and animals. Pasteurization, or rapid heating, kills harmful bacteria in milk. Drinking water is purified to remove bacteria and other microorganisms. Sewage is treated so that it will not pollute water supplies. Sometimes bacteria help to clean up sewage. Helpful bacteria break down material in the sewage so that it does not harm people.

- Living and nonliving things have different properties.

- Living things are different from nonliving things in two main ways. Living things are made of cells. Nonliving things are not. Living things can carry out all the basic life activities. Nonliving things cannot.

- Biology is the study of living things, or organisms.

- Living things are divided into five kingdoms to make them easier to study. The kingdoms are plants, animals, protists, fungi, and monerans.

- Plants make their own food and do not move around from place to place. They have many cells that are organized into tissues and sometimes organs.

- Animals eat other organisms for food. They can move around to get their food. They have many cells that are organized into tissues and organs.

- Protists include algae, seaweeds, and protozoans. Most are one-celled. They have properties of both animals and plants. Some make their own food. Others absorb their food. Some do both.

- At one time, fungi were classified as plants. But fungi do not make their own food. They absorb their food from other organisms or the remains of other organisms. Some are parasites.

- Monerans are bacteria. They are one-celled organisms that do not have organelles. Some make their own food and others absorb it.

Science Words		
algae, 37		moneran, 39
biology, 36		organism, 33
cilia, 38		parasite, 38
decompose, 38		property, 32
flagella, 38		protist, 37
fungus, 38		protozoan, 37
kingdom, 36		pseudopod, 38
microorganism, 37		

Vocabulary Review

Number your paper from 1 to 13. Then choose the word from the Word Bank that best completes each sentence. Write the answer on your paper.

WORD BANK
algae
biology
cilia
decompose
fungi
kingdom
microorganism
moneran
organism
parasite
property
protist
protozoan

1. _____ is the study of living things.

2. The hardness of a rock is a _____.

3. Some protozoans use hair-like structures called _____ to move.

4. Mushrooms are in the fungi _____.

5. Another word for a living thing is an _____.

6. Fungi release chemicals that _____ matter.

7. _____ break down dead plants and animals.

8. An organism that is too small to be seen without a microscope is a _____.

9. Protists that make their own food and usually live in water are _____.

10. An organism that lives on a living organism and harms it is a _____.

11. A _____ is an animal-like protist.

12. An organism that has one cell and does not have organelles is a _____.

13. One type of _____ is a protozoan.

Concept Review

Number your paper from 1 to 6. Then choose the answer that best completes each sentence. Write the letter of the answer on your paper.

1. Nonliving things do not have _____.

   a. cells   **b.** properties   **c.** color

2. Most animals need to _____ to get food.

   a. move   **b.** reproduce   **c.** breathe

3. Plants can make their own _____.

   a. minerals   **b.** food   **c.** flagella

4. A new kingdom was discovered when _____ were seen under a microscope.

   a. plants   **b.** fungi   **c.** microorganisms

5. _____ were once classified as plants, but they do not make their own food.

   a. Fungi   **b.** Algae   **c.** Animals

6. Bacteria are organisms in the _____ kingdom.

   a. monera   **b.** fungi   **c.** protist

Critical Thinking

What are some of the properties that are used to divide living things into kingdoms? Give some examples.

Test Taking Tip   When answering multiple-choice questions, read the sentence completely using each choice. Then choose the choice that makes the most sense when the entire sentence is read.

Classifying Animals

How would you describe the birds shown in the photo? How are they alike? How are they different? You can see that the birds share certain features that help them survive around water. But some of the birds have features that the other birds do not have. Such similarities and differences allow biologists to organize birds and other living things into groups. In this chapter, you will learn how biologists group animals. You will also learn some of the features of the major groups of animals.

ORGANIZE YOUR THOUGHTS

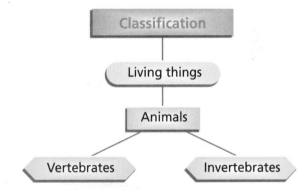

Classification

Living things

Animals

Vertebrates   Invertebrates

Goals for Learning

▶ To learn how biologists classify and name animals
▶ To identify the features of different groups of vertebrates
▶ To identify the features of different groups of invertebrates

Biologists have identified more than one million different kinds of animals in the world. More kinds of animals are added to the list every day. To deal with such a large list, biologists need a way to divide it into smaller groups.

Classifying Based on Similarities

Look at the vehicles in the photo. How could you **classify** the cars, or divide them into groups? One way would be to think of how some of the cars are similar. For example, you could put the passenger cars in one group and the trucks in another group. You could then divide the passenger cars and the trucks by their size. You might divide each of those groups into smaller groups based on color.

Classify

Group things based on the features they share.

You can classify these cars based on their similar features.

Biologists divide animals into groups based on their similarities too. For example, falcons, sparrows, and geese are classified as birds because they all have feathers. All birds have feathers, but no other type of animal does.

The bird group is divided into smaller groups based on other features. Falcons are birds of prey. All members of that group have feet with sharp claws that can grab prey. Sparrows are perching birds. Their feet have toes that are good for gripping branches. Geese are waterbirds. Like other waterbirds, geese use their webbed feet for swimming. Try to match these three bird groups with the bird feet shown in the photos.

Which groups of birds have feet like these?

Taxonomy
The science of classifying organisms based on the features they share.

Biologists classify all organisms based on their similar features. The science of classifying organisms according to their similarities is called **taxonomy**.

The Seven Levels of Classification

Recall the example of organizing vehicles into groups. In that example, there were three levels of organization. The highest level contained two groups, which were passenger cars and trucks. The middle level contained groups based on the sizes of the cars. The lowest level contained groups based on color.

Biologists also use different levels to classify living things. The diagram shows that there are seven levels in the classification system of organisms: kingdom, **phylum**, class, order, family, genus, and species.

Phylum

Subdivision of a kingdom.

Kingdoms represent the highest level in the classification system. You learned in Chapter 2 that biologists classify all organisms into five kingdoms. The animal kingdom is one of the five kingdoms. Each kingdom is divided into groups called phyla (plural of *phylum*). The phyla represent the second-highest level of classification. More organisms are included in a kingdom than in any one of its phyla. Each phylum is divided into classes, each class is divided into orders, and so on.

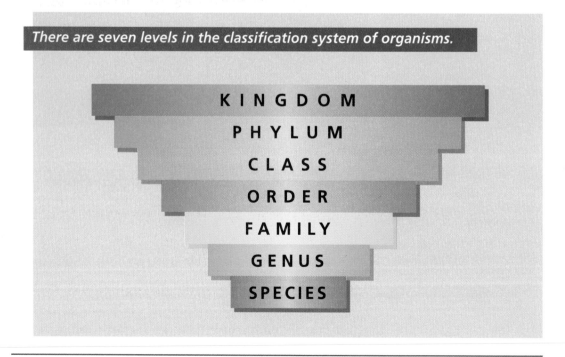

There are seven levels in the classification system of organisms.

KINGDOM

PHYLUM

CLASS

ORDER

FAMILY

GENUS

SPECIES

The lowest level in the classification system is the **species**. Each species represents a single type of organism. Members of the same species can breed and produce offspring like themselves.

A Place for Every Organism

Every organism that has been identified has its own place in the classification system. The diagram shows how biologists classify four species of animals. Notice that the African elephant, the red tree mouse, and the heather mouse belong to the same phylum. The boll weevil belongs to a different phylum. This means that these three animals are more similar to each other than they are to the boll weevil. Notice also that the two mice belong to the same order. The elephant belongs to a different order. Thus, the red tree mouse and the heather mouse are more similar to each other than they are to the elephant. Organisms that are very similar belong to the same genus. Which animals in the diagram belong to the same genus?

Classification of Four Animals

Some classification groups contain a large number of species. For example, the order Coleoptera contains about 500,000 species, including the boll weevil. Other orders may have just a few species. For example, the African elephant and the Asian elephant are the only two species in the order Proboscidea.

Kingdom		Animalia	
Phylum	Arthropoda	Chordata	
Class	Insecta	Mammalia	
Order	Coleoptera	Proboscidea	Rodentia
Family	Curculionidae	Elephantidae	Cricetidae
Genus	*Anthonomus*	*Loxodonta*	*Phenacomys*
Species	*grandis*	*africana*	*longicaudus*	*intermedius*
	Boll weevil	**African elephant**	**Red tree mouse**	**Heather mouse**

Scientific Names

Most people call animals by their common names, such as mockingbird and mountain lion. However, using common names can be confusing. The mountain lion in the picture has at least four other common names—puma, cougar, catamount, and American panther. All five names refer to the same species. People who use one of these names may not know that the other names refer to the same species. The opposite problem occurs with the common name "June bug." At least a dozen different beetle species have that name. When someone says "June bug," you have no way of knowing which species that is. The same animal may have different names in different languages too. For example, an owl is called *gufo* in Italian, *hibou* in French, and *búho* in Spanish.

The scientific name of human beings is *Homo sapiens*. The scientific name of chimpanzees is *Pan troglodytes*. Do human beings and chimpanzees belong to the same genus?

Scientific name

The name given to each species, consisting of its genus and its species label.

To overcome these problems, biologists give each species a **scientific name**. An organism's scientific name consists of two words. The first word is the organism's genus, and the second word is its species label. For example, the scientific name of the mountain lion is *Felis concolor*. Thus, the mountain lion belongs to the genus *Felis* and the species *concolor*. Look again at the diagram on page 49. What is the scientific name of the African elephant?

The mountain lion has several common names but only one scientific name: **Felis concolor.**

The scientific name given to each species is unique. This means that different species have different scientific names, even if they have the same common name. Scientific names are in Latin, so they are recognized by biologists around the world. For example, *Felis concolor* means the same thing in France, the United States, and Mexico. As you may have noticed, scientific names are always printed in *italics* or are underlined. The first word in the name is capitalized, but the second word is not.

Has everything been classified?

You may think that every kind of organism on the earth has already been studied, classified, and named. In fact, biologists continue to discover species that no one has identified before. Many of the newly found species are insects. Some biologists think there could be millions of insect species that still have not been identified.

Some new species may be useful in finding new medicines. Others may help control pests that damage crops. To learn how a new species might be useful, biologists must study the organism closely. They must learn how it carries out its life activities. Then they can classify the organism.

Self-Check

1. On what do biologists base their classification of organisms?
2. List the seven levels of classification of organisms, from highest to lowest.
3. What is a species?
4. The banana slug and the cuttlefish belong to the same phylum. The clownfish belongs to a different phylum. Is the banana slug or the clownfish more similar to the cuttlefish?
5. The barn owl belongs to the genus *Tyta* and the species *alba*. What is the barn owl's scientific name?

INVESTIGATION

Classifying Objects

Materials

✓ assortment of objects found in a classroom

Purpose
To make a classification system for objects found in a classroom

Procedure
1. Form a team with two or three other students. On a sheet of paper, make a list of objects in your classroom. Include objects that may be on shelves or in drawers and cabinets.

2. Divide the objects on your list into groups based on their similarities. Name each group.

3. Make up a classification system for the objects on your list. Your system should have several levels. Each level should include all of the groups in the next-lower level.

4. Write your classification system on a sheet of paper. List the objects that belong in each group. Show how the different levels are related to each other.

5. Compare your classification system with the system made up by other student teams.

Questions
1. What were the names of the groups your team came up with?

2. How many levels did your classification system have?

3. How did your classification system differ from the systems of other student teams?

4. How does this investigation show the value of having a single system for classifying organisms?

Cartilage
A soft material found in vertebrate skeletons.

Vertebra
One of the bones or blocks of cartilage that make up a backbone.

Vertebrate
An animal with a backbone.

The animals that are probably most familiar to you are animals with backbones. These animals are called **vertebrates**. Vertebrates include tiny hummingbirds and enormous blue whales. Humans also are vertebrates. Altogether, there are nearly 50,000 species of vertebrates.

Features of Vertebrates

Vertebrates have three features that set them apart from other animals. First, all vertebrates have an internal skeleton, which is inside their body. The skeleton of vertebrates is made of bone or a softer material called **cartilage**. Some other animals also have an internal skeleton, but it is made of different materials.

The second feature of vertebrates is their backbone. A backbone is made up of many small bones or blocks of cartilage. For example, the human backbone contains twenty-six bones. Each bone or block of cartilage in the backbone is called a **vertebra**. That is why animals with backbones are known as vertebrates.

The third feature of vertebrates is the skull. The skull surrounds and protects the brain. Look for the backbone and skull in the skeleton of a cow.

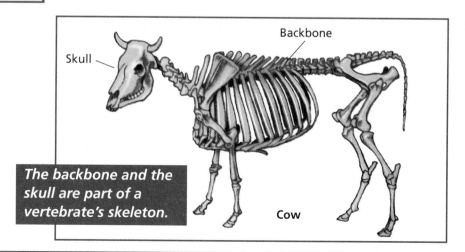

Skull

Backbone

The backbone and the skull are part of a vertebrate's skeleton.

Cow

A bony fish is covered with scales.

Vertebrates are divided into seven classes. Three of the classes consist of different types of fishes. The other four classes are amphibians, reptiles, birds, and mammals.

Fishes

Biologists have identified about 24,000 species of fishes. There are more species of fishes than of any other kind of vertebrate. All fishes live in water and breathe with structures called **gills**.

Most fishes have a skeleton made of bone and are called bony fishes. They include bass, trout, salmon, and many others. You can see in the photo that the body of a bony fish is covered with scales that overlap like roof shingles. The scales protect the fish and give it a smooth surface. Many bony fishes have an organ called a **swim bladder** that is filled with gas. By changing the amount of gas in its swim bladder, the fish can move up or down in the water.

What kind of fishes do you usually eat? Do those fishes have skeletons made of bone or cartilage?

Sharks, rays, and skates have a skeleton made of cartilage instead of bone. Many of these fishes have powerful jaws and rows of sharp teeth. Their tiny, toothlike scales make their skin feel like sandpaper. Lampreys and hagfishes also have a skeleton made of cartilage, but they have no jaws or scales.

Amphibian
A vertebrate that lives at first in water and then on land.

Gill
A structure used by some animals to breathe in water.

Metamorphosis
A major change in form that occurs as some animals develop into adults.

Swim bladder
A gas-filled organ that allows a bony fish to move up and down in the water.

Amphibians

Amphibians include about 4,000 species of frogs, toads, and salamanders. The word *amphibian* comes from two Greek words meaning "double life." This refers to the fact that many amphibians spend part of their life in water and part on land. Recall from Chapter 1 that frogs begin their life as tadpoles that live in water. After a while, a tadpole grows legs, loses its gills and tail, and develops into an adult frog. This change is called **metamorphosis**. The frog may spend much of its life on land.

Adult amphibians breathe with lungs or through their skin. The skin is thin and moist. To keep from drying out, amphibians must stay near water or in damp places. Since amphibian eggs do not have shells, they must be laid in water or where the ground is wet.

Reptiles

Reptile

An egg-laying vertebrate that breathes with lungs.

Snakes, lizards, turtles, alligators, and crocodiles are **reptiles**. There are about 7,000 species of reptiles. Some reptiles, such as sea turtles, live mostly in water. Others, such as tortoises, live on land. The skin of reptiles is scaly and watertight, so reptiles can live in dry places without drying out. Some tortoises, for example, live in deserts where water is scarce. Most reptiles lay eggs on land. The eggs have a soft shell that keeps the young inside from drying out. All reptiles breathe with lungs. Reptiles that live in water must come to the surface to breathe.

Dinosaurs were reptiles. The first dinosaurs appeared about 235 million years ago. Some dinosaurs were taller than a four-story building and heavier than ten elephants. However, many dinosaurs were no bigger than a house cat. All dinosaurs became extinct about 65 million years ago.

Amphibians have smooth, moist skin. The skin of reptiles is dry and scaly.

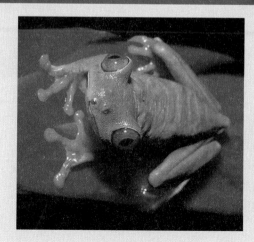

Birds

There are more than 9,000 species of birds, and almost all of them can fly. Feathers make flight possible by providing lift and streamlining the body. Birds also have hollow bones, which keep their skeleton light. Flying requires a lot of energy, so birds cannot go long without eating. Feathers act like a warm coat that keeps heat inside the bird's body. All birds breathe with lungs and have a horny beak. Birds lay eggs that are covered by a hard shell.

Mammals

Mammary gland
A milk-producing structure on the chest or abdomen of a mammal.

Mammals are named for their **mammary glands**, which are milk-producing structures on the chest or abdomen. As shown in the photo, female mammals nurse their young with milk from these glands. Mammals also have hair covering most of their body. Hair helps keep in body heat. Most mammals live on land, but some, such as whales and porpoises, live in water. All mammals have lungs.

Most of the 4,400 species of mammals have young that develop inside the mother. These mammals include bears, elephants, mice, and humans. About 300 species of mammals, including opossums and kangaroos, have young that develop in a pouch on the mother. The duck-billed platypus and the spiny anteater are the only mammals that lay eggs.

Mammals feed their young with milk produced by mammary glands.

Self-Check

1. What three features do all vertebrates have?
2. How does a trout's skeleton differ from a shark's skeleton?
3. What happens during metamorphosis in a frog?
4. Why are a reptile's eggs able to survive in dry places?
5. What two features do mammals have that other vertebrates do not have?

Cnidarian
An invertebrate animal that includes jellyfish, sea anemones, corals, and hydras.

Invertebrate
An animal that does not have a backbone.

Radial symmetry
An arrangement of body parts that resembles the arrangement of spokes on a wheel.

Tentacle
An armlike body part in invertebrates that is used for capturing prey.

Every animal that is not a vertebrate is called an **invertebrate**. An invertebrate is an animal that does not have a backbone. Invertebrates make up about 97 percent of all animal species and belong to more than thirty phyla. You will learn about eight of those phyla in this lesson.

Sponges

Sponges are the simplest animals. Their bodies consist of two layers of cells without any tissues or organs. All of the 10,000 species of sponges live in water. Sponges strain food particles out of the water as the water moves through their body. The water enters through pores in the body wall. If you use a natural bath sponge, you are using the skeleton of a dead sponge.

Cnidarians

Cnidarians include animals such as jellyfish, sea anemones, corals, and hydras. There are about 10,000 species of cnidarians. All live in water. Cnidarians have a type of body symmetry known as **radial symmetry**. In radial symmetry, body parts are arranged like spokes on a wheel. You can see the radial symmetry of a sea anemone in the photo. Cnidarians have armlike **tentacles** with stinging cells. The tentacles capture small prey and push them into the body, where they are digested.

The tentacles of this sea anemone show radial symmetry.

Did You Know?

Doctors sometimes use leeches to remove blood from the wounds of patients who have had surgery.

Flatworms

As their name suggests, **flatworms** are flat and thin. Their bodies have a left half and a right half that are the same. This type of body plan is known as **bilateral symmetry**. There are more than 18,000 species of flatworms. Most are parasites that live on or inside other animals. An example of a flatworm that is a parasite is the tapeworm. Tapeworms live in the intestines of vertebrates, including humans. In the intestine, tapeworms absorb nutrients through their skin. People can get tapeworms when they eat infected meat that has not been cooked completely.

Roundworms

Roundworms have long, round bodies that come to a point at the ends. Like flatworms, roundworms have bilateral symmetry. Most of the 80,000 species of roundworms are not parasitic. They may live in the soil or in water. Some soil-dwelling roundworms help plants by eating insect pests. About 150 species of roundworms are parasites, and many of them live in humans. For example, hookworms settle in the intestine and feed on blood. Hookworms enter the body by boring through the skin. That usually happens when people walk barefoot in places that are not clean.

Segmented Worms

Segmented worms have a body that is divided into many sections, or segments. These worms may live in the soil, in freshwater, or in the ocean. The earthworm is the most familiar of the 15,000 species of segmented worms. Earthworms tunnel through the soil, eating small food particles. Their tunnels loosen the soil and allow air to enter it, which helps plants grow. Leeches are another kind of segmented worm. Many leeches eat small invertebrates, but some leeches are parasites. Leeches that are parasites attach to the skin of a vertebrate and feed on its blood. While feeding, leeches release a chemical that keeps the blood flowing.

Mollusks

There are more than 112,000 species of mollusks. Some live on land, while others live in freshwater or in the

A squid uses its tentacles to capture prey.

Arthropods shed their external skeleton as they grow.

ocean. Snails and slugs make up the largest group of mollusks. Snails have a coiled shell, but slugs have no shell at all. Another group of mollusks includes clams, scallops, and oysters. Their shell is made of two hinged pieces that can open and close. Squids and octopuses have no outer shells. These mollusks can swim quickly as they hunt for fish and other animals. As you can see in the photo, they capture prey with their tentacles.

Arthropods

Arthropods are the largest group of invertebrates. They make up more than three-fourths of all animal species. The major groups of arthropods are crustaceans, arachnids, centipedes, millipedes, and insects. Arthropods are segmented animals with jointed legs. Most arthropods also have antennae, which they use to feel, taste, or smell.

Arthropod
A member of the largest group of invertebrates, which includes insects.

All arthropods have an external skeleton that supports the body and protects the tissues inside. If you ever cracked open the claw of a crab, you know how hard this skeleton can be. Arthropods can bend their bodies because they have joints in their legs and between their body segments. However, an external skeleton is not able to grow as an internal skeleton does. For that reason, an arthropod must shed its skeleton to grow in size. The shedding process is called **molting**, which is shown in the photo. An arthropod begins to produce a new skeleton before it molts. After the animal molts, the skeleton takes a few days to harden completely. The soft-shelled crabs served in restaurants are crabs that have just molted.

Echinoderms

Echinoderms include sea stars, sea urchins, sand dollars, and sea cucumbers. All 7,000 species of echinoderms live in the ocean. Like cnidarians, echinoderms have radial symmetry. Find the echinoderm's **tube feet** in the photo. The tube feet attach firmly to surfaces. Echinoderms use their tube feet to move.

Echinoderms, such as this sea star, are invertebrates with tube feet and radial symmetry.

Arachnid

A class of arthropods that includes spiders, scorpions, mites, and ticks.

Crustacean

A class of arthropods that includes crabs, lobsters, crayfish, and sow bugs.

Many people fear spiders. How are spiders helpful to humans?

Crabs, lobsters, and crayfish are **crustaceans**. Most of the 40,000 species of crustaceans live in rivers, lakes, and oceans. Crustaceans have five pairs of legs. Some of the legs have small claws that help the animal handle food. The two legs closest to the head usually have powerful claws used for protection. Sow bugs and pill bugs are crustaceans that live on land. You can often find them under rocks and in other moist places.

Spiders, scorpions, mites, and ticks are **arachnids**. There are about 70,000 species of arachnids. Almost all arachnids live on land. They have four pairs of legs. Spiders produce threads of silk to spin webs and build nests. Most spiders eat insects, but some also catch small fish or frogs. Spiders capture their prey by injecting it with a poison. Scorpions also use poison to capture prey. They use a stinger to inject the poison. Mites and ticks include species that live on the human body. Mites feed on hair and dead skin. Ticks pierce the skin and feed on blood.

All of the 2,500 species of centipedes and the 10,000 species of millipedes live on land. Their bodies have up to 175 segments. Notice in the photo that centipedes have one pair of legs on each body segment. They can run quickly because their legs are long. Centipedes use their poison claws to kill insects and other prey. Millipedes have two pairs of legs on each body segment. Their legs are short, so millipedes move slowly. Most millipedes eat dead plant matter in the soil.

Centipedes have a pair of legs on each body segment.

Insects

The 700,000 species of insects live almost everywhere except in the deep ocean. Insects include mosquitoes, flies, ants, and beetles. Insects have three pairs of legs. Most have one or two pairs of wings. Insects are the only invertebrates that can fly. Like frogs, most insects go through metamorphosis. Study the metamorphosis of a butterfly in the diagram.

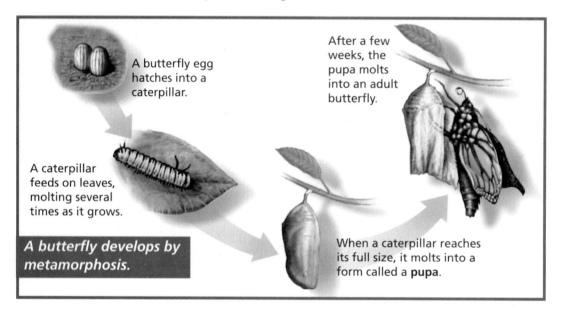

A butterfly egg hatches into a caterpillar.

After a few weeks, the pupa molts into an adult butterfly.

A caterpillar feeds on leaves, molting several times as it grows.

A butterfly develops by metamorphosis.

When a caterpillar reaches its full size, it molts into a form called a **pupa**.

Pupa

A stage in the development of some insects that leads to the adult stage.

Many insects are pests. Grasshoppers and caterpillars destroy crops. Fleas and mosquitoes may carry microorganisms that cause diseases. However, many insects are helpful to humans. Bees and other insects spread pollen from flower to flower. Without pollen, the flowers could not produce fruits. Insects also make useful products, such as honey, wax, and silk.

Self-Check

1. How do sponges feed?
2. Contrast radial symmetry and bilateral symmetry.
3. Give an example of a flatworm, roundworm, and segmented worm.
4. How do echinoderms move?
5. Explain why arthropods molt.

- Biologists classify animals based on the animals' similar features.
- The classification system used by biologists has seven levels.
- Every species has a two-word scientific name consisting of its genus and its species label.
- Vertebrates are animals that have a backbone.
- Fishes live in water and breathe with gills.
- Amphibians live in water or in damp places on land.
- Reptiles can live in dry places because their skin is watertight.
- Birds have feathers and hollow bones. These features make flight possible.
- Mammals have hair and feed their young with milk from mammary glands.

- Invertebrates are animals without a backbone.
- Sponges have no tissues or organs.
- Cnidarians have radial symmetry and use tentacles to capture prey.
- Most flatworms and some roundworms are parasites.
- Segmented worms have a body that is divided into many segments.
- Many mollusks have a hard shell. Squids and octopuses capture prey with their tentacles.
- Echinoderms have radial symmetry and use tube feet to move.
- Arthropods have a segmented body, external skeleton, and jointed legs.

Science Words

amphibian, 54	gill, 54	scientific name, 50
arachnid, 61	invertebrate, 57	segmented worm, 58
arthropod, 59	mammary gland, 56	species, 49
bilateral symmetry, 58	metamorphosis, 54	swim bladder, 54
cartilage, 53	molting, 60	taxonomy, 47
classify, 46	phylum, 48	tentacle, 57
cnidarian, 57	pupa, 62	tube foot, 60
crustacean, 61	radial symmetry, 57	vertebra, 53
flatworm, 58	reptile, 55	vertebrate, 53
	roundworm, 58	

Vocabulary Review

Number your paper from 1 to 8. Then choose the word or words from the Word Bank that best complete each sentence. Write the answer on your paper.

WORD BANK
bilateral symmetry
invertebrates
mammary glands
metamorphosis
scientific name
swim bladder
taxonomy
vertebrates

1. Animals that have a backbone are called _____.

2. A fish uses its _____ to move up or down in the water.

3. Animals with _____ have bodies with a left half and right half that are the same.

4. An animal's _____ consists of its genus and its species label.

5. The science of classifying organisms according to their similarities is called _____

6. Female bears produce milk from their _____

7. The change of a tadpole into a frog is an example of _____

8. Sponges, cnidarians, and mollusks are all _____

Concept Review

Number your paper from 1 to 10. Then choose the answer that best completes each sentence. Write the letter of the answer on your paper.

1. In the classification system of organisms, the level of _____ is between phylum and order.

    a. kingdom   **b.** class   **c.** genus

2. The genus of the western rattlesnake, *Crotalus viridis,* is _____.

    a. *viridis*   **b.** *Crotalus*   **c.** western

3. Squids capture prey with their _____.

    a. tentacles   **b.** tube feet   **c.** shells

4. Sharks have _____ scales.

    a. smooth   **b.** large   **c.** toothlike

5. _____ allows crustaceans to grow larger in size.

    a. Bilateral symmetry **b.** Molting   **c.** Metamorphosis

6. The bodies of _____ are made of segments.

    a. insects   **b.** flatworms   **c.** cnidarians

7. A bird's feathers and _____ help it to fly.

    a. beak   **b.** hollow bones   **c.** feet

8. All vertebrates have _____ skeleton.

    a. an internal   **b.** an external   **c.** a bony

9. _____ allow animals to live on land.

    a. Gills   **b.** Lungs   **c.** Scales

10. Fishes, sponges, and mollusks belong to the same _____.

    a. kingdom   **b.** phylum   **c.** class

Critical Thinking

Write the answer to each of the following questions.

1. A biologist is studying vertebrates in the desert. Would she be more likely to find amphibians or reptiles during her studies? Explain your answer.

2. Suppose you found a small arthropod under a rock. Using only a hand lens, how could you tell whether the animal is an arachnid or an insect?

Test Taking Tip | Answer all questions you are sure of first. Then go back and answer the others.

Chapter 4

Classifying Plant Groups

W here have you seen plants today? You probably passed many of them on your way to school. Plants come in all shapes and sizes. They include tiny moss smaller than your fingernail and giant redwood trees 30 stories tall! These plants are very different from one another. However, they are alike in some ways. In this chapter, you will learn how plants are alike and how they are different.

ORGANIZE YOUR THOUGHTS

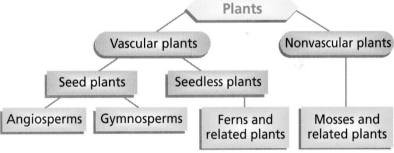

Plants
- Vascular plants
  - Seed plants
    - Angiosperms
    - Gymnosperms
  - Seedless plants
    - Ferns and related plants
- Nonvascular plants
  - Mosses and related plants

Goals for Learning

▶ To understand that plants are classified according to their similar structures

▶ To explain the difference between vascular and nonvascular plants

▶ To explain the differences and similarities between plants with seeds and seedless plants

▶ To describe angiosperms, gymnosperms, ferns, and mosses

After reading this lesson, you should be able to

▶ explain how plants are classified.

▶ describe the history of the classification of plants.

▶ tell the difference between vascular and nonvascular plants.

Genus
A group of living things that includes separate species.

Vascular plant
A plant that has tubelike cells.

Vascular tissue
A group of plant cells that form tubes through which food and water move.

Scientists have discovered over 300,000 kinds of plants. That sounds like a lot. However, scientists think even more kinds have yet to be discovered. About 1,000,000 kinds of plants may exist that have not been found and named. Most of these plants live in the tropical rain forests.

Scientists divide this huge number of plants into groups to make them easier to study. They classify plants according to whether they have body parts such as seeds, tubes, roots, stems, and leaves. The three main groups of plants are seed plants, ferns, and mosses. The groups that contain ferns and mosses also contain related plants. However, ferns and mosses form the greatest number in each of these groups.

History of Classification

The classification of plants started more than 2,000 years ago. The Greek philosopher Aristotle first classified plants and animals. He and his student Theophrastus listed the names of almost 500 plants. In 1753, Carolus Linnaeus, a Swede, developed a new method to classify plants and animals. Today, organisms are classified based on his system.

Under this system, organisms have a two-word name. The first word is the **genus**. For example, maple trees belong to the genus *Acer*. The scientific name of all maple trees begins with the word *Acer*. The second word is the species. Each kind of maple tree has its own species name. The scientific name of the sugar maple tree is *Acer saccharum*. The scientific name of the red maple is *Acer rubrum*.

Vascular and Nonvascular Plants

Seed plants and ferns are vascular plants. **Vascular plants** have tubelike cells. *Vascular* means "vessel" or "tube." These cells form tissue called **vascular tissue**. The tissue

Did You Know?

The tallest living thing in the world is one of California's redwood trees. It is 112 meters (368 ft.) tall. The oldest living thing in the world is a 4,060-year-old bristlecone pine tree in California.

forms tubes that transport food and water through the plant. Vascular plants have well-developed leaves, stems, and roots.

Vascular tissue is important in two ways. First, it allows food and water to be transported over a distance. Plants can grow in places where water is not always present. Second, vascular tissue is thick and provides support for a plant. This also allows plants to grow tall.

The veins of a leaf are vascular tissue.

Nonvascular plant
A plant that does not have tubelike cells.

Mosses are nonvascular plants. **Nonvascular plants** do not have tubelike cells. These plants are short and must have constant contact with moisture. They do not have tubes to transport water or to support them. These small plants usually grow in damp, shady places on the ground and on the sides of trees and rocks. Unlike vascular plants, nonvascular plants do not have true leaves, stems, or roots.

Self-Check

1. What are the three main groups of plants?
2. Who developed the classification system of organisms that is used today?
3. What two groups make up the scientific name of each kind of organism?
4. How are vascular and nonvascular plants different?
5. What are two ways that vascular tissue is important?

Angiosperm
A flowering plant.

Embryo
A beginning plant.

Seed
A plant part that contains a beginning plant and stored food.

What are some seeds that you eat?

Recall that scientists classify plants into three main groups. Seed plants are different from the other plant groups because they use seeds to reproduce. A **seed** is a plant part that contains a beginning plant and stored food. The beginning plant is called an **embryo**. A seed has a seed coat that holds in moisture. When conditions are right, the embryo grows into a full-sized plant.

Seed plants have the most advanced vascular tissue of all plants. They have well-developed leaves, stems, and roots.

Seed plants have many sizes and shapes. The duckweed plant that floats on water may be just one millimeter long. Giant redwood trees are the largest plants in the world. A pine tree has long, thin needles. A rose has soft petals. The different sizes and shapes of seed plants help them to live in many different places. Grass, trees, garden flowers, bushes, vines, and cacti are all seed plants.

Seed plants are the largest group of plants. They are divided into two subgroups. These are flowering plants and nonflowering plants.

Angiosperms

Most species of plants are **angiosperms**, or flowering plants. The word *angiosperm* is made from the Greek words *angeion*, "capsule," and *sperma*, "seed." A capsule, or fruit, protects the seeds of angiosperms. The fruit forms from part of the flower. Flowers come in many shapes and colors.

The flowers of some plants are colorful and showy.

Dicots and Monocots

Angiosperms are divided into two kinds, monocots and dicots. Most angiosperms are dicots. **Dicots** have two "seed leaves" or two leaves on the embryo inside the seed. You can see this by looking at a bean, which is a large dicot seed. If you split a bean apart, you may be able to see the two leaves on the tiny embryo. When a bean is planted, the plant appears with two leaves. If you look closely at the leaves, you will see that the veins are crisscrossed. This crisscross pattern of veins is another property of dicots.

The number of species of dicots is more than 165,000. Some dicots, such as oak and ash, are trees that provide shade or produce wood for furniture. Animals eat dicots in the form of fruits and vegetables. Most flowering plants are dicots. Examples are roses and sunflowers.

Monocots have only one seed leaf. When a monocot starts growing from a seed, a single leaf appears. The veins in the leaf of a monocot are parallel. This means they all go in the same direction. You can see parallel veins in a blade of grass, for example. There are more than 50,000 species of monocots. They include corn, wheat, and rice. Grasses that cattle eat are monocots. Some flowers, such as lilies and orchids, are monocots.

Dicot
An angiosperm that has two seed leaves.

Monocot
An angiosperm that has one seed leaf.

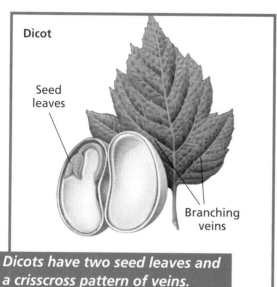

Dicot

Seed leaves

Branching veins

Dicots have two seed leaves and a crisscross pattern of veins.

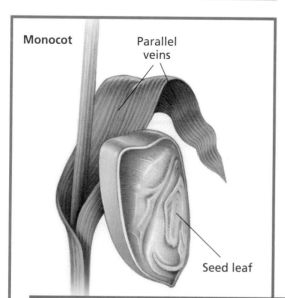

Monocot

Parallel veins

Seed leaf

Monocots have one seed leaf and a parallel pattern of veins.

Gymnosperms

Nonflowering seed plants are called **gymnosperms**. They do not produce flowers. The word *gymnosperm* means "naked seed." The seeds of gymnosperms are not surrounded by a fruit. The seeds are produced inside cones. For example, the seeds of pine trees form on the scales of cones.

Conifers and Other Gymnosperms

There are about 700 species of gymnosperms. The major group of gymnosperms is conifers. **Conifers** are cone-bearing gymnosperms. There are about 600 species of conifers. All conifers are woody shrubs or trees. They make up most of the forests around the world. Pines, spruces, and firs are conifers. Plants such as junipers, yews, and spruces decorate the landscape of many homes. Conifers are a major source of lumber. For example, people make the wood frame of many houses out of pine. Conifers are the main source of paper and other wood products.

Most conifers have green leaves all year. Therefore, they are called evergreens. They lose only some of their leaves at any time. The leaves of conifers are shaped like needles. They do not lose water as easily as the broad leaves on other trees do. This makes it easier for conifers to live in dry places where trees must store water for a long time.

Conifers have cones and needle-shaped leaves.

Conifers grow in places where other plants cannot grow, such as shallow, rocky soil and along seashores.

Besides conifers, there are other gymnosperms. The ginkgo tree is one of the most familiar. Ginkgo trees have peculiar fan-shaped leaves. These trees are planted along many city streets because they are able to survive pollution better than other trees. Ginkgo trees also are more resistant to disease than other trees. Other types of gymnosperms are tropical trees that look like palm trees or ferns.

The leaves of the ginkgo tree are shaped like fans.

Self-Check

1. What are other names for flowering plants and nonflowering seed plants?
2. What are the differences between dicots and monocots?
3. Name two plants that are dicots and two that are monocots.
4. Why are the seeds of gymnosperms called "naked seeds"?
5. Why are conifers able to live where other plants cannot?

INVESTIGATION

Identifying Angiosperms and Gymnosperms

Materials

✓ 5 different kinds of leaves

✓ pencil

✓ paper

Purpose

To identify angiosperms and gymnosperms by looking at their leaves

Procedure

1. Copy the data table below on a sheet of paper.

Leaf	Shape	Angiosperm or gymnosperm	Vein pattern	Monocot or dicot
Leaf 1				
Leaf 2				
Leaf 3				
Leaf 4				
Leaf 5				

2. Look at the leaves that your teacher shows you. On another sheet of paper, draw each leaf. Be sure to include some of the veins in your sketch. Number the leaves 1 through 5.

3. Examine the shape of each leaf. Is it needle-shaped? Is it round and flat? Is the edge smooth or ragged? You might think of other ways to describe the leaf. Record what you see in the first column on your table.

4. Classify each leaf as belonging to an angiosperm or gymnosperm. Use the shape of the leaf to decide. Record your answer on your table.

5. Observe the vein pattern in each leaf. Are the veins crisscross or parallel? Record your findings on your table. If you cannot see veins in a leaf, leave its box blank.

6. Classify each leaf that belongs to an angiosperm as a dicot or a monocot. Use the vein pattern of the leaf to decide. Record your answer on your table.

7. Draw a line through any empty boxes that remain on your table.

Questions

1. How do the leaves of gymnosperms differ from the leaves of angiosperms?

2. Compare the shapes of the leaves of monocots to the leaves of dicots.

3. After you were done, did any empty boxes remain on your table? Why?

4. What are some other ways that the leaves you examined are different?

Explore Further

Make a leaf collection. Collect leaves from houseplants and plants in your yard or a park, or ask permission to collect leaves in a garden store. Dry the leaves between layers of newspaper stacked under heavy books. Mount each leaf on a piece of paper. Identify each leaf as you did in the Investigation. Use reference books to find the two-word scientific names of the plants.

Objectives

After reading this lesson, you should be able to

▶ list vascular and nonvascular plants that are seedless.

▶ describe similarities and differences between ferns and seed plants.

▶ describe mosses and how they grow.

There are two main groups of seedless plants. The largest group includes ferns and related plants. Like seed plants, ferns are vascular plants. Unlike seed plants, they do not have seeds. The second group of seedless plants is mosses and related plants. They are different from ferns because they are nonvascular plants.

Ferns

The largest group of seedless vascular plants is **ferns**. There are about 9,000 species of ferns in the world. Many of them are tropical plants. They range in size from tiny, filmy plants to large tree-like plants. Like other vascular plants, ferns have well-developed leaves, stems, and roots.

Ferns are used as decorative plants because of their leaves. You may have seen ferns in flower arrangements or in pots. The leaves, or **fronds**, usually are large and flat. They are divided into small sections, or leaflets, that spread out from a center rib. If you look closely, you can see new fronds that are curled up. They uncurl as they grow.

Fern
A seedless vascular plant.

Frond
A large feathery leaf of a fern.

Sori
Clusters of reproductive cells on the underside of a frond.

Spore
The reproductive cell of some organisms.

On the underside of fronds, you can see small dots called **sori**. Sori are clusters that contain the reproductive cells of ferns. These cells are called **spores**. When the spores are ripe, the sori burst open and release the spores into the air.

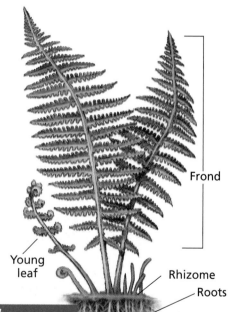

Young leaf

Frond

Rhizome

Roots

Young fern fronds uncoil as they grow.

After they are released, spores must land in a moist place. If not, they will dry up because they do not have a seed coat to hold in moisture. Spores that drop in a moist place produce a tiny plant. The plant must have constant moisture to grow. Seeds, on the other hand, carry moisture and food inside their seed coats. Seeds usually survive longer than spores when conditions are dry. This explains why there are more seed plants than seedless plants.

Mosses

Moss
A nonvascular plant that has simple parts.

Rhizoid
A tiny root-like thread of a moss plant.

Scientists have found about 14,000 species of mosses. A **moss** is a nonvascular plant that has simple leaf-like and stem-like parts. It does not have well-developed leaves, stems, and roots. Mosses do not have vascular tissue to transport water. They must live in moist, shady places.

Mosses grow best where the air is full of moisture and the soil is wet. They get water through root-like threads called **rhizoids**. Woodlands and the edges of streams are common homes for mosses. Mosses look like little trees and often form carpet-like mats on the forest floor.

Like ferns, mosses reproduce by means of spores. Millions of tiny spores form inside spore cases on special stalks. The spore case breaks open when it is ripe. It shoots the spores into the air. The spores make new plants when they fall on moist soil. One reason for moss survival is that mosses produce great numbers of spores. Some spores have been known to survive for many years and still grow moss plants.

Mosses can form a carpet-like mat.

Humus
Decayed plant and animal matter that is part of the topsoil.

Soil and Bog Builders

Because mosses are so tiny, they can grow in places where other plants cannot take root. Mosses grow within the bark of fallen trees, within cracks in rocks, and in thin soils. In this way, they help to form soil. When moss plants die, they form humus. **Humus** is the part of the soil made by dead plant and animal matter. It is very rich and helps plants to grow.

Mosses of the genus *Sphagnum* are known as bog builders. A bog is wet, spongy ground that is formed from rotted moss and other plant matter. Air does not reach the dead plants. The lack of oxygen keeps the plants from breaking down, or decaying, quickly. Over time, this plant matter becomes tightly pressed together and forms peat. Most of the plant matter in peat is sphagnum moss. Peat moss is mixed with soil to improve gardens.

SCIENCE IN YOUR LIFE

Energy from ferns and mosses

Ferns that lived millions of years ago are important to your life today. About 300 million years ago, forests and swamps contained many ferns, some the size of trees. Over time, these ferns died, and layers of dead ferns and other plants built up. Pressure and heat on the deep layers of plant material caused coal to form. Coal is burned to produce steam in power plants, which produce electricity.

Peat is also used as a source of energy, especially in parts of Europe. In Ireland, for example, peat is cut into loaf-sized chunks and burned in stoves and fireplaces. The peat burns slowly, like charcoal.

Self-Check

1. What groups of plants do not have seeds?
2. What does *nonvascular* mean?
3. Why are there more seed plants than seedless plants?
4. Why do spores need a moist place to land?
5. Where do mosses need to live and why?

- Plants are classified according to whether they have body parts such as seeds, tubes, roots, stems, and leaves.

- The three main groups of plants are seed plants, ferns and related plants, and mosses and related plants.

- Vascular plants have vascular tissue that forms tubes for transporting food and water.

- Nonvascular plants do not have vascular tissue, so they cannot transport water far.

- Flowering plants are called angiosperms. The seeds of angiosperms are surrounded by a fruit.

- Angiosperms are divided into two groups. Dicots have two seed leaves. Their leaves have a crisscross pattern. Monocots have one seed leaf. The veins in their leaves are parallel.

- Gymnosperms are nonflowering plants that have seeds. Their seeds are not surrounded by a fruit.

- The major group of gymnosperms is conifers.

- Conifers bear cones and have needle-like leaves. Most are evergreen.

- Gingko trees are another kind of gymnosperm. They have fan-shaped leaves.

- Ferns and mosses have no seeds. Ferns are vascular plants. Mosses are nonvascular plants.

- Ferns and mosses reproduce by spores.

Science Words		
angiosperm, 70	monocot, 71
conifer, 72	moss, 77
dicot, 71	nonvascular plant, 69
embryo, 70	rhizoid, 77
fern, 76	seed, 70
frond, 76	sori, 76
genus, 68	spore, 76
gymnosperm, 72	vascular plant, 68
humus, 78	vascular tissue, 68

Chapter 4 REVIEW

Vocabulary Review

Number your paper from 1 to 14. Then choose the word or words from the Word Bank that best complete each sentence. Write the answer on your paper.

WORD BANK

angiosperm

conifer

dicot

embryo

fern

frond

gymnosperm

monocots

moss

nonvascular
  plants

rhizoids

seed

spores

vascular plant

1. Mosses get water through root-like threads called _____.

2. _____ is a nonvascular plant.

3. The large feathery leaf of a fern is called a(n) _____.

4. A(n) _____ has a protective coat around a plant embryo.

5. Mosses are examples of _____.

6. The leaves of _____ have parallel veins.

7. A nonflowering seed plant is a(n) _____.

8. The seeds of a(n) _____ are usually surrounded by fruit.

9. A(n) _____ is a cone-bearing gymnosperm.

10. A(n) _____ is a seedless, vascular plant.

11. _____ are reproductive cells of ferns and mosses.

12. An angiosperm that has two seed leaves is called a(n) _____.

13. A plant that has tissue that forms tubes is called a(n) _____.

14. A seed contains stored food and a(n) _____.

Concept Review

Number your paper from 1 to 4. Then choose the answer that best completes each sentence. Write the letter of the answer on your paper.

1. Vascular tissue forms _____ that transport food and water.

   a. tubes   **b.** hollows   **c.** leaves

2. All angiosperms have _____.

   a. one seed leaf   **b.** two seed leaves   **c.** flowers

3. Most conifers have _____ that are green all year round.

   a. broad leaves   **b.** flowers   **c.** needle-shaped leaves

4. Plants that must live in moist, shady places are _____.

   a. angiosperms   **b.** mosses   **c.** conifers

Critical Thinking

Write the answer to each of the following questions.

1. The scientific name of a certain apple tree is *Malus domestica*. What is the genus and species of the apple tree?

2. Suppose a plant does not have seeds. Can you tell if the plant is vascular or nonvascular? Explain your answer.

Test Taking Tip | When choosing answers from a word bank, answer all of the questions you know first. Then, study the remaining words to choose the answers for the questions you are not sure about.

Chapter

5

Bacteria, Protists, and Fungi

Name a harsh environment where you think no organism can survive. Chances are, bacteria live there. Some bacteria live in hot, acid waters of sulfur springs. Some live in extremely salty waters, such as the Dead Sea in the Middle East. Some bacteria live where there is no oxygen, such as at the bottom of this swamp. Bacteria live almost every other place too. In fact, bacteria, protists, and fungi are all around you, even if you do not notice them.

ORGANIZE YOUR THOUGHTS

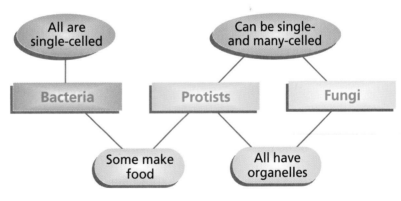

All are single-celled

Can be single- and many-celled

Bacteria

Protists

Fungi

Some make food

All have organelles

Goals for Learning

▶ To identify the properties of bacteria

▶ To explore the features and different kinds of protists

▶ To describe the properties and life activities of fungi

The greatest number of organisms in the world are bacteria. They are members of the kingdom Monera. More than 10,000 known species of bacteria live almost everywhere on Earth.

Properties of Bacteria

Bacteria are single-celled organisms. Most bacterial cells are very small. They can be seen only by using a microscope. The cells of other organisms are usually at least 50 times larger.

Bacteria are the simplest organisms. The inside of a bacterial cell lacks organelles. Recall that organelles are tiny structures in cells that do particular jobs. All other organisms have organelles. This characteristic sets bacteria apart from all other organisms.

Fossil evidence suggests that bacteria appeared on earth at least 3.5 billion years ago. For about 1 billion years, they were the only form of living thing on Earth. Some modern-day bacteria may be like those first bacteria.

One way that biologists classify bacteria is by their shape. Bacteria can look like rods, spirals, or spheres. Spherical, or round, bacteria often form long chains. Some form clusters that look like a bunch of grapes.

Most bacteria are shaped like rods, spirals, or spheres.

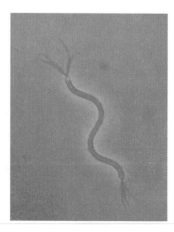
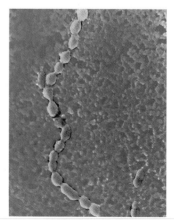

Life Activities of Bacteria

Although bacteria are single-celled and simple, they are complete organisms. Each bacterial cell carries out all of the basic functions of life. For example, bacteria use many different ways to obtain energy. Some bacteria break down dead organisms or waste matter. Others use sunlight to make food. Still other bacteria get energy from minerals, such as iron. In fact, bacteria have more different ways to get energy than any other kind of organism.

Bacteria in this hot spring trap sunlight to make food and give the water a blue-green color.

Many kinds of bacteria need oxygen to carry out respiration. However, some bacteria are poisoned by oxygen. They live only where oxygen is not present, such as at the bottom of swamps. These bacteria produce methane out of hydrogen and carbon dioxide. The methane bubbles out of the water as marsh gas.

Binary fission
Reproduction in which a bacterial cell divides into two cells that look the same as the original.

Saprophyte
An organism that decomposes dead organisms or waste matter.

Bacteria reproduce by a process called **binary fission**. The bacterial cell divides into two cells that look the same as the original cell. Some bacteria can reproduce every 20 minutes.

Helpful Bacteria

Many bacteria are helpful to other organisms in two ways. First, some bacteria recycle nutrients, such as carbon and nitrogen. They break down, or decompose, dead organisms or waste matter. Organisms that do this are called **saprophytes**. Some of the broken-down nutrients are returned to the soil. Plants use them. Animals get these nutrients by eating the plants or by eating other animals that eat plants.

The swellings on the roots of this pea plant contain bacteria that change nitrogen into ammonia.

Second, bacteria help plants to get nitrogen. Nitrogen is plentiful in the atmosphere. However, plants cannot absorb, or take it in, from the air. The nitrogen must be changed into ammonia before the plants can use it. Some kinds of bacteria change the nitrogen into ammonia. They live inside the roots of particular plants. In return, the plants provide the bacteria with food. The plants and the bacteria benefit, or help, each other. A closeness in which two organisms live together and help, each other is called **mutualism**.

Many bacteria are useful to humans in two ways. First, bacteria help to produce some of the food we eat. Do you ever eat cheese, sour cream, or yogurt? Bacteria break down milk to produce these foods. Bacteria also change cucumbers into pickles and cabbage into sauerkraut.

Second, bacteria can produce many different materials that are helpful to humans. For example, chemical companies use bacteria to make vitamins. Some bacteria make antibiotics, materials that kill other kinds of bacteria. Scientists can change some bacteria to make particular chemicals. For example, scientists have caused some bacteria to produce a drug called insulin. Many people with the disease diabetes need this drug.

Harmful Bacteria

Some bacteria cause food to spoil. For example, pasteurized milk still contains some bacteria. They are harmless but eventually will sour the milk. Refrigerating food helps to prevent spoiling. Bacteria grow slowly at low temperatures. Food that looks or tastes bad must usually be thrown away instead of eaten.

Other bacteria are more than just a nuisance. Some bacteria cause disease. *Salmonella* can get into food and cause serious illness if eaten. The food usually does not look or taste bad. One way to kill *Salmonella* is to cook meat thoroughly.

The table below lists several other diseases that bacteria cause. Some bacteria harm the body by producing poisons called **toxins**. Bacterial toxins are among the most powerful poisons known. A single gram of botulism toxin can kill a million people.

Toxin

A poison produced by bacteria or other organisms.

Diseases Caused by Bacteria

Disease	Type of bacteria	Way of transmission
Botulism	*Clostridium botulinum*	incorrectly preserved food
Gonorrhea	*Neisseria gonorrhoeae*	sexual contact
Lyme disease	*Borrelia burgdorferi*	tick bites
Tetanus	*Clostridium tetani*	dirty wounds
Strep throat	*Streptococcus pyogenes*	close physical contact

What products that contain antibacterial agents have you used?

Doctors prescribe, or give, antibiotics, such as penicillin to fight bacterial diseases. However, bacteria often develop ways to resist the antibiotic. Household products, such as dish soaps, often contain antibacterial agents. They also may cause bacteria to become resistant. As more bacteria become resistant, scientists must search for new materials to kill the bacteria.

Self-Check

1. Explain how bacteria are different from all other organisms.
2. What are the three shapes that most bacteria have?
3. How do bacteria obtain energy?
4. How do bacteria reproduce?
5. Name two ways in which bacteria are useful to humans.

The Protist kingdom contains more than 60,000 species of organisms. Protists may have features like those of plants, animals, or fungi. However, all plants and animals and most fungi have many cells. Most protists are single-celled, like bacteria. What makes protists different from bacteria? Unlike bacteria, the cells of protists have organelles inside their cells. The cells of plants, animals, and fungi also have organelles.

Algae

Plantlike protists are known as algae. Like plants, algae use the energy in sunlight to make food from carbon dioxide and water.

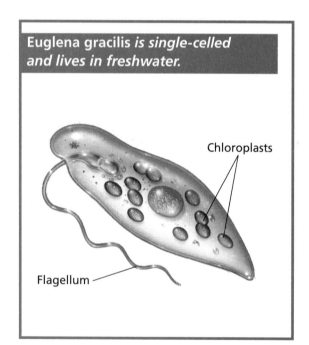

Euglena gracilis *is single-celled and lives in freshwater.*

Chloroplasts

Flagellum

Most algae are aquatic, which means they live in freshwater or salt water. Most are single-celled. Tiny algae float or swim near the surface of the water in vast numbers. Although each is only a single cell, together they produce nearly half the world's carbohydrates. Algae provide food for all the other organisms that live in lakes or the sea. Algae also release oxygen as they make food. About half the oxygen that enters the atmosphere comes from algae.

One kind of single-celled alga is *Euglena gracilis*. Inside its cell are many **chloroplasts**. These structures capture the light energy from the sun that is used to make food. All other algae also have chloroplasts. *Euglena gracilis* moves through the water with a long, whiplike structure called a flagellum.

Chloroplast
A structure that captures the light energy from the sun to make food.

Diatom
Microscopic alga that has a hard shell.

Did You Know?

When you brush your teeth, you may feel the crunch of shells from diatoms. Diatoms are used in making toothpaste.

Other kinds of single-celled algae are **diatoms**. They are found in great numbers in freshwater and in the ocean. They have hard shells that contain silica. This is the same material found in glass. As diatoms die, their shells build up in deposits at the bottom of lakes and the sea. These deposits are mined to make metal polish, soaps, and scouring powders.

Although most algae are single-celled, some are many-celled. One familiar example is seaweed. One kind of seaweed is commonly called sea lettuce. Its blades look like lettuce leaves and can grow up to 60 cm long. Giant seaweeds known as kelps are even larger. Their bodies may stretch 100 m from a shallow ocean floor to the surface. Kelps are harvested and used to thicken food.

Kelps are large, many-celled algae.

Not all algae live in water. Some live in moist places on land, such as in soil or on stones. Algae in the genus *Protococcus* often grow on trees and fence posts. The next time you walk in the woods, look for these algae on the shaded side of tree trunks.

Protozoans

Animal-like protists are called protozoans, which means "first animals." All protozoans are single-celled and can be seen only under a microscope. They live in water, on land, and inside other organisms. Like animals, protozoans cannot make their own food. Instead, they eat bacteria, other protists, or dead organisms. Protozoans are divided into four groups by the way they move.

Amebas are protozoans that move by pushing out parts of their cell. The pushed-out part is called a pseudopod. *Pseudopod* means "false foot." It looks like a foot and pulls the ameba along. In this way, amebas change their shape. Amebas also use their pseudopods to surround and trap other protists for food. Amebas live on rocks and plants in ponds.

An ameba (blue-green) pushes out pseudopods to move and to capture food.

Another group of protozoans is covered with short, hairlike structures known as cilia. A **paramecium** is a common example of a protozoan that has cilia. Like amebas, paramecia often are found in ponds. The cilia on a paramecium move back and forth like tiny oars. They all move in the same direction at the same time. For example, when the cilia push backward, the paramecium moves forward. You can see a picture of a paramecium on page 92.

A third group of protozoans uses flagella to push or pull themselves around. These protozoans include *Giardia lamblia*, which is a parasite in the intestines of animals.

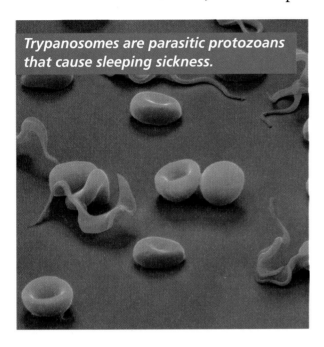

Trypanosomes are parasitic protozoans that cause sleeping sickness.

Humans can get this parasite from water that contains wastes from infected humans or animals. The disease causes tiredness, weight loss, and diarrhea. It is usually not fatal. A much more serious disease is sleeping sickness. This disease is caused by **trypanosomes**. These protozoans live as parasites in the blood of humans and other mammals. They have a flagellum that moves them through the blood. Trypanosomes are spread by the bite of tsetse flies, which live only in Africa. Sleeping sickness is fatal unless treated.

Sporozoan
A protozoan that is a parasite, which lives in blood and causes malaria.

Trypanosoma
A protozoan that is a parasite, which lives in blood and causes sleeping sickness.

The fourth group of protozoans has no means of moving as adults. They reproduce by forming spores, so they are called **sporozoans**. All sporozoans are parasites. They live in the blood of their hosts. The sporozoan *Plasmodium* causes malaria. Mosquitoes in the genus *Anopheles* spread malaria when they draw blood from an infected person. The sporozoans enter the mosquito and reproduce. The mosquito transfers the sporozoans when it bites another person. Malaria can be deadly. Every year, it affects half a billion people and kills nearly three million.

Self-Check
1. How are protists different from bacteria?
2. List two reasons why aquatic algae are important.
3. How are diatoms and kelps different from each other?
4. Describe the three ways that protozoans move.
5. Explain what causes malaria and how the disease is spread.

Anal pore
The opening through which undigested food leaves a paramecium.

Food vacuole
A bubblelike structure where food is digested inside a protozoan.

Gullet
The opening through which a paramecium takes in food.

Like all other organisms, protists must carry out all of the basic life activities. Though most protists are single-celled, their cells are not simple. Each cell must perform the duties of tissues and organs in a plant or animal.

Getting and Digesting Food

You have already learned that algae make their own food but protozoans do not. However, some algae can change the way they feed themselves. For example, *Euglena gracilis* uses its chloroplasts to make food when sunlight is present. In the dark, it acts like a protozoan and eats its food.

Different kinds of protozoans have different ways of getting food. As you read earlier, amebas trap other protists with their pseudopods. Paramecia use their cilia to sweep food particles over their surface. The food moves into an opening called the **gullet** on the paramecium's side. The gullet is like the mouth of an animal.

The diagram shows what happens to the food that enters a paramecium's gullet. The gullet encloses the food within a bubblelike structure called a **food vacuole.** These small packets of food travel all through the paramecium. Chemicals in each food vacuole break down the food. The food then leaves the food vacuole to be used by the paramecium. Food that is not digested leaves the paramecium through an opening called the **anal pore**. Amebas and other protozoans also digest food inside food vacuoles.

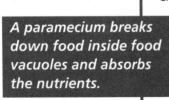

A paramecium breaks down food inside food vacuoles and absorbs the nutrients.

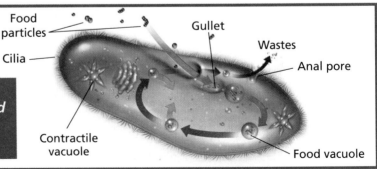

Food particles — Cilia — Gullet — Wastes — Anal pore — Contractile vacuole — Food vacuole

Maintaining Water Balance

Most protists live in a watery environment. Water moves easily through the **cell membrane**. The cell membrane is a thin layer that surrounds and holds a cell together. This movement of water creates a problem. To understand how, consider a single-celled protist that lives in freshwater. The water inside the protist is mixed with many other chemicals. The water outside the protist contains few chemicals but more water molecules. The water molecules are more concentrated, or crowded together. This difference in concentration causes water to move into the protist from the outside. **Osmosis** is the movement of water through a cell membrane. Water molecules move from an area of high concentration to an area of low concentration.

Protists need some water to survive. However, too much water causes the cell to burst. The diagram shows what would happen if the cell could not get rid of some of the water. As more water entered, the protist would grow larger and larger. At some point, the cell membrane would stretch to its breaking point. The protist would burst and die.

Cell membrane
A thin layer that surrounds and holds a cell together.

Contractile vacuole
A structure in a protist that removes water that is not needed.

Osmosis
The movement of water through a cell membrane.

When you add milk to a bowl of dry cereal, the cereal swells. Is the concentration of water higher in the dry cereal or in the milk?

Water enters a protist by osmosis. Too much water would cause the protist to swell and burst.

Water

To avoid bursting, protists release water that is not needed. Structures called **contractile vacuoles** collect the water. They contract, or pull together, to squeeze the water out of the protist. Find a contractile vacuole in the diagram of the paramecium on page 92. Contractile vacuoles carry out the same function that your kidneys perform when you drink too much water. Maintaining water balance is an important function for all organisms.

Sensing and Reacting

All organisms must be able to sense and react to signals in their environment. Many protists have an **eyespot**, which can sense changes in the brightness of light. The eyespot allows algae to move to areas where the light is brighter. With brighter light, they can make food more quickly.

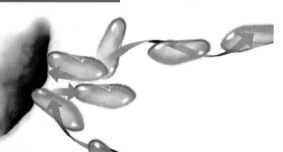

After bumping into an object, a paramecium backs up and changes direction.

Protozoans can sense food in their environment and move toward it. Protozoans also can detect and move away from harmful chemicals. They can move away from objects that are in their way. For example, when a paramecium bumps into an object, it reverses the movement of its cilia. This causes the paramecium to back up. The paramecium then spins briefly and heads off in a new direction.

Reproduction

Many single-celled protists reproduce by dividing into two cells. The result is two protists that look the same as the original cell. This process is an example of asexual reproduction.

Some protists also can reproduce in pairs. Each member of the pair gives some hereditary material to the offspring. The offspring are different from either parent. *Hereditary* refers to properties that are passed from parent to offspring. This type of reproduction is known as sexual reproduction.

Self-Check

1. Describe the path of food in a paramecium.
2. Why is living in freshwater a problem for single-celled protists?
3. What is the function of contractile vacuoles?
4. How are eyespots useful to algae?
5. Describe one way that protists reproduce asexually.

Objectives

After reading this lesson, you should be able to

▶ identify the properties of fungi.

▶ describe the features of several types of fungi.

▶ list ways in which fungi are helpful and harmful.

Hypha
A thin, tubelike thread that is produced by a fungus. Plural is hyphae.

Mycelium
A mass of hyphae. Plural is mycelia.

More than 100,000 species belong to the kingdom Fungi. These organisms grow in the coldest and the hottest places on Earth. They inhabit water and soil. Fungi even live on and inside other organisms, including humans. Whenever you eat mushrooms or bread made with yeast, you are eating fungi.

Properties of Fungi

What features set fungi apart from organisms in other kingdoms? Unlike animals, fungi do not move from place to place. They live in one spot the way plants do. But unlike plants, fungi cannot make their own food. They have no chloroplasts as algae and plants do. Fungi reproduce by releasing spores. You will learn more about reproduction in fungi later in this chapter. Most fungi are many-celled. A few are single-celled.

Most fungi grow in moist, dark, warm places. Because they cannot make food, they must absorb it. Most are saprophytes because they decompose waste or dead matter. Fungi do not grow tall or make any woody tissue. They grow by producing fine tubelike threads called **hyphae**. These hyphae extend into the soil or the material they feed on. A mass of hyphae is called a **mycelium**. You can see a picture of hyphae and a mycelium on page 102. Mycelia often look white and fuzzy. The hyphae in a mycelium transport nutrients through the fungus.

Can people get rid of the fungi growing in their lawns by removing the mushrooms they see?

Club Fungi

Club fungi are the most familiar fungi because they are often the easiest to see. They come in many colors. White and brown are the most common. They also can be black, purple, red, and yellow. Club fungi also are called mushrooms. However, a mushroom is just the aboveground part. Most of the fungus is a mycelium that grows underground. A single mycelium may be quite large and produce dozens of mushrooms.

A mushroom is made of a stalk that supports a cap. On the underside of the cap are rows of gills. The gills are not used for breathing. Their job is to release millions of spores into the air.

Mushrooms are the aboveground part of club fungi.

Rusts and Smuts

Rusts and smuts are fungi that live as parasites on plants. They often grow on cereal plants, such as wheat, corn, barley, and rye. Although they are related to club fungi, they do not produce mushrooms. Rusts get their name because they are reddish brown, the color of rust. Smuts are noted because they stink. They change plant organs into dark masses of spores. Both rusts and smuts can kill the plants that serve as their hosts.

Corn smut, a parasitic fungus, produced the gray masses on this ear of corn.

Molds

What happens if you leave a slice of bread uncovered for several days? If the bread doesn't become too dry, it will probably develop a fuzzy coating. That coating is a fungus called bread mold. Other kinds of mold may form on old books or clothes stored in a damp basement. Molds will grow on just about any food or object made from something living.

Bread mold looks fuzzy because it produces thousands of hyphae. At the top of each hypha is a small knob that releases spores. You can see these knobs in the hyphae shown on page 95. The spores scatter in the air. They can survive freezing or drying for months. If they land on moist food, such as a slice of bread, they produce mycelia. The bread you buy in stores often contains preservatives that slow the growth of mold.

The mold that grows on bread is a fungus.

Yeasts

Yeasts live in liquid or moist environments, such as plant sap and animal tissues. Yeasts are normally single-celled. Under some conditions, however, some yeasts can develop mycelia.

Bakers have used the yeast *Saccharomyces cerevisiae* for centuries. This yeast digests carbohydrates to produce carbon dioxide and other substances. The carbon dioxide released by the yeast in bread dough makes bread rise.

Helpful Fungi

Many fungi are useful to humans and other organisms. You learned that yeasts are used to make bread. Many mushrooms can be eaten and are quite tasty, although many are poisonous. Fungi known as truffles and morels are considered delicacies. Some cheeses owe their special flavors to particular species of molds.

Cyclosporine
A drug that is produced from mold and that helps prevent the rejection of transplanted organs.

Fungi also are used to make products besides food. For example, molds called *Penicillium* produce the antibiotic penicillin. Another species of mold produces **cyclosporine**. This drug helps prevent the rejection of transplanted organs. Yeasts make alcohol, which is added to gasoline to create gasohol.

These fungi make this dead tree's nutrients ready for use by other organisms.

Like bacteria, fungi play an important role in the recycling of nutrients. They break down dead leaves, dead animals, and other waste matter for food. As the material is broken down, some of it is returned to the soil. Plants can absorb the nutrients from the soil and use them to grow. When a plant dies, fungi begin immediately to decompose it, continuing the cycle.

Harmful Fungi

Fungi can grow on nearly anything made from something living. You already know that molds spoil bread and other foods. Rusts and smuts cause millions of dollars of damage to crop plants every year. Fungi break down the wood in buildings and the leather in boots. They can even digest the images on photographs and negatives.

Some fungi cause disease in humans. The skin disease known as ringworm is caused by a fungus, not a worm. Fungi also cause the itching and burning of athlete's foot. Many people are allergic to fungal spores. Fungi can cause deadly diseases, especially in people who are not healthy to begin with.

Some fungi are extremely poisonous. Some molds produce chemicals called **aflatoxins**, which cause liver cancer. These molds can grow on poorly stored peanuts or grains, such as corn. Some mushrooms in the genus *Amanita* contain a toxin that destroys the liver. Their common names are "death cap" and "destroying angel." Eating one of these mushrooms is enough to kill you.

The mushroom Amanita muscaria *is poisonous.*

SCIENCE IN YOUR LIFE

Can a fungus save your life?

You have already read that scientists can cause bacteria to make specific chemicals. Scientists have had similar successes with yeasts. Like bacteria, yeasts are single-celled and easy to grow in the laboratory. They also reproduce rapidly. In addition, yeasts are more similar to humans than bacteria are.

Scientists used the yeast *Saccharomyces cerevisiae* to develop a vaccine for hepatitis B. Hepatitis B is a life-threatening disease caused by a virus. The scientists inserted genetic material from the virus into the yeast. The yeast cells then produced proteins that are normally part of the virus. People who are injected with these proteins become immune to hepatitis B.

Self-Check

1. How are fungi different from animals and plants?
2. What do the gills of a mushroom do?
3. Why does bread mold look fuzzy?
4. How do fungi help to recycle nutrients?
5. What are two diseases that fungi cause?

INVESTIGATION

Observing Paramecia

Materials

✓ safety goggles
✓ medicine droppers
✓ methyl cellulose
✓ microscope slide
✓ paramecium culture
✓ coverslip
✓ compound light microscope
✓ stopwatch
✓ distilled water
✓ paper towel
✓ salt water

Purpose

To study the function of contractile vacuoles in paramecia

Procedure

1. Copy the data table below on a sheet of paper.

	Number of contractions per minute		
	Culture medium	Distilled water	Salt water
Paramecium #1			
Paramecium #2			
Paramecium #3			
Average			

2. Put on the safety goggles.

3. Use a medicine dropper to place a drop of methyl cellulose on a microscope slide. Add one drop of paramecium culture to the methyl cellulose drop. Cover both drops with a coverslip.

4. Place the slide on the microscope stage. Using low power, find the paramecia and observe their movement.

5. Switch to high power and examine the structure of a paramecium. Locate one of the contractile vacuoles, using the diagram on page 92.

6. Count how many times the contractile vacuole contracts in one minute. Record the number in your table. Repeat for two other paramecia.

7. Use a clean medicine dropper to put a drop of distilled water at one edge of the coverslip. Touch a paper towel to the opposite edge of the coverslip. That will draw the distilled water under the coverslip.

8. Repeat step 6 with three more paramecia.

9. Repeat step 7 with salt water.

10. Repeat step 6 with three more paramecia.

11. Calculate the average number of contractions per minute in culture medium, distilled water, and salt water. To do this, add the counts in each column and divide by three. Record the averages in your table.

12. Clean up your work space.

Questions

1. How did distilled water affect the activity of the contractile vacuoles?

2. How did salt water affect the activity of the contractile vacuoles?

3. In distilled water, the concentration of water is *higher* than it is in culture medium. In salt water, the concentration of water is *lower* than it is in culture medium. Using this information, explain the effects of distilled water and salt water.

Digestive enzyme
A chemical that helps break down food.

You might think that fungi are placed in their own kingdom because they do not fit anywhere else. However, fungi have special ways of feeding, reproducing, and living with other organisms. The organisms in the fungi kingdom are alike in many ways.

Getting and Digesting Food

As you know, fungi get food by breaking down waste and dead matter. Some animals and protists also feed on dead matter. But there is a difference. Animals and protists digest their food after it enters their body. Fungi digest their food outside their body. Fungi release **digestive enzymes** onto their food. Digestive enzymes are chemicals that help break down food. The food is then small enough to be absorbed by the fungi. Fungi use the nutrients in the food for energy and growth.

Although fungi cannot hunt food, they can grow their hyphae quickly into a food source. The hyphae branch to reach all parts of the food. The hyphae provide a large surface for absorbing nutrients.

The hyphae of a mycelium branch all through a food source, such as this orange.

Reproduction

When conditions are good for growth, fungi usually reproduce asexually. The most common way of asexual reproduction is the release of spores. Each spore usually contains a single cell. If it lands in a moist place containing food, the spore produces a mycelium. The mycelium looks the same as the fungus that released the spore.

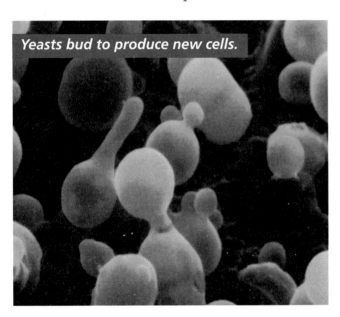

Yeasts bud to produce new cells.

Yeasts use another way of asexual reproduction, called **budding**. During budding, part of a yeast cell pinches off to make a smaller cell. The smaller cell grows rapidly to the same size as the first cell. Both cells look the same.

Many fungi also reproduce sexually, especially when growing conditions are poor. Fungi do not have male and female sexes. They have opposite mating types called "plus" and "minus." When a plus hypha touches a minus hypha, the two can join. The joined hyphae then form a structure that releases spores. These spores will produce new mycelia that are different from either parent.

Budding
Reproduction in which part of an organism pinches off to form a new organism.

Mycorrhiza
A mutualism between a fungus and the roots of a plant. Plural is mycorrhizae.

Living With Other Organisms

Some fungi live close to the roots of plants. The fungus absorbs minerals from the soil and shares them with the plant. In exchange, the plant provides the fungus with some of the food it makes. The plant and the fungus benefit. This example of mutualism is called a **mycorrhiza**.

Lichen

An organism that is made up of a fungus and an alga or a bacterium.

Some scientists call lichens "pioneer organisms." How is a lichen like a pioneer?

More than 90 percent of plants have mycorrhizae on their roots. The next time you see an oak or pine tree, look for mushrooms around its base. They probably sprouted from fungi that have formed mycorrhizae with the tree.

Another type of mutualism is two organisms that grow together. Algae or certain bacteria grow in a tangle among the hyphae of fungi. The two organisms together are called a **lichen**. The algae or bacteria use sunlight to make food and provide it to the fungi. In return, the fungi provide moisture and shelter for the other organism. In lichens that grow on rocks, the fungi produce acids that release minerals from the rock. Both organisms use the minerals for growth.

Lichens can withstand great extremes of temperature. They can grow where other organisms cannot survive, such as on rocks. For this reason, lichens are often the first organisms to inhabit a new area. They break down rock and begin to form soil for other organisms to use.

The colorful patches on this rock are lichens.

Lichens are sensitive to air pollution. They absorb water from moist air. They can be killed by air that contains pollutants. The presence of healthy lichens in an area usually means that the air is clean.

Self-Check

1. What is the function of digestive enzymes?
2. Describe asexual reproduction in yeasts.
3. How do fungi produce offspring that are not identical?
4. What is a mycorrhiza?
5. How do lichens show air quality?

- Bacteria are very small, single-celled organisms. They do not have organelles inside their cells.

- Bacteria reproduce by splitting into two cells that look the same.

- Some bacteria are used to produce food and different kinds of chemicals. Others spoil food and cause diseases.

- Bacteria play an important role in recycling nutrients.

- Protists include plantlike algae and animal-like protozoans.

- Algae make their own food by using the energy in sunlight. Most algae are single-celled and live in water.

- Protozoans are single-celled and must absorb their food. They move by using pseudopods, flagella, or cilia.

- Protists use contractile vacuoles to remove water that is not needed. They can sense and respond to their environment. They can reproduce asexually and sexually.

- Most fungi are many-celled. They absorb nutrients by growing hyphae into food.

- Like bacteria, some fungi spoil food and cause diseases. Others are highly poisonous. Some fungi are used to produce food and medicines.

- Fungi are important nutrient recyclers.

- Fungi reproduce by releasing spores. The spores may be produced by asexual or sexual reproduction.

- Mycorrhizae and lichens are examples of mutualism between fungi and other organisms.

Science Words		
	contractile vacuole, 93	mutualism, 86
	cyclosporine, 98	mycelium, 95
aflatoxin, 99	diatom, 89	mycorrhiza, 103
ameba, 90	digestive enzyme, 102	osmosis, 93
anal pore, 92	eyespot, 94	paramecium, 90
binary fission, 85	food vacuole, 92	saprophyte, 85
budding, 103	gullet, 92	sporozoan, 91
cell membrane, 93	hypha, 95	toxin, 87
chloroplast, 88	lichen, 104	trypanosoma, 91

Vocabulary Review

Number your paper from 1 to 8. Match each word in Column A with the correct phrase in Column B. Write the letter of the correct phrase on your paper.

Column A

_____ **1.** alga

_____ **2.** chloroplast

_____ **3.** cilia

_____ **4.** contractile vacuole

_____ **5.** flagellum

_____ **6.** lichen

_____ **7.** mycelium

_____ **8.** mycorrhiza

Column B

a. short, hairlike structures

b. mass of hyphae

c. fungus around plant roots

d. a plantlike protist

e. structure used to make food

f. long, whiplike structure

g. fungus with alga or bacterium

h. removes water from a cell

Concept Review

Number your paper from 1 to 8. Then choose the answer that best completes each sentence. Write the letter of the answer on your paper.

1. Bacteria are _____.

   a. single-celled   **b.** many-celled   **c.** not made of cells

2. Most disease-causing bacteria harm the body by producing _____.

   a. antibiotics   **b.** nitrogen   **c.** toxins

3. Single-celled algae with hard shells that contain silica are called _____.

   a. kelps   **b.** diatoms   **c.** amebas

4. The disease sleeping sickness is caused by _____.

   a. bacteria   **b.** protozoans   **c.** fungi

5. A paramecium moves away from an object by _____.

   a. pushing out a pseudopod
   b. pushing with its flagellum
   c. reversing the movement of its cilia

6. The gills on the underside of a mushroom are used for _____.

   a. releasing spores   **b.** breathing   **c.** digestion

7. Yeasts reproduce by a process called _____.

   a. binary fission   **b.** budding   **c.** mutualism

8. The fungus in a lichen provides _____.

   a. food   **b.** light   **c.** moisture

a.

b.

Use the photos to answer questions 9 and 10.

 9. Which organism makes its own food?

10. Which organism reproduces by releasing spores?

Critical Thinking

Write the answer to each of the following questions.

1. Biologists used to classify *Euglena gracilis* as a protozoan. Explain why they may have classified it that way.

2. Why might producing an antibiotic such as penicillin be useful to a fungus?

Test Taking Tip | When answering multiple-choice questions, first identify the choices you know are untrue.

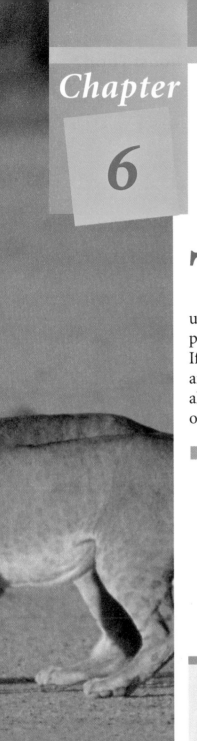

How Animals Stay Alive

These lions use caution to hunt down a porcupine. The porcupine could jab its quills into the lions, causing great pain. Both kinds of animals are using their body systems to stay alive. If the lions kill the porcupine, they will get the energy they need for fuel. If the porcupine gets away, it will continue to live. All animals must carry out the same basic activities to stay alive. In this chapter, you will learn how different kinds of animals achieve this task.

ORGANIZE YOUR THOUGHTS

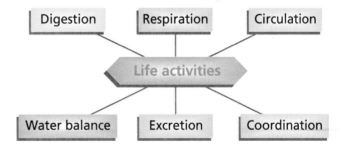

Goals for Learning

▶ To understand how animals obtain and digest food
▶ To explore respiration and circulation in animals
▶ To explain how animals preserve water balance and excrete wastes
▶ To describe the functions of the endocrine system and the nervous system

Objectives

After reading this lesson, you should be able to

▶ describe three main ways animals get food.

▶ explain the importance of digestion.

▶ tell the difference between a gastrovascular cavity and a digestive tract.

Filter feeding
Getting food by straining it out of the water.

Unlike plants, algae, and some bacteria, animals cannot make their own food. Animals must get food from other organisms. Different animals have different ways of getting food.

Filter Feeding

Many animals that live in water get food by filtering, or straining, it. This way of getting food is called **filter feeding.** In Chapter 3, you read about animals that use filter feeding. Sponges strain bacteria and protists from the water that passes through their body. Recall that sponges cannot move around as adults. Filter feeding allows them to gather food without chasing it. Barnacles also remain in place. They collect food particles with their legs. The legs act as screens. Mollusks, such as clams and oysters, tend to remain in one spot. They use their gills to strain food out of the water. Some filter-feeding animals do move. Many whales harvest millions of tiny animals by swimming with their mouths open.

Feeding on Fluids

Some animals get food from the fluids of plants or other animals. The fluids are rich in nutrients. Aphids and cicadas are insects that have piercing mouthparts. They draw sap from roots and stems. Bees, butterflies, and hummingbirds draw nectar from flowers. Spiders and assassin bugs capture insects and suck the fluid from their bodies. Leeches, mosquitoes, and horseflies feed on the blood of vertebrates, including humans.

Are human teeth suited for eating plants, animals, or both? Explain your answer.

Consuming Large Pieces of Food

Most animals consume, or eat, large pieces of solid food. Sometimes they eat entire organisms. Such animals use different kinds of body structures to capture and consume their food. For example, hydras, jellyfish, and other cnidarians have tentacles armed with stinging cells. The tentacles catch small animals in the water and bring them to the mouth. Cnidarians consume their food whole.

Many insects have mouthparts that are suited for cutting and chewing. The mouthparts turn the food into pieces that are small enough to swallow. Grasshoppers, termites, and beetles use their chewing mouthparts to feed on plants. Animals that eat plants are known as **herbivores**. Dragonflies and praying mantises also have chewing mouthparts but eat other insects. Animals that eat other animals are called **carnivores**.

Vertebrates are the only animals that have teeth. Mammals have teeth of different shapes and sizes. Each kind of tooth does a certain job. Chisel-like teeth at the front of the mouth cut food into pieces. Long, pointed teeth grip and pierce food. Teeth that have a flat surface grind and crush food. A mammal's teeth tell what kind of food it eats. Carnivores have sharp, pointed teeth that tear flesh. Herbivores have large teeth that have a flat surface. These teeth are suited for grinding plants.

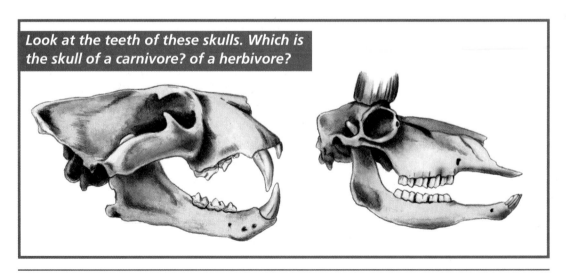

Look at the teeth of these skulls. Which is the skull of a carnivore? of a herbivore?

Digesting Food

Foods usually contain fats, proteins, and carbohydrates. These chemicals provide the energy an animal needs. However, they are too large for most animal cells to absorb, or take in. These large chemicals must be broken down into smaller chemicals before cells can absorb them. The process of breaking down food into small chemicals is digestion. Animals digest food by secreting digestive enzymes. An enzyme is a substance that speeds up chemical changes. **Secrete** means to form and release.

In sponges, the digestive enzymes work inside cells. These cells line the inside of the sponge. The cells trap food that enters the sponge. They package the food in food vacuoles like those in paramecia. Digestive enzymes break down the food into small chemicals. The cells then absorb the chemicals.

Digesting food inside cells has one drawback. The food must be small enough to fit inside food vacuoles. This means that sponges can eat only tiny food particles. Most other animals digest their food outside of cells. They have a space where digestion begins. These animals can eat much larger foods.

Gastrovascular Cavities

Cnidarians and flatworms digest food in a hollow space called a **gastrovascular cavity**. This space has only one opening, the mouth. Food enters through the mouth. Special cells line the gastrovascular cavity. These cells secrete digestive enzymes. The enzymes break down the food into small particles. The cells can then absorb the particles. Material that is not digested leaves through the mouth.

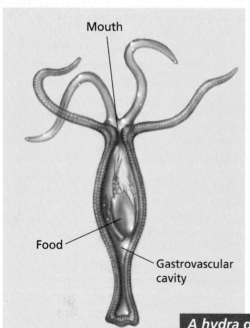

Mouth

Food

Gastrovascular cavity

A hydra digests food in its gastrovascular cavity.

Anus
The opening through which material that is not digested leaves the digestive tract.

Crop
The part of the digestive tract of some animals where food is stored.

Digestive tract
A tubelike digestive space with an opening at each end.

Gizzard
The part of the digestive tract of some animals that grinds food.

Digestive Tracts

Animals that are more developed have a **digestive tract**. This is a tubelike digestive space with an opening at each end. Food moves through a digestive tract in one direction. Different parts of the tract carry out different functions. The main functions of digestive tracts are storing food, digesting food, and absorbing nutrients.

Most digestive tracts are organized the same way. The digestive tract of a bird provides a good example. Food enters the digestive tract through the mouth. It passes down the esophagus to the **crop**, where it is stored. In the stomach, the food mixes with acid and digestive enzymes. The mixture moves to the **gizzard**. The gizzard grinds it into a watery paste. More digestive enzymes are added in the intestine. Here, digestion is completed. The walls of the intestine absorb the small chemicals. Material that is not digested leaves the digestive tract through an opening called the **anus**.

The digestive tracts of animals have some differences. For example, humans do not have a crop or a gizzard. The human stomach carries out the functions of those organs. You will learn more about the human digestive tract in Chapter 8.

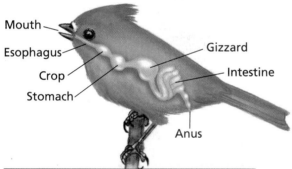

Mouth
Esophagus
Crop
Stomach
Gizzard
Intestine
Anus

The different parts of a digestive tract carry out different functions.

Self-Check

1. Name three kinds of animals that use filter feeding to get food.
2. How are cicadas different from dragonflies in the way they feed?
3. Why must animals digest their food?
4. Name and describe the type of digestive space found in a cnidarian.
5. What functions does the digestive tract perform?

Chapter 6

INVESTIGATION

Studying Feeding in Hydras

Materials

- ✓ microscope well slide
- ✓ hydra culture
- ✓ 2 medicine droppers
- ✓ stereo-microscope
- ✓ water flea culture
- ✓ filter paper
- ✓ scissors
- ✓ forceps
- ✓ beef broth
- ✓ dish labeled "used hydras"

Purpose

To observe feeding behavior in a simple animal

Procedure

1. Copy the data table below on a sheet of paper.

Stimulus	What happened?
Water fleas	
Moving filter paper	
Touched by filter paper	
Beef broth on filter paper	

2. Use a medicine dropper to place a hydra on a well slide. Make sure the hydra is in water.

3. Use another medicine dropper to add some water fleas to the slide. Water fleas are small crustaceans on which hydras often feed.

4. Place the slide on the microscope stage. Using high power, observe the feeding responses of the hydra. Record your observations. If the hydra does not respond after several minutes, get another hydra and try again.

5. Place any hydras you have used in the dish labeled "used hydras." Rinse the slide with water.

6. Place a new hydra on your slide. Move the slide to the microscope stage.

7. Use scissors to cut a small piece of filter paper. Using forceps, move the filter paper in the water near the hydra. Be careful not to touch the hydra. You are testing the hydra's response to water vibrations. Record your observations.

8. Gently touch different parts of the hydra with the filter paper. You are testing the hydra's response to touch. Record your observations.

9. Dip the filter paper in beef broth. Hold the filter paper in the water near the hydra. Again, do not touch the hydra. You are testing the hydra's response to chemicals. Record your observations.

10. Place the hydra in the dish labeled "used hydras." Clean up your work space.

Questions

1. How were the hydra's responses to water vibrations, touch, and chemicals different?

2. Which of these stimuli probably triggers feeding responses when a hydra consumes a water flea?

Explore Further

Look for dead water fleas on the bottom of their culture dish. Find out if a dead water flea will trigger a feeding response in a hydra. Do the results of this test support your answer to question 2?

How Do Animals Respire and Transport Materials?

Diffusion
The movement of materials from an area of high concentration to an area of low concentration.

Respire
Take in oxygen and give off carbon dioxide.

To obtain the energy in food, all animals must carry out chemical reactions. In these reactions, food molecules join with oxygen. Energy is released. Carbon dioxide forms as a waste product. Thus, animals must bring oxygen into their body. They must eliminate carbon dioxide. This process of gas exchange is called respiration. Animals **respire** in different ways.

Gas Exchange in Simple Animals

The body wall of sponges and cnidarians is made of just two cell layers. Water outside the animal touches the cells in one layer. Water inside the animal touches cells in the other layer. Both layers of cells get oxygen and get rid of carbon dioxide by **diffusion**. Diffusion is movement from an area of high concentration to an area of low concentration. The concentration of oxygen is higher in the water than in the cells. Therefore, oxygen diffuses from the water into the cells. The concentration of carbon dioxide is higher in the cells than in the water. Therefore, carbon dioxide diffuses from the cells into the water.

Flatworms have very thin body walls too. Most cells touch water, either outside or in the gastrovascular cavity. Gas exchange in flatworms also happens by diffusion.

Carbon dioxide

Oxygen

All cells in a hydra can exchange oxygen and carbon dioxide with the surrounding water.

Gas Exchange in Other Animals

Most animals are not just two cell layers thick. They contain many cells deep inside the body. These cells cannot exchange gases directly with the outside environment. Animals like these must have a special organ for gas exchange. Such organs come in many different forms.

Animals that live in water usually have gills. Fish have one type of gills. Tadpoles, lobsters, and clams also have gills. Gills often have a feathery structure. This structure

The gills on this brown trout provide a large surface area for exchanging gases.

provides a large surface area. This allows diffusion to happen quickly. Oxygen diffuses from the water into the gills. Carbon dioxide diffuses in the opposite direction.

Land animals exchange oxygen and carbon dioxide with the air. Insects use a system of tubes to carry air into the body. The tubes have very fine branches that reach almost all of the animal's cells. The entrances to the tubes are scattered over the insect's body. Watch a bee that has landed on a flower. You will see its abdomen move in and out. It is pumping air into and out of the tubes.

Most other land animals use lungs for gas exchange. Lungs are like balloons inside the body. When you inhale, or breathe in, you draw air into your lungs. Exhaling, or breathing out, forces the air back out. Like gills, lungs provide a large surface area for gas exchange.

Circulatory
Flowing in a circle.

Closed circulatory system
A system in which blood stays inside vessels at all times.

Open circulatory system
A system in which blood makes direct contact with cells.

What type of circulatory system do you have?

Did You Know?

A shrew's heart can beat as fast as 1,300 times per minute. An elephant's heart beats only about 25 times per minute.

Circulatory Systems

Animals must transport oxygen from their gills or lungs to the rest of their body. They must transport carbon dioxide from the rest of their body to their gills or lungs. A **circulatory** system performs these jobs. Circulatory means flowing in a circle. This system moves blood through the body. In the gills or lungs, oxygen enters the blood. Carbon dioxide leaves. As the blood circulates, it delivers oxygen and picks up carbon dioxide. Blood also carries nutrients from the digestive tract to cells.

All circulatory systems have a set of tubes and one or more pumps. The tubes are called blood vessels. The pumps are called hearts. When a heart contracts, or pulls together, it squeezes blood through the blood vessels.

Arthropods and most mollusks have an **open circulatory system**. In this system, blood leaves one set of vessels. It enters spaces around the organs. The blood flows slowly through the spaces. It makes direct contact with cells. It then enters another set of vessels and returns to the heart.

Annelids, vertebrates, and some mollusks have a **closed circulatory system**. The blood stays inside vessels at all times. The smallest vessels have very thin walls. Oxygen and carbon dioxide diffuse into or out of the blood across these walls.

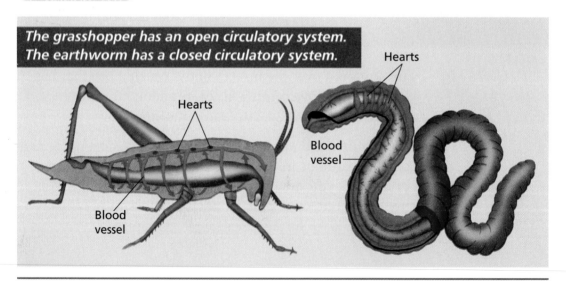

The grasshopper has an open circulatory system. The earthworm has a closed circulatory system.

Hearts

Hearts

Blood vessel

Blood vessel

Vertebrate Circulatory Systems

The circulatory system of a vertebrate includes a single heart. The heart is divided into enclosed spaces called chambers. The **atria** are chambers that receive blood that returns to the heart. The **ventricles** are chambers that pump blood out of the heart. Fish have one atrium and one ventricle. Amphibians and most reptiles have two atria and one ventricle. Birds, mammals, and some reptiles have two atria and two ventricles.

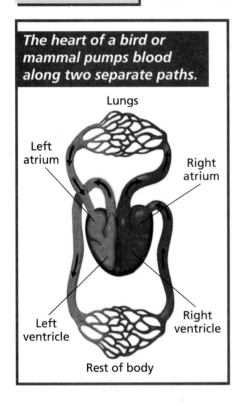

The heart of a bird or mammal pumps blood along two separate paths.

Lungs

Left atrium

Right atrium

Left ventricle

Right ventricle

Rest of body

The diagram shows how blood circulates through the body of a mammal or bird. The left atrium receives blood from the lungs. This blood has a lot of oxygen that was picked up in the lungs. The blood has little carbon dioxide. The left atrium sends the blood to the left ventricle. The left ventricle pumps it to the rest of the body. The blood delivers oxygen to body tissues. It picks up carbon dioxide that has formed as waste. The blood returns to the right atrium. The blood has little oxygen and a lot of carbon dioxide. The blood moves from the right atrium to the right ventricle. The right ventricle pumps the blood to the lungs. In the lungs, oxygen enters the blood. Carbon dioxide leaves the blood. The carbon dioxide is exhaled as waste. The blood returns to the left atrium, completing the cycle.

Self-Check

1. How are gases exchanged in a sponge?
2. Describe the system that insects use to respire.
3. What is the difference between an open and a closed circulatory system?
4. What is the function of the atria in a vertebrate heart?
5. In a bird's heart, where does blood go from the right ventricle?

What happens if you exercise hard on a hot day? You sweat a lot. You drink fluids to replace the water you lost. What happens if you drink too much water? You get rid of it by producing more urine. Your body works to keep a normal balance of water. Other animals also have ways to maintain, or keep, water balance.

Water Balance in the Sea

Seawater is water and salt. The fluids of animals also contain water and salt. The more salt a fluid has, the lower its water concentration is. Recall from Chapter 5 that water will move into an area where its concentration is lower. This is called osmosis. This movement can cause problems if too much water gets into an animal.

Most sea invertebrates avoid getting too much water in their bodies. The water concentration in their fluids equals the water concentration in seawater. Therefore, water does not move between their bodies and the surrounding seawater. The same is true for sharks, rays, and skates.

In bony fishes, their body fluids have a higher water concentration than seawater. As a result, water moves from their bodies into the sea. Like all animals, bony fishes need some water. If all the water left their bodies, they would shrink and die. These fishes drink seawater to replace the water they lose by osmosis. Drinking seawater brings a lot of salt into their bodies. They **excrete** the extra salt through their gills. To excrete means to get rid of wastes or substances that are not needed.

Bony fishes in the sea drink seawater and excrete salt from their gills.

Water, salt

Water

Salt

Water Balance in Freshwater

Animals that live in freshwater have too much water coming into their bodies. You may recall that protists have this same problem. The concentration of water outside their bodies is higher than the concentration inside. Therefore, water constantly moves into them.

Freshwater animals use special organs to remove excess, or too much, water. Flatworms have a system of tiny tubes all through their bodies. The tubes are connected to cells called **flame cells**. These cells got their name because they have a tuft of cilia. When the cilia move, they look like a flickering flame. Flame cells collect excess water inside the flatworm. Their cilia push the water along the tubes. Water leaves the tubes through pores, or openings, in the body wall.

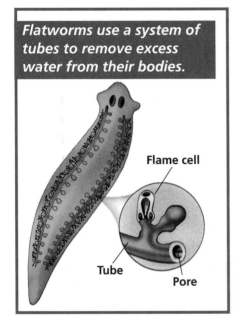

Flatworms use a system of tubes to remove excess water from their bodies.

Flame cell

Tube

Pore

Freshwater bony fishes have the opposite problem that saltwater bony fishes have. In a lake or stream, water enters through the gills of a fish at all times. To get rid of the excess water, the fish use their **kidneys** to excrete urine. Kidneys are organs of excretion found in vertebrates. Excretion means getting rid of wastes from the body. The urine is mostly water, but it also contains some salt. The fish must replace the salt. The fish absorbs salt with its gills.

Water

Salt

Water, salt

Freshwater bony fishes excrete water and some salt with their kidneys. They take up salt with their gills.

Water Balance on Land

In land animals, the biggest problem with water balance is drying out. Animals have ways to limit water loss. Land snails withdraw into their shell. Insects have a waxy layer that covers their outside skeleton. The wax stops water from evaporating from their body. Reptiles, birds, and mammals have a watertight skin.

Suppose you go several hours without drinking anything. Will your urine have a higher or a lower water concentration than normal?

The entire body of a land animal cannot be watertight. Animals have to respire. They give off water when oxygen and carbon dioxide are exchanged. Land animals also lose water in their urine, feces, and sweat.

Most land animals can maintain water balance by drinking water. If open water is scarce, animals may get water by eating leaves, fruits, or roots. Some animals are especially suited for getting water from food. For example, the kangaroo rat of the American Southwest never drinks water. It gets its water from seeds and other plant matter.

Kidneys are the main organs in keeping water balance in mammals and birds. Suppose too much water gets into the body. The kidneys excrete urine with a high water concentration. In this way, they remove excess water. Suppose the water concentration in the body is too low. The kidneys excrete urine with a low water concentration. This keeps more water in the body.

Excreting Wastes

If an animal needs to save water, why does it produce urine? Producing urine does more than maintain water balance. It also removes dangerous wastes from the body. One type of waste is ammonia. It is formed when proteins break down. Ammonia is poisonous to cells. Animals need a way to get rid of it.

In most animals that live in water, the ammonia moves out into the water. The ammonia does not build up inside the body. Animals that live on land must get rid of ammonia in another way. They change ammonia into chemicals that are less poisonous. Then they excrete these chemicals in their urine.

Self-Check

1. How do most sea invertebrates maintain water balance?
2. What is the function of flame cells?
3. How do freshwater fishes maintain water balance?
4. List three ways some land animals limit water loss.
5. Why is the breakdown of proteins a problem for animals?

SCIENCE IN YOUR LIFE

Can you live without kidneys?

Kidneys are important organs. They constantly filter wastes from the blood. Although they weigh only 300 grams, they receive about 1½ liters of blood every minute. You can survive just fine with only one kidney. A person who loses both kidneys, though, cannot survive without help.

A dialysis machine, or artificial kidney, can remove wastes from blood. In this machine, the patient's blood circulates on one side of a very thin membrane. Dialysis fluid circulates on the other side. The membrane allows wastes to move from the blood into the dialysis fluid. Patients typically must use the machine for four to six hours three times a week.

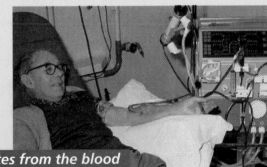

A dialysis machine removes wastes from the blood of a person whose kidneys no longer function.

How Do Animals Coordinate Their Bodily Activities?

Objectives

After reading this lesson, you should be able to

▶ explain how the endocrine system coordinates activities.

▶ explain how messages travel through the nervous system.

▶ describe the features of some invertebrate nervous systems.

▶ describe the organization of the vertebrate nervous system.

Coordinate
Work together.

Hormone
A chemical signal that glands produce.

All of the parts of an animal have to work together. Animals must **coordinate** the activities of their cells, tissues, and organs. To coordinate means to work together. Most animals have two systems for coordinating the activities of their parts. Both systems use chemicals. The chemicals act as signals to tell tissues and organs what to do.

The Endocrine System

One system that coordinates some activities is the endocrine system. This system is made of glands that secrete chemicals called **hormones**. The circulatory system carries the hormones all through the body. The hormones touch every cell. However, the hormones affect only certain cells. The cells must have a particular type of protein. The hormone binds to the protein. This causes the cell to change its activity. There are many different hormones. Each hormone may work on different kinds of cells. Hormones are found in vertebrates and invertebrates.

Let's look at an example of how the endocrine system works. Mammals produce a hormone called vasopressin. This hormone is made when a mammal's body does not have enough water. A gland at the base of the brain secretes vasopressin. The blood transports this hormone all through the body. The hormone binds to proteins in kidney cells. This causes the kidney to excrete urine with a low water concentration. Less water leaves through the urine. More water stays in the body.

Blood vessel

Hormone   Protein   Cell

Gland

Hormones travel through the blood. They affect only those cells that have the right proteins.

The movement of hormones through the body takes a while. Hormones must get from glands to cells or organs. The endocrine system is suited to control activities that happen slowly. For example, hormones control the metamorphosis of a tadpole into a frog.

The Nervous System

The second system that coordinates activities in animals is the nervous system. The nervous system carries its messages directly to parts of the body. It does not need the circulatory system. Instead, nerve cells carry the messages. Nerve cells have long, thin branches at the ends. Some nerve cells are very long. For example, some nerve cells reach from your lower back to the tips of your toes.

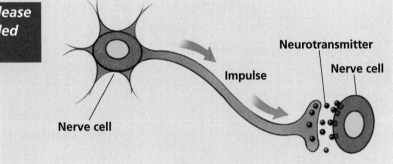

Many nerve cells release chemical signals called neurotransmitters.

Neurotransmitter

Impulse

Nerve cell

Nerve cell

Impulse
A message that a nerve cell carries.

Neurotransmitter
A chemical signal that a nerve cell releases.

People who severely injure their spinal cord in their upper back cannot move their arms or legs. Why?

Messages that travel along nerve cells are called **impulses**. One end of a nerve cell starts an impulse. The impulse travels across the cell to the other end. At this end, the impulse causes the cell to release a chemical signal. This signal is called a **neurotransmitter**. It binds to proteins on nearby nerve cells. These cells change their activity. They continue to move impulses from cell to cell. This is the way messages travel from one nerve cell to another.

Impulses travel quickly along nerve cells. The fastest impulses can reach speeds of 120 meters per second. The nervous system is suited to control activities that happen quickly. For example, your nervous system directs the movements of your fingers when you type at a keyboard.

Nerve net

A bunch of nerve cells that are loosely connected.

Invertebrate Nervous Systems

Except for sponges, all animals have a nervous system. Cnidarians, such as hydras, have the simplest nervous system. They do not have brains. They have a bunch of nerve cells that are loosely connected. This is called a **nerve net**. This is all cnidarians need to control their simple activities. The nerve net causes a hydra to shrink if it is touched. It controls the movement of tentacles when a hydra feeds.

Flatworms, segmented worms, and arthropods are more highly developed. They have structures to sense their environment. The front end of the animal contains eyes and sometimes antennae. The front end also has clusters of nerve cells. These serve as a simple brain. The brain receives information from the sense structures. In segmented worms and arthropods, each body segment also has a cluster of nerve cells. The clusters are connected to each other and to the brain. The nervous system of these invertebrates coordinates movement, feeding, reproduction, and other activities.

Of all the invertebrates, squids and octopuses have the most highly developed nervous systems. Their brains contain millions of nerve cells. Octopuses can be taught to solve simple problems. They also can learn to recognize objects based on their shape or feel.

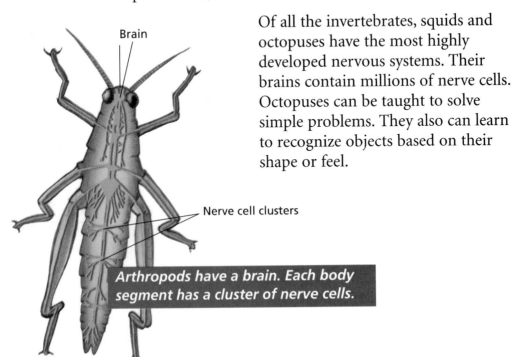

Brain

Nerve cell clusters

Arthropods have a brain. Each body segment has a cluster of nerve cells.

The Vertebrate Nervous System

The nervous system is organized the same way in all vertebrates. The nervous system is divided into two parts. One part is the **central nervous system**. It includes the brain and spinal cord. The second part is the **peripheral nervous system**. Peripheral means outer. This part is made up of nerves. The nerves connect the central nervous system with the rest of the body. The diagram shows how these parts are arranged in a frog.

Bones protect the brain and the spinal cord. The skull protects the brain. The backbone protects the spinal cord. Nerves pass through holes in the skull and backbone.

The brain is the control center for the vertebrate nervous system. The brain interprets messages from the sense organs. It directs the movement of muscles. It controls how fast the heart beats. It controls how fast an animal breathes. It helps maintain balance when an animal walks. In some vertebrates, the brain is the center of emotions and reasoning.

The spinal cord links the brain and the body below the neck. It relays information from the body to the brain. It carries the brain's commands back to the body.

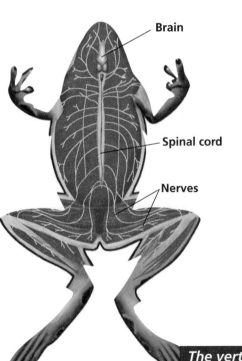

Brain

Spinal cord

Nerves

The vertebrate nervous system is made up of the brain, the spinal cord, and nerves.

Comparing Vertebrate Brains

The brains of different types of vertebrates are different. One difference is the size of the brains. The brains of fish, amphibians, and reptiles are small compared to the rest of their body. Birds and mammals have much larger brains for their body size. The brain of a 100-gram mammal is about ten times bigger than the brain of a 100-gram fish.

Another difference is the size of the different parts of the brain. A part called the **cerebrum** is especially large in birds and mammals. This part controls thought, memory, and learning. These functions are more highly developed in birds and mammals than in other vertebrates.

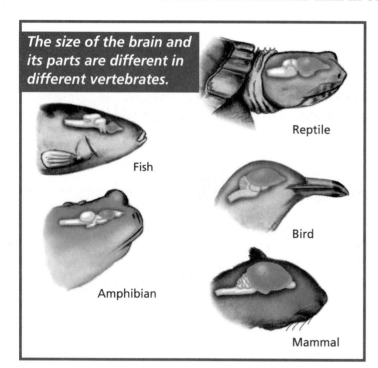

The size of the brain and its parts are different in different vertebrates.

Fish

Amphibian

Reptile

Bird

Mammal

In some mammals, the surface of the cerebrum is highly folded. The folds increase the surface area of the cerebrum. Since nerve cells are located near the surface, folding makes room for more nerve cells. The more nerve cells an animal has, the more it can learn and remember. Porpoises and humans have brains with the greatest number of folds.

Self-Check

1. How do hormones move through the body?
2. What is the function of neurotransmitters?
3. What is a nerve net?
4. What are the parts of the vertebrate central nervous system?
5. What is the importance of having a highly folded cerebrum?

- Animals feed by filtering food, sucking fluids, or consuming large pieces of food.

- Animals digest food in their cells, in a gastrovascular cavity, or in a digestive tract.

- Most animals that live in water use gills to exchange oxygen and carbon dioxide. Land animals use lungs or tubes.

- In an open circulatory system, blood leaves the vessels and makes direct contact with cells. In a closed circulatory system, blood stays inside vessels.

- Bony fishes in the sea drink seawater to replace the water they lose by osmosis. Freshwater bony fishes use their kidneys to excrete water gained by osmosis.

- Land animals lose water by respiration and in their sweat, urine, and feces. They replace lost water by drinking or eating.

- Animals must excrete the ammonia they produce when they break down proteins.

- The endocrine system uses hormones, which are carried by the blood.

- The nervous system uses chemical signals called neurotransmitters, which are released by nerve cells.

- Cnidarians have a simple nervous system called a nerve net. Most other invertebrates have a brain that is connected to nerve cells.

- The vertebrate nervous system is made of the central nervous system and the peripheral nervous system.

Science Words		
anus, 113	crop, 113	kidney, 121
atrium, 119	diffusion, 116	nerve net, 126
carnivore, 111	digestive tract, 113	neurotransmitter, 125
central nervous system, 127	excrete, 120	open circulatory system, 118
cerebrum, 128	filter feeding, 110	peripheral nervous system, 127
circulatory, 118	flame cell, 121	respire, 116
closed circulatory system, 118	gastrovascular cavity, 112	secrete, 112
coordinate, 124	gizzard, 113	ventricle, 119
	herbivore, 111	
	hormone, 124	
	impulse, 125	

Vocabulary Review

Number your paper from 1 to 10. Then choose the word or words from the Word Bank that best complete each sentence. Write the answer on your paper.

WORD BANK
closed circulatory system
digestive tract
filter feeding
flame cells
gastrovascular cavity
gizzard
herbivore
hormones
nerve net
ventricle

1. The circulatory system carries chemical signals known as _____.

2. A tubelike digestive space with an opening at each end is called a _____.

3. A chamber that pumps blood out of a vertebrate heart is called a _____.

4. Flatworms remove excess water through a system of tubes connected to _____.

5. Blood stays inside vessels at all times in a _____.

6. An animal that eats plants is called a _____.

7. Cnidarians have a simple nervous system known as a _____.

8. A _____ is a digestive space with a single opening.

9. In most animals, a _____ grinds food into a watery paste.

10. A sponge gets food by _____.

Concept Review

Number your paper from 1 to 8. Choose the answer that best completes each sentence. Write the letter of the answer on your paper.

1. Leeches get food by _____.
   a. filter feeding   b. sucking fluids
   c. eating solid pieces of food

2. Animals break down food by secreting _____.
   a. digestive enzymes   b. hormones
   c. neurotransmitters

3. Insects use a system of _____ to carry air into the body.
   a. gills   **b.** lungs   **c.** tubes

4. In a mammal's heart, blood goes from the left atrium to the _____.
   a. left ventricle   **b.** right atrium   **c.** lungs

5. Most sea invertebrates have an inside water concentration that is _____ the water concentration in seawater.
   a. less than   **b.** equal to   **c.** greater than

6. When proteins are broken down in the body, _____ is formed as a waste product.
   a. oxygen   **b.** fat   **c.** ammonia

7. The endocrine system works best to control activities that happen _____.
   a. slowly   **b.** quickly   **c.** only once

8. The brain and spinal cord make up the _____ nervous system.
   a. peripheral   **b.** central   **c.** invertebrate

Critical Thinking

Write the answer to each of the following questions.

1. What method of feeding is used by the animals shown in the photo? Explain your reasoning.

2. Some animals live in water that has a low oxygen concentration. They often have large gills. Why would large gills be helpful to these animals?

Test Taking Tip   Make sure you have the same number of answers on your paper as the number of items on the test.

How Plants Live

Imagine living your life stuck to one spot. How would you get water or food? It would be hard for you to survive that way. But plants live in one spot and survive quite well. That is because plants do not have to get their food from other sources. They make their own food right where they are. A plant's roots, stems, and leaves allow it to pull what it needs from the soil and air around it. In this chapter, you will learn how a plant's parts work together to help make food and reproduce.

ORGANIZE YOUR THOUGHTS

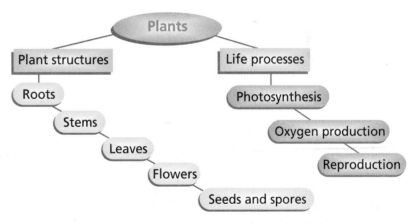

Plants

Plant structures

Roots

Stems

Leaves

Flowers

Seeds and spores

Life processes

Photosynthesis

Oxygen production

Reproduction

Goals for Learning

▶ To identify the main parts of a plant
▶ To explain how plants make food, transport food and water, and produce oxygen
▶ To describe how plants reproduce

To make food and survive, plant roots take water and minerals from the soil. Plant leaves collect light from the sun and carbon dioxide from the air. A vascular system of tiny tubes runs through the roots, leaves, and stems of most plants. It connects all parts of the plant. Without this system, the parts of the plant could not do their jobs.

What Roots Do

Have you ever tried to pull a weed out of the ground? You were probably surprised by how hard you had to pull. You discovered an important function of roots. They hold plants firmly in the ground. Roots also have three other functions. First, they absorb water and minerals from the soil. Roots push their way through the soil to reach the water and minerals they need. Second, roots store water and minerals. They can also store food that is made in leaves. Third, the root vascular system brings water and minerals to other parts of the plant.

Roots hold a plant in the ground, absorb water and minerals, and store food.

Annual growth ring

Annual growth ring
Rings in a tree trunk formed by the growth of wood in layers.

Phloem
The vascular tissue in plants that carries food from leaves to other parts of the plant.

Xylem
The vascular tissue in plants that carries water and minerals from roots to stems and leaves.

The Parts of a Root

The tip of a root is always growing. As it grows, it pushes its way through the soil.

Millions of tiny root hairs cover the tip of each root. It is the root hairs that absorb water and minerals from the soil. Roots can store the water and minerals until needed. Water and minerals can also move to the stems and leaves through the root's vascular tissue. **Xylem** vascular tissue forms tubes that carry water and minerals from roots to stems and leaves. The leaves use the water and minerals to make food. **Phloem** vascular tissue forms tubes that carry food from leaves to stems and roots. The roots can also store food.

What Stems Do

Stems are the parts of plants that connect the leaves with the roots. Most stems are above the ground. Stems have three functions. First, stems support the leaves. They hold the leaves up so that they can receive sunlight. Second, stems transport food, water, and minerals through the plant. Third, stems can store food.

The Parts of a Stem

Like roots, stems contain xylem and phloem. They also contain a special layer of growth tissue. It produces new layers of xylem and phloem cells. These layers build up in some plants, so stems become thicker as they get taller. In trees, these layers become wood. In a tree trunk, one layer forms a new ring each year. You can count these rings, called **annual growth rings**, to tell the tree's age.

Xylem and phloem form the annual growth rings of trees.

Petiole
The stalk that attaches a leaf to a stem.

Stoma
A small opening in a leaf that allows gases to enter and leave; plural is stomata.

What are some leaves that you might eat?

What Leaves Do

Leaves are the parts of the plant that trap sunlight. Leaves have four functions. First, they make food. Second, they store food. Third, they transport food to stems. Fourth, they allow gases to enter and leave the plant.

The Parts of a Leaf

Leaves have three main parts: the petiole, the blade, and the veins. The **petiole**, or stalk, attaches the leaf to a stem or a branch. The blade is the main part of the leaf. It collects light from the sun to make food. Many leaves are thin and have flat surfaces. A tree full of leaves can gather large amounts of energy from the sun.

The veins are part of the plant's vascular system. They are thin tubes that are arranged in a pattern. Veins run throughout the blade. They also run through the petiole to the stem. The veins of leaves transport food and water between the stem and the leaf.

The underside of each leaf has many small openings called stomata. Each opening is called a **stoma**. Stomata allow gases, such as carbon dioxide and oxygen, to enter and leave the leaf. Water vapor also leaves through stomata.

The parts of a leaf are the petiole, the blade, and the veins.

Self-Check

1. What are the functions of roots?
2. What is the difference between xylem and phloem tissue?
3. How are annual growth rings made?
4. What are the main parts of a leaf?
5. What do stomata do?

All plants make food in a process called **photosynthesis**. Why is this important to you? To live, people need the food that plants make. Much of the food you eat comes directly from plants. The rest comes from animals that eat plants or that feed on plant-eating animals.

The Process of Photosynthesis

During photosynthesis, plants use the energy of sunlight to turn carbon dioxide and water into simple sugars (food) and oxygen. How do plants get the energy, carbon dioxide, and water they need for photosynthesis? Carbon dioxide comes from the air. It enters the leaves through the stomata. Water comes up from the roots through the xylem. The minerals that the roots absorb also help the plant make food.

Plants use energy, water, and carbon dioxide to make food.

Photosynthesis
The process in which a plant makes food.

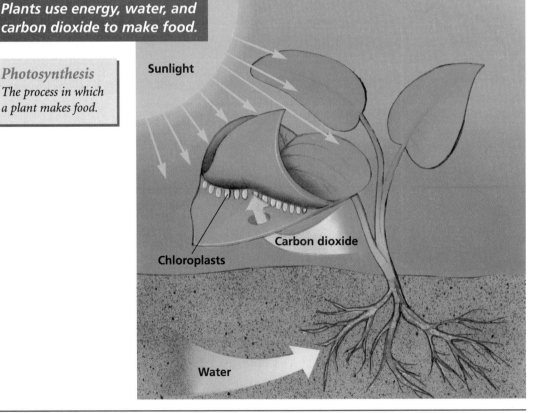

Sunlight

Carbon dioxide

Chloroplasts

Water

Chlorophyll
The green pigment in plants that captures light energy for photosynthesis.

Pigment
A chemical that absorbs certain types of light.

Plants get the energy they need when light shines on their chloroplasts. Chloroplasts are organelles in plant cells where photosynthesis takes place. Chloroplasts contain a green pigment called **chlorophyll**. A **pigment** is a chemical that absorbs certain types of light. The cells of the green parts of plants, such as leaves, contain many chloroplasts. When sunlight hits chloroplasts in the leaves, the chlorophyll absorbs light. The sunlight then supplies the energy for photosynthesis.

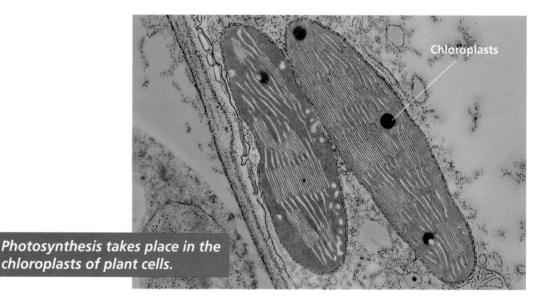

Chloroplasts

Photosynthesis takes place in the chloroplasts of plant cells.

Plants use the energy to split water into hydrogen and oxygen. The oxygen leaves the plant through the stomata and goes into the air. The hydrogen combines with the carbon dioxide to make simple sugar. Plants store the energy of sunlight in the sugar as chemical energy.

Chemical Energy

Chemical energy is energy stored in the bonds that hold a chemical's molecules together. When the chemical breaks apart, the energy is released. Glucose is the simple sugar that plants make during photosynthesis. Glucose contains stored chemical energy. Plants and animals that eat plants use that stored energy. In Lesson 3, you will learn how plants and animals use this energy.

The Chemical Equation for Photosynthesis

You can write a chemical equation that shows how photosynthesis works. In an equation, the left side and the right side are equal. Each side of this equation has the same number of oxygen, hydrogen, and carbon atoms. The chemical equation for photosynthesis looks like this:

$$6CO_2 + 6H_2O + \text{light energy} \longrightarrow C_6H_{12}O_6 + 6O_2$$

carbon dioxide + water + light energy makes sugar + oxygen

The substances to the left of the arrow are those needed for photosynthesis: carbon dioxide (CO_2), water (H_2O), and light from the sun. The substances to the right of the arrow are the products of photosynthesis: sugar ($C_6H_{12}O_6$) and oxygen (O_2). In photosynthesis, six molecules of carbon dioxide ($6CO_2$) join with six molecules of water ($6H_2O$). They form one molecule of sugar ($C_6H_{12}O_6$) and six molecules of oxygen ($6O_2$).

Self-Check

1. Why are leaves green?
2. What is photosynthesis and where does it occur?
3. What do plants need to make food?
4. What is the source of the chemical energy stored in plants?
5. What is the chemical equation for photosynthesis?

Objectives

After reading this lesson, you should be able to
- ▶ identify the importance of oxygen for all living things.
- ▶ describe how plants produce and release oxygen.

Oxygen is a gas that all living things need. You breathe in oxygen thousands of times each day. Most of that oxygen was released by plants during photosynthesis.

Properties of a Gas

Gases make up the air around you. Fan yourself with a piece of paper. The breeze you feel on your face is moving air. Why can you not see or hold air? The tiny, invisible particles of the gases in air are far apart. There is a lot of space between them. The particles move around quickly. You cannot hold or touch a gas such as air. In a solid, such as your desk, the particles are packed tightly together. They hardly move. That is why you can touch the desk.

Cellular respiration
The process in which cells break down food to release energy.

The Importance of Oxygen

Two of the most important gases in the air that you breathe are carbon dioxide and oxygen. Oxygen is important to most living things. They use oxygen to break down food to release the chemical energy stored in it. This process is called **cellular respiration**.

Photosynthesis happens only in plants. Respiration happens in both plants and animals. Cellular respiration is a special low-temperature kind of burning that breaks down glucose. Glucose is the simple sugar that plants make during photosynthesis. Glucose is also your body's main source of energy. You get that energy when your cells burn sugars and starches that come from plants you eat. Your body cells use oxygen to break apart the sugar molecules. During cellular respiration, oxygen combines with hydrogen to make water. Carbon dioxide is released as a waste product. Does this sound familiar? It is the opposite of photosynthesis.

Photosynthesis and respiration are part of the carbon dioxide–oxygen cycle. Plants take in carbon dioxide and water and give off oxygen during photosynthesis. Plants and animals take in oxygen and give off carbon dioxide and water during respiration. This cycle is necessary for life on Earth.

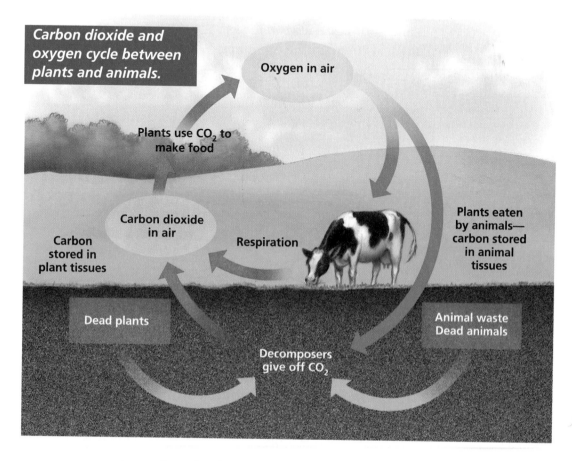

Carbon dioxide and oxygen cycle between plants and animals.

Oxygen in air

Plants use CO$_2$ to make food

Carbon dioxide in air

Carbon stored in plant tissues

Respiration

Plants eaten by animals— carbon stored in animal tissues

Dead plants

Animal waste Dead animals

Decomposers give off CO$_2$

Producing Oxygen

The oxygen that plants produce comes from water. During photosynthesis, plants use water and carbon dioxide to make sugars. Photosynthesis splits water into hydrogen and oxygen. The hydrogen combines with the carbon dioxide to make sugar and more water. The oxygen becomes oxygen gas. The plant uses some of the oxygen for cellular respiration. A plant, however, makes more oxygen than it needs. The rest of the oxygen leaves the plant and goes into the air.

Guard cell
A cell that opens and closes stomata.

Releasing Oxygen

The oxygen that goes out of the plant into the air leaves through the stomata. Remember that stomata are small openings on a leaf. Each stoma has two special cells called **guard cells.** The size and shape of the guard cells change as they take up and release water. When the guard cells take up water and swell, the stomata open. Oxygen, carbon dioxide, and water vapor can move in and out of the leaf through the openings. When the guard cells lose water, the stomata close.

During droughts, stomata are closed most of the time. How would this affect the rate of photosynthesis? How would this affect the growth of crop plants?

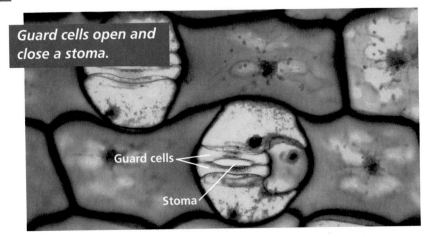

Guard cells open and close a stoma.

Guard cells

Stoma

The amount of light affects the opening and closing of stomata. The stomata of most plants close at night. They open during the day when photosynthesis takes place. The amount of water also affects the opening and closing of stomata. When the soil and air are dry, stomata close, even during the day. This prevents the plant from losing water during short dry periods.

Self-Check

1. Why can you not see or feel a gas?
2. Why do living things need oxygen?
3. How is respiration the opposite of photosynthesis?
4. What happens to water during photosynthesis?
5. What do guard cells do?

Asexual reproduction
Reproduction that involves one parent and no egg or sperm.

Sexual reproduction
Reproduction that involves two parents, an egg, and sperm.

Zygote
A fertilized cell.

Plants can reproduce by sexual reproduction or by asexual reproduction. **Sexual reproduction** involves two parents. The female parent provides the egg. The male parent provides the sperm. The sperm and egg cells join to form a new plant. **Asexual reproduction** involves only one parent and no egg or sperm. Many plants can reproduce sexually and asexually.

Reproduction in Seedless Plants

Mosses and ferns are seedless plants. They reproduce asexually and sexually. Asexual reproduction happens when a small piece of the parent plant breaks off. That piece forms a new plant.

Seedless plants reproduce sexually from spores. A spore is a reproductive cell with a thick protective coating. Spores develop into tiny plants that are male, female, or both male and female. The plants produce sperm and eggs. A sperm cell swims to an egg cell through the moisture around the plants. The egg and sperm come together during fertilization. The fertilized cell is called a **zygote**. The zygote is the beginning of a new plant. When the plant matures, it produces spores that produce a new generation of plants.

Reproduction in Seed Plants

There are two types of seed plants, flowering plants and nonflowering plants. Seed plants can reproduce asexually. New plants can grow from a piece of a plant called a cutting. A single leaf or stem can grow roots and become a new plant. However, seed plants usually reproduce sexually.

Seedless plants such as ferns reproduce from spores.

Sexual Reproduction in Angiosperms

Some plants can grow from a single leaf. Is this sexual or asexual reproduction?

Flowering plants are angiosperms. The flower is the part of an angiosperm that contains eggs and sperm. In a flower, the **stamens** are the male organs of reproduction. They produce the **pollen**, which contain sperm. The **pistil** is the female organ of reproduction. The lower part of the pistil is the **ovary**, which contains eggs.

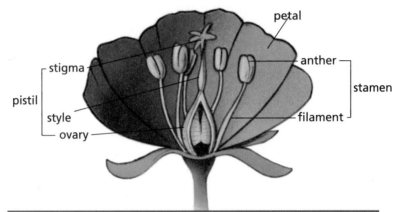

Flowers are the reproductive organs of angiosperms.

For reproduction to take place, the sperm in pollen must fertilize the egg. Flowers have many colors and shapes to attract insects and birds. They land on flowers to drink **nectar**, which is a sweet liquid that many kinds of flowers produce. While insects and birds drink, pollen sticks to their bodies. They carry the pollen to the pistil of other flowers or the same flower. Wind also spreads pollen. The process in which pollen is transferred from the stamen to the pistil is called **pollination**.

Fertilization

After pollination, the pollen grain grows a tube. The tube reaches down through the pistil to the eggs in the ovary. When the pollen inside the tube meets an egg, fertilization takes place. A new plant forms. The ovary grows and becomes a fruit with seeds inside. The fruit protects the seeds.

Germinate
To start to grow into a new plant; sprout.

Seeds

Seeds contain the embryo, or beginning stages of a new plant. If the temperature and amount of water are just right, the seed **germinates**. That means it starts to grow into a new plant. Seeds also contain stored food. The young plant uses this food until it can make its own. If the new plant is fertilized, a new set of seeds develops in the ovary.

Sexual Reproduction in Gymnosperms

Gymnosperms are nonflowering plants. The largest group of gymnosperms are conifers, or cone-bearing plants.

How are male and female cones different?

Most evergreen trees are gymnosperms. The reproductive organs of gymnosperms are in cones, not flowers. Some cones are male. Some are female. Male cones are usually smaller than female cones.

During reproduction, male cones release millions of pollen grains into the air. Some of the pollen reaches female cones. As in flowering plants, the pollen grain grows a tube that reaches eggs in the ovary. When the pollen and egg meet, fertilization takes place. But unlike angiosperms, a fruit does not cover gymnosperm seeds. The uncovered seeds are under the scales of the cones.

Self-Check

1. What is the difference between sexual reproduction and asexual reproduction?
2. Which types of plants use spores to reproduce?
3. Describe the process of fertilization in angiosperms.
4. What happens when a seed germinates?
5. Describe the process of reproduction in a conifer.

Chapter 7

INVESTIGATION

Growing an African Violet From a Leaf

Materials

✓ African violet plant
✓ water
✓ 2 paper cups
✓ aluminum foil
✓ pencil
✓ potting soil

Purpose
To grow a plant, using asexual reproduction

Procedure

1. Have your teacher cut a leaf with a long stem from the African violet plant.

2. Fill a cup with water, then cover it with aluminum foil. With a pencil, poke a hole in the center of the foil.

3. Insert the leaf into the hole. The end of the stem should be in the water.

4. Place the leaf and cup in a window where the leaf will get sunlight.

5. Change the water in the cup every few days. As you do, observe the end of the stem. Observe and record any changes.

6. When roots appear and begin to grow, plant your leaf in a cup of potting soil. Bury the roots and part of the stem in the soil. Water the soil.

7. Place the potted leaf on a windowsill. Keep the soil moist. What eventually happens?

Questions

1. What was the first change that you observed in the leaf? Describe your observation.

2. Why do you think the plant produced this type of new growth?

3. How does the plant change after the leaf is planted in soil?

4. What type of reproduction occurred in this investigation? Explain your answer.

Explore Further

Many plants will grow from leaf or stem cuttings. Try to grow some other plants this way. You may want to use a book on houseplants as a reference.

What makes a fruit a fruit?

If someone asked you to name a fruit, would you think of a tomato? Probably not. You are more likely to think of an apple, an orange, or a banana. We usually think of fruits as plant parts that contain sugar and taste sweet. But a fruit is a ripened ovary. It is usually the part of the plant that protects the seeds. According to that definition, a tomato is a fruit. So are cucumbers, squashes, and string beans.

The presence of seeds is usually a clue that the food is a fruit. Today, however, some fruits are specially raised so that they have no seeds. Many types of navel oranges have been developed to be seedless. There are also seedless grapes and watermelons. The bananas we eat do not have seeds because the fruit grows without fertilization.

The fruits of plants are an important part of a well-balanced diet. They provide important nutrients such as vitamins A, B, and C, and potassium. Fresh fruits are also a good source of fiber, a substance that aids digestion. A healthy diet includes two to four servings of fruit each day.

- Roots hold plants in the ground and absorb water and minerals.

- Food is moved from the leaves and stems back to the roots through phloem vascular tissue. Food can be stored in the roots.

- Stems support the leaves, store food, and transport food, water, and minerals through the plant.

- Most leaves are thin and flat with three main parts: the petiole, the blade, and the veins.

- Plants make food in the green parts of the plant. The cells in these parts contain chloroplasts, where photosynthesis takes place.

- Plants need carbon dioxide and water to make food. Food stores chemical energy. The process of releasing energy from food is cellular respiration.

- Plants give off oxygen gas. All living things need oxygen for cellular respiration.

- The oxygen a plant produces leaves the plant through the stomata.

- Plants can reproduce by sexual reproduction, which involves two parents, or by asexual reproduction, which involves only one parent.

- Plants reproduce asexually by growing new plants from parts or cuttings. Mosses and ferns reproduce sexually by forming spores. Seed plants reproduce sexually by producing seeds.

- Angiosperms use flowers to reproduce sexually. Pollen from the stamen fertilizes an egg in the pistil. A fruit surrounds the seed.

- In gymnosperms, male and female organs are in different cones or in different trees. A fruit does not surround the seed.

Science Words		
	guard cell, 142	pollen, 144
	nectar, 144	pollination, 144
annual growth rings, 135	ovary, 144	sexual reproduction, 143
asexual reproduction, 143	petiole, 136	
cellular respiration, 140	phloem, 135	stamen, 144
chlorophyll, 138	photosynthesis, 137	stoma, 136
germinate, 145	pigment, 138	xylem, 135
	pistil, 144	zygote, 143

Vocabulary Review

Number your paper from 1 to 14. Then choose the word or words from the Word Bank that best complete each sentence. Write the answer on your paper.

WORD BANK
asexual reproduction
cellular respiration
chlorophyll
germinate
guard cell
phloem
photosynthesis
pistil
pollen
pollination
sexual reproduction
stamen
stigma
stomata
xylem

1. In _____, there is only one parent.

2. The type of cell that opens and closes a stoma is a(n) _____.

3. Food moves around in a plant through _____ .

4. Water and minerals move in a plant through _____.

5. Gases move in and out of a leaf through _____.

6. Plants make simple sugars during _____.

7. Pollen is transferred from the stamen to the top of the pistil in the process of _____.

8. The male part of a flower is the _____.

9. The sperm of seed plants is contained in grains of _____.

10. Reproduction that involves egg and sperm is _____.

11. Oxygen is used and carbon dioxide is given off during _____.

12. The green pigment, _____, captures light energy for photosynthesis.

13. The female part of a flower is the _____.

14. When conditions are right, a seed will _____, or start growing into a new plant.

Concept Review

Number your paper from 1 to 4. Then choose the answer that best completes each sentence. Write the letter of the answer on your page.

1. The main parts of a plant are roots, stems, and _____.

    a. leaves   **b.** stomata   **c.** pollen

2. Water vapor, carbon dioxide, and oxygen enter and leave a plant through the _____.

    a. roots   **b.** flowers   **c.** stomata

3. The food that is made during photosynthesis contains _____ energy.

    a. chemical   **b.** light   **c.** cellular

4. The process in which a sperm joins with an egg is _____.

    a. pollination   **b.** fertilization   **c.** respiration

Critical Thinking

Write the answer to each of the following questions.

1. The chemical formula for glucose is $C_6H_{12}O_6$. How many carbon, hydrogen, and oxygen atoms does one molecule of glucose have?

2. Explain how energy for animals comes from the sun.

Test Taking Tip   When answering multiple choice questions, be sure to read all the choices.

Chapter

8

Human Body Systems

I f someone asked you to name the most amazing machine, what would your answer be? Suppose you got some hints. This machine has a strong, yet light, frame. It can move from place to place. If it gets a scratch, it fixes itself in a day or two. The machine carries food to its working parts. It lasts an average of 75 years. Its command center works like a computer. It has many systems that work together. You have probably figured out already that the most amazing "machine" is the human body—you.

ORGANIZE YOUR THOUGHTS

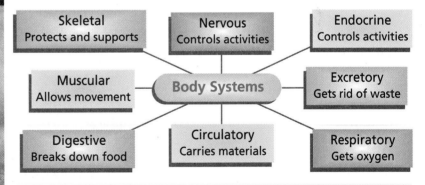

Skeletal
Protects and supports

Nervous
Controls activities

Endocrine
Controls activities

Muscular
Allows movement

Body Systems

Excretory
Gets rid of waste

Digestive
Breaks down food

Circulatory
Carries materials

Respiratory
Gets oxygen

Goals for Learning

▶ To identify eight systems of the human body
▶ To describe the structure and function of each human body system
▶ To recognize that body systems work together to carry out basic life activities

Digestion

Your body is made up of several systems that work together to maintain your good health. One of these systems is your digestive system, which breaks down food for your body to use. Food contains energy for your body's cells. However, this food is too large to enter cells. The food must be broken down into smaller pieces. This process is called digestion. Food contains carbohydrates, proteins, and fats. In digestion, these nutrients are broken down into a form that your cells can use for energy. As you read about digestion, refer to the drawing of the digestive system shown below.

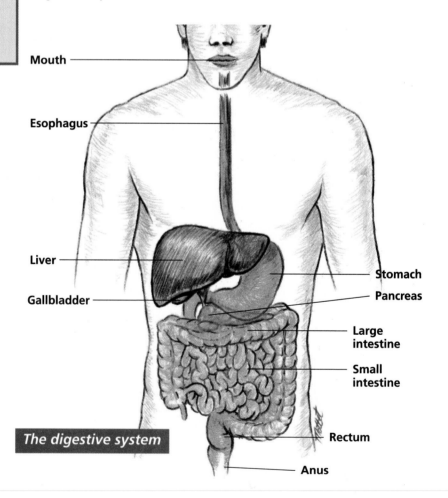

Mouth

Esophagus

Liver

Gallbladder

Stomach

Pancreas

Large intestine

Small intestine

Rectum

Anus

The digestive system

Why do you think chewing your food well helps your digestion?

Digestion Begins Inside Your Mouth

Your teeth and jaws chew and crush food while your tongue turns it over. This mechanical action makes pieces of food smaller. As you chew, salivary glands secrete saliva, a fluid that has a digestive enzyme. An enzyme is a protein that causes chemical changes. The enzyme in saliva changes carbohydrates into sugars as you chew. Digestive enzymes help to break down food. Each part of the digestive system has its own special digestive enzymes.

Digestion begins in the mouth.

Salivary glands

Tongue

The Esophagus

As you chew, food moves around in your mouth. When you swallow, the food moves into your pharynx, or throat. From there, it moves into the esophagus. This long tube connects the mouth to the stomach. Smooth muscles in the esophagus contract, or squeeze together, to push food toward the stomach. This movement is called **peristalsis**.

Chyme
Liquid food in the digestive tract that is partly digested.

Peristalsis
The movement of digestive organs that pushes food through the digestive tract.

The Stomach

Digestion continues in the stomach. Strong muscles of the stomach walls contract. This action churns and mixes the food. The stomach walls secrete digestive juices. These juices are hydrochloric acid and digestive enzymes. A special moist lining protects the stomach from being eaten away by the acids. The acid and enzymes break down large molecules of food. Solid food becomes liquid. This liquid food is called **chyme**.

The Small Intestine

Peristalsis squirts chyme from the stomach into the small intestine. The small intestine is a coiled tube that is about 4 to 7 meters long. This is where most digestion takes place.

Two organs and a gland close to the small intestine aid digestion. These are the liver, the gallbladder, and the pancreas. The liver makes a fluid called **bile**. Bile breaks apart fat molecules. The **gallbladder** stores the bile. The bile enters the small intestine through a tube called a bile duct. The pancreas is a gland that secretes enzymes that complete the digestion of carbohydrates, proteins, and fats.

By this time, the food molecules are ready to be absorbed, or taken in, by body cells. They are absorbed through tiny, fingerlike structures called **villi**. Thousands of villi line the small intestine. Villi make the surface area of the intestine larger. Many food molecules can be absorbed through the blood vessels of the villi. Blood carries the food molecules to cells all through the body.

Did You Know?

If the villi in the small intestine could be laid out flat, the area would be as big as a baseball diamond.

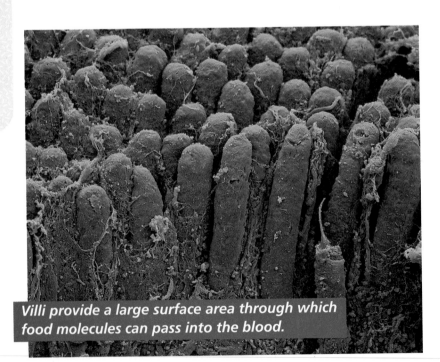

Villi provide a large surface area through which food molecules can pass into the blood.

The Large Intestine

Peristalsis moves material that cannot be digested to the large intestine. The main function of the large intestine is to remove water from undigested material. The water is returned to the body. The undigested material forms a solid mass called **feces**. Feces are stored in the rectum for a short time. The **rectum** is the last part of the large intestine. Smooth muscles line the large intestine. They contract and push the feces out of the body through an opening called the anus. The journey of food through your digestive system takes about 24 to 33 hours.

Feces
Solid waste material remaining in the large intestine after digestion.

Rectum
Lower part of the large intestine where feces are stored.

Self-Check

1. What does the digestive system do?
2. Where and how does digestion begin?
3. Describe the path that food takes through the digestive system.
4. Why are villi shaped the way they are?
5. How do feces leave the body?

Body cells must have a way to get oxygen and nutrients. They must get rid of wastes. The circulatory system performs these functions. The circulatory system consists of the heart and blood vessels. The heart pumps blood throughout the body through blood vessels. Blood carries food and oxygen to all the body cells. Blood also carries away wastes from the body cells.

The Heart

The main organ of the circulatory system is the heart. The heart is about the size of a human fist. It is located between the lungs in the chest cavity. The heart is the most powerful organ in the body. It is made mostly of muscle tissue called **cardiac** muscle. The heart contracts and relaxes in a regular rhythm known as the heartbeat. The heartbeat is automatic. A person does not have to think about it to make it happen.

The heart beats about 70 times a minute in adults who are sitting or standing quietly. The heart beats faster in children and teenagers. The heart beats even faster when a person runs, swims, or does other physical activities. Each time the heart contracts, it squeezes blood out of itself and into blood vessels. Pressure increases inside the walls of certain blood vessels, and they bulge. This bulge can be felt at the wrist and on the side of the neck as the pulse.

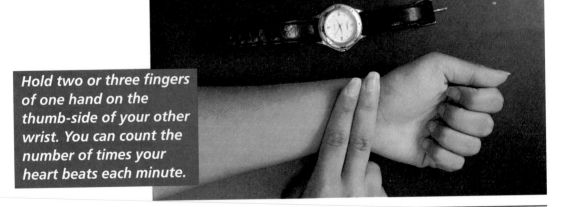

Hold two or three fingers of one hand on the thumb-side of your other wrist. You can count the number of times your heart beats each minute.

How Blood Circulates

Look at the picture of the heart below. Notice that it has two sides, left and right. Each side has an upper chamber called the atrium and a lower chamber called the ventricle. Use your finger to trace over the picture as you read how blood moves through the heart.

The right atrium receives blood from the rest of the body. The blood is low in oxygen and high in carbon dioxide. The blood moves into the right ventricle. The right ventricle pumps the blood to the lungs. In the lungs, the blood is filled with oxygen. Carbon dioxide leaves the blood and is exhaled, or breathed out. From the lungs, blood that is high in oxygen goes back to the heart. It goes first to the left atrium and then to the left ventricle. The left ventricle is a thick, powerful muscle. It sends the blood surging out through a large vessel called the aorta. The blood then moves to the rest of the body.

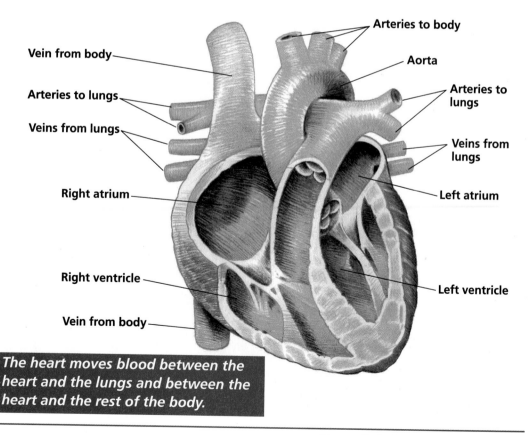

Vein from body

Arteries to lungs

Veins from lungs

Right atrium

Right ventricle

Vein from body

Arteries to body

Aorta

Arteries to lungs

Veins from lungs

Left atrium

Left ventricle

The heart moves blood between the heart and the lungs and between the heart and the rest of the body.

Why does blood shoot out in spurts if you cut an artery?

Blood Vessels

Blood travels in only one direction to form a circle pattern. Blood vessels that carry blood away from the heart are called arteries. Arteries carry blood full of oxygen. The aorta is the largest artery. The aorta leads to the rest of the body. The arteries become smaller as they move away from the heart. Only one artery carries blood high in carbon dioxide. This artery carries blood from the right ventricle to the lungs.

Tiny arteries branch into blood vessels called capillaries. The walls of the capillaries are only one cell thick. Oxygen and food molecules pass easily through the capillary walls to cells. Wastes, such as carbon dioxide, move into the capillaries from cells. The body has so many capillaries that each of its millions of cells is next to a capillary wall.

Capillaries that branched out from arteries join up again to form veins. Veins are blood vessels that carry blood to the heart. They carry carbon dioxide from the cells. Veins become larger as they move toward the heart. Pressure from the heart is not as great in veins as in arteries. Veins have one-way valves that keep the blood from flowing backward. Some veins are squeezed by muscles. This helps blood flow back to the heart. For example, when you walk, the muscles in your legs help blood to flow from your legs back to your heart. Only one vein carries blood high in oxygen. This vein carries blood from the lungs into the heart.

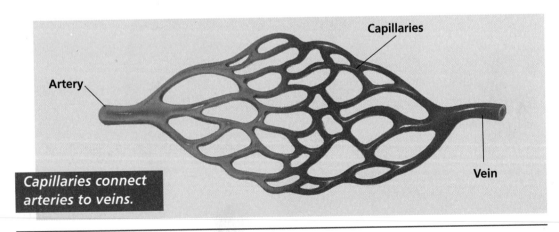

Capillaries connect arteries to veins.

Blood Pressure

Blood pressure is the force of blood against the walls of blood vessels, usually arteries. When your heart beats, blood is pushed into the arteries. This forces the artery walls to bulge for a moment. The heart works hard to pump blood so that it reaches every part of the body. If blood vessels lose their ability to stretch, blood pressure rises. If blood pressure goes up too high, the heart can be damaged.

Blood and Its Parts

Blood does more than deliver oxygen and carry wastes to the lungs. As you recall from Lesson 1, it also delivers nutrients from the digestive system to cells. Food molecules pass through blood vessels in the villi. Blood carries waste products to the kidneys. You will learn more about that in Lesson 4. Blood also contains materials that fight infections and heal wounds.

Blood has a liquid part and a part that contains cells. The liquid part of blood is called **plasma**. Plasma is mostly water. It makes up half of your blood. Plasma contains dissolved substances including oxygen, food molecules, minerals, and vitamins.

Some proteins in plasma fight disease. These proteins are called **antibodies**. Antibodies help a person to be immune to, or resist, disease. Antibodies fight harmful microorganisms and cancer cells. Your body makes antibodies against these foreign substances. It makes one kind of antibody for each different foreign substance.

Red blood cells make up almost half of the blood. These cells are filled with **hemoglobin**, which is a protein that carries oxygen in the blood. Oxygen plus hemoglobin gives blood its bright red color. Hemoglobin easily gives up oxygen to the cells. It picks up carbon dioxide. In the lungs, hemoglobin exchanges carbon dioxide for oxygen.

White blood cells are larger than red blood cells. However, they are fewer. There is only about one white blood cell for every 700 red cells. Like antibodies, white blood cells protect the body against foreign substances. White blood cells move through the walls of capillaries to where they are needed. Some wrap themselves around invaders and trap them. Others make chemicals that kill harmful germs. Some white blood cells work with antibodies to destroy invaders. One kind of white blood cell makes antibodies.

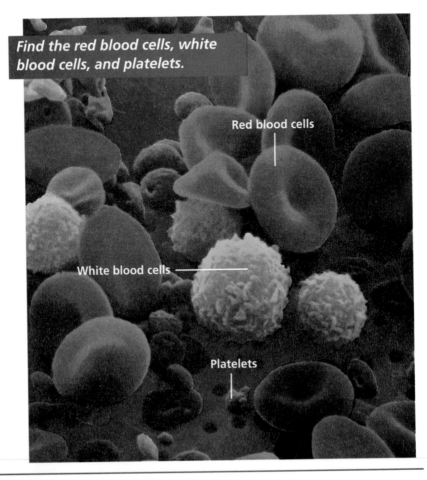

Find the red blood cells, white blood cells, and platelets.

Red blood cells

White blood cells

Platelets

Platelet
A tiny piece of cell that helps form clots.

Platelets are tiny cell pieces that help blood to clot. A clot is a thick mass of blood. Platelets do not have a regular shape like red and white blood cells. Platelets collect at the place where skin is cut. They stick to each other and to the broken blood vessel. Red blood cells stick to the platelets. This mass of platelets and red blood cells forms a clot.

Blood Types

People have one of four blood types. These are Type A, Type B, Type AB, and Type O. Different blood types are caused by different proteins in the red blood cells. Sometimes people who are injured or who have certain illnesses need blood. They may receive a blood transfusion to replace lost blood. Blood banks with the different blood types are set up to provide blood. Before a transfusion, health care workers must identify the patient's blood type. If the wrong blood type is given, the person's blood clumps. This blocks the tiny capillaries. Oxygen does not get to cells. Without oxygen, cells die.

Self-Check

1. What are the two main parts of the circulatory system?
2. What is the difference between arteries and veins?
3. What does blood do?
4. What are the functions of red blood cells, white blood cells, and platelets?
5. Why is it important to know your blood type?

INVESTIGATION

How Does Exercise Change Heart Rate?

Materials

✓ watch or clock with a second hand

✓ paper and pencil

✓ graph paper

Purpose

To observe the changes in heart rate during different amounts of activity

Procedure

1. Copy the table below on a sheet of paper.

2. Sit quietly for three minutes. Then find your pulse as shown on page 158.

3. Take your pulse. To do this, count the number of times you feel your pulse for 15 seconds. Multiply this number by 4. Your answer is your pulse for one minute. Record this number as your resting heart rate.

Activity	Heart rate
Sitting (resting heart rate)	
Standing up	
After running in place	
Resting 30 seconds	
Resting 1 minute	
Resting 1½ minutes	
Resting 2 minutes	
Resting 2½ minutes	
Resting 3 minutes	

4. Stand up and immediately take your pulse again. Record this number.

5. Run in place for 200 steps. Then immediately take your pulse and record it.

6. Sit quietly for 30 seconds and take your pulse again. Record this number.

7. Repeat step 6 until you have taken your pulse every 30 seconds for three minutes. Remember to record your data.

8. Graph all of your data. Set up the graph so that time is on the x-axis (the line that runs the same direction as the bottom of the page). Put your heart rate on the y-axis (which runs the same direction as the side of the page).

Questions

1. How does the amount of activity affect heart rate?

2. Describe the demands on your heart when the heart rate was lowest and when it was highest.

3. Why does the heart rate change as the amount of activity changes?

Explore Further

Find out what "mild" activities increase heart rate. Try taking your pulse after talking, coughing, drinking, or eating.

Alveolus
A tiny air sac where respiration happens. Plural is alveoli.

Bronchiole
A tube that branches off the bronchus.

Bronchus
A tube that connects the trachea and lungs. Plural is bronchi.

Trachea
The tube that carries air to the bronchi.

The Respiratory System

The function of the respiratory system is to get oxygen into the body and to get rid of carbon dioxide. Lungs are the most important organs in the respiratory system. They connect your body to the outside air. The circulatory system then carries the oxygen from your lungs to the rest of your body. You have two lungs. One is in the right side of your chest, and one is in the left side. Your heart lies between them.

How Air Moves to the Lungs

Look at the picture on page 167. Air comes into your body through your nose and mouth. It travels through the pharynx. Air and food share this passageway. From the pharynx, the air moves through the larynx, or voice box. A flap of tissue covers the larynx when you swallow. This tissue prevents food from going into your airways. From the larynx, air moves into a large tube called the **trachea**, or windpipe. The trachea branches into two smaller tubes called **bronchi**. One bronchus goes into each lung. In the lungs, each bronchus branches into smaller tubes called bronchial tubes. The bronchial tubes continue to branch and become **bronchioles.**

Respiration

At the end of each bronchiole are tiny sacs that hold air. They are so small that you need a microscope to see them. These microscopic air sacs are called **alveoli**. The walls of alveoli are only one cell thick. They are always moist. Many tiny capillaries act like nets and wrap around the alveoli.

Blood returning to the heart from the rest of the body is full of carbon dioxide. The right ventricle pumps blood through an artery to the lungs. Recall that this is the only artery in the body that is high in carbon dioxide instead of oxygen. It is called the pulmonary artery. *Pulmonary* means "lung." The carbon dioxide passes out of the capillaries around the alveoli. Carbon dioxide leaves the body when you exhale, or breathe out.

When you inhale, or breathe in, oxygen comes into the lungs. The oxygen moves through the walls of the alveoli. Oxygen then moves through the walls of the tiny capillaries and into the blood. The exchange of carbon dioxide and oxygen is called respiration.

A vein carries the blood that is high in oxygen to the left atrium. This vein is called the pulmonary vein. Recall that it is the only vein that carries blood high in oxygen.

Breathing

At rest, you usually breathe about 12 times a minute. With each breath, the lungs stretch and you take in about half a liter of air. A strong muscle below your lungs helps you breathe. This muscle is called the diaphragm. It separates the lung cavity from the abdominal cavity.

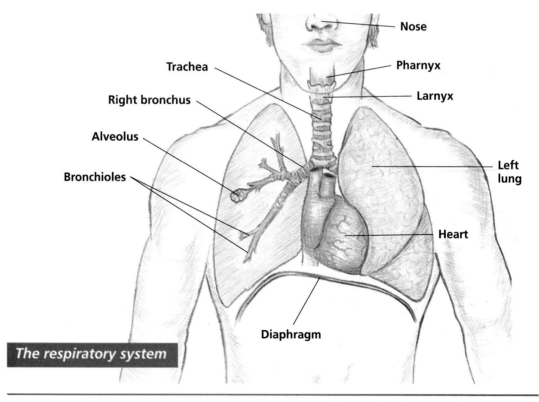

Nose

Trachea

Pharnyx

Right bronchus

Larnyx

Alveolus

Left lung

Bronchioles

Heart

Diaphragm

The respiratory system

Breathing happens partly because the pressure inside the chest cavity changes. When the diaphragm contracts, or tightens, it moves down. The ribs move upward. This movement increases the volume of the chest cavity. Air is inhaled, or pulled in, to fill this larger volume. When the diaphragm relaxes, it moves up. The ribs move downward. This movement reduces the volume of the chest cavity. Air is exhaled, or forced out of the lungs. Just like the heartbeat, breathing is automatic.

Self-Check

1. What is the function of the respiratory system?
2. Describe the path of air from the nose to the alveoli.
3. What is respiration?
4. Where and how does respiration take place?
5. How does the diaphragm move when you inhale and exhale?

SCIENCE IN YOUR LIFE

Cardiopulmonary resuscitation (CPR)

Every day in the United States, about 700 people experience cardiac arrest. This means that the heart stops beating and there is no pulse. Cardiac arrest may occur because of heart disease, electrical shock, poisoning, a drug overdose, drowning, or choking. The circulatory system stops working. Without oxygen, organs begin to shut down. The respiratory system begins to fail. A person can die within minutes if these systems are not working.

A procedure called cardiopulmonary resuscitation (CPR) can fill in temporarily for the heart and lungs. A person performing CPR provides oxygen to the victim until emergency help arrives. In CPR, a person uses rescue breathing and chest compressions.

CPR saves thousands of lives each year in the United States. However, CPR should be performed only by a person who is trained to use it. Find out where you can get CPR training in your community. Call the American Heart Association, the American Red Cross, a fire department, a hospital, a park district, or a library.

Objectives

After reading this lesson, you should be able to

▶ explain how perspiration gets rid of wastes.

▶ describe the function of kidneys.

▶ explain how urine leaves the body.

Perspiration
Liquid waste made of heat, water, and salt released through the skin.

Why is it necessary to drink plenty of fluids if you are perspiring a lot?

Did You Know?

Perspiration by itself does not have an odor. Body odor occurs when bacteria living on the skin break down the wastes in perspiration.

You know that when you exhale, you get rid of carbon dioxide. Carbon dioxide is one of the wastes that cells make when they use oxygen and food to release energy. Other wastes that your cells make include water, heat, salt, and nitrogen. Exhaling releases some of the extra water and heat.

Perspiration

Many wastes leave your body through its largest organ, the skin. Your blood carries heat, water, and salt to sweat glands in your skin. These wastes form a salty liquid called **perspiration**. Thousands of sweat glands in the skin release perspiration through pores onto the skin's surface. Perspiration cools your body as the water evaporates from the skin.

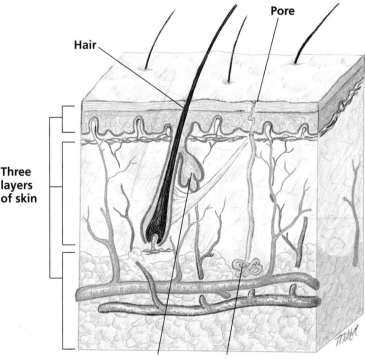

Hair · Pore · Three layers of skin · Oil gland · Sweat gland

One function of the skin is to release wastes.

The Excretory System

Your cells make nitrogen wastes, which are poisonous. The **excretory system** gets rid of these wastes. The **kidneys** are the main organs of the excretory system. The body has two kidneys, located in the lower back. Kidneys filter nitrogen wastes out of the blood. The kidneys also remove some extra water and salt from the blood.

The filtered wastes form a liquid called **urine**. Tubes called **ureters** carry urine from each kidney. The urine collects in the urinary bladder. This muscular bag stretches as it fills. When the urinary bladder is almost full, you feel the need to urinate. When you do, the urinary bladder squeezes urine out of your body through a tube called the **urethra**. Follow the path of urine through the excretory system in the drawing.

Excretory system
A series of organs that gets rid of cell wastes in the form of urine.

Kidney
The organ in the excretory system where urine forms.

Ureter
A tube that carries urine from the kidney to the urinary bladder.

Urethra
The tube that carries urine out of the body.

Urine
Liquid waste formed in the kidneys.

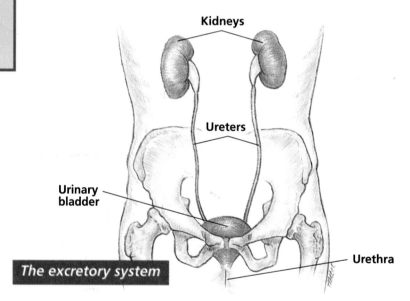

Kidneys

Ureters

Urinary bladder

Urethra

The excretory system

Self-Check

1. List four wastes that your cells produce.
2. What is perspiration?
3. What is the function of kidneys?
4. What is urine made of?
5. Describe how urine travels through the excretory system.

How Does the Nervous System Control the Body?

Objectives

After reading this lesson, you should be able to

▶ identify the structures and functions of the nervous system.

▶ describe how impulses travel.

▶ explain how the eyes "see" objects.

▶ trace a sound wave as it travels through the ear.

▶ describe how the senses of taste and smell work together.

Your body systems constantly work together to keep you healthy and functioning. For your systems to work, however, they have to be coordinated. All the different parts have to know what to do and when to do it. Your body has to respond to changes in the environment. For example, if you run, the heart has to know to pump faster. Your nervous system coordinates all of your body parts. It is your body's communication network.

The Nervous System

The nervous system is divided into two main parts. The central nervous system is made of the brain and the spinal cord. This system controls the activities of the body. The peripheral nervous system is made of nerves outside the central nervous system. This system carries messages between the central nervous system and other parts of the body.

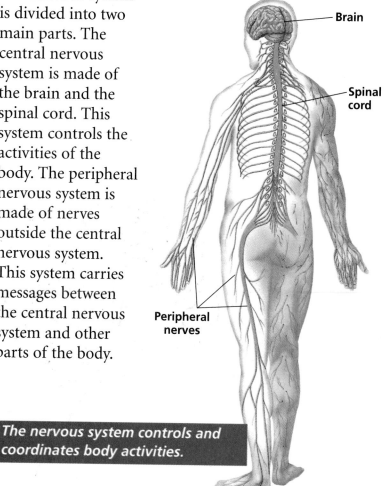

Brain

Spinal cord

Peripheral nerves

The nervous system controls and coordinates body activities.

The Brain

The three parts of the brain are the cerebrum, the cerebellum, and the brain stem. The largest part is the cerebrum, as the drawing shows. The cerebrum controls the way you think, learn, remember, and feel. It controls muscles that let you move body parts, such as your arms and legs. It interprets messages from the sense organs, such as the eyes and ears. The cerebrum is divided into two halves. The left half controls activities on the right side of the body. The right half controls activities on the left side of the body.

The cerebellum lies beneath the cerebrum. The cerebellum controls balance. It helps muscles work together so that you walk and write smoothly.

Under the cerebellum is the brain stem. It connects the brain and the spinal cord. The brain stem controls the automatic activities of your body. This includes heart rate, gland secretions, digestion, respiration, and circulation. The brain stem coordinates movements of muscles that move without you thinking about them, such as your stomach muscles.

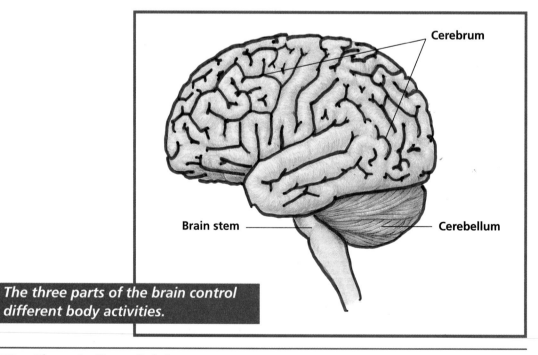

Cerebrum

Brain stem

Cerebellum

The three parts of the brain control different body activities.

Neuron
A nerve cell.

Synapse
A tiny gap between
neurons.

The Spinal Cord

The spinal cord is a thick bunch of nerves that start at the brain stem and go down the back. The spinal cord is protected inside a backbone. The brain sends and receives information through the spinal cord. Thirty-one pairs of spinal nerves branch off from this cord. The spinal nerves send nerve messages all over the body. The spinal cord and brain are the central controls of the sense organs and body systems.

Neurons

Nerve cells are called **neurons**. They send messages in the form of electrical signals all through the body. These messages are called impulses. An impulse carries information from one nerve cell to the next. Neurons do not touch each other. Impulses must cross a small gap, or **synapse**, between neurons. How does this happen? An impulse travels from end to end of a neuron. When the impulse reaches the end of the cell, a chemical is released. The chemical moves out into the synapse and touches the next neuron. This starts another impulse. Information moves through your body by traveling along many neurons.

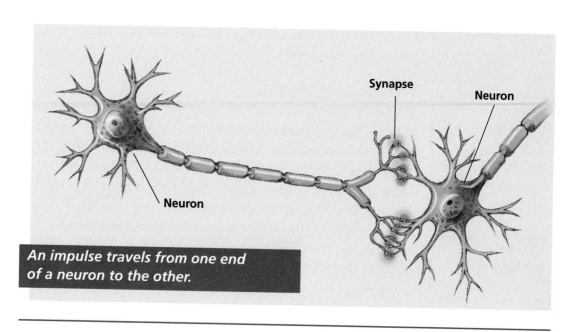

Synapse

Neuron

Neuron

An impulse travels from one end of a neuron to the other.

There are three kinds of neurons in your nervous system. Sensory neurons carry impulses from sense organs to the spinal cord or the brain. Motor neurons carry impulses from the brain and spinal cord to muscles and glands. Associative neurons carry impulses from sensory neurons to motor neurons.

Reflex Actions

Why is it important that your brain control many functions automatically?

Sneezing, coughing, and blinking are reflex actions. They happen automatically. What happens if you touch a hot frying pan? Sensory neurons send the "It is hot!" message to the spinal cord. Inside the spinal cord, associative neurons receive the impulses and send them to the motor neurons. All of this happens in an instant, as you feel the heat. You pull your hand away quickly. You have been saved from a serious burn. Many other reflex actions protect the body from injury. For example, if an object comes flying toward your eyes, you blink without thinking.

Sense Organs

The body connects with the outside world through sense organs. The five main sense organs are the eyes, ears, skin, nose, and tongue. **Receptor cells** in these organs receive information about the outside world. Receptor cells send impulses to your brain through sensory neurons. Your brain makes sense of the impulses. Then you see, hear, feel, smell, and taste.

Cornea
A clear layer of the eye that light passes through.

Iris
The part of the eye that controls the amount of light that enters.

Receptor cell
A cell that receives information about the environment and starts nerve impulses to send that information to the brain.

The Sense of Sight

Your eyes are your organs of sight. Review the drawing on page 175 as you read about how the eye works. Light enters the eye through a clear layer called the **cornea**. A tough, white outer layer surrounds the cornea. This layer is the white of the eye. The colored part of the eyes is the **iris**. It is made of tiny muscles arranged in a ring. The black hole in the center of the iris is an opening called the pupil. Light passes from the cornea through the pupil. The iris controls the amount of light that enters by making the pupil larger or smaller. The pupil opens wide in a dark room. The larger opening lets in more light and you can see more clearly. Likewise, the pupil becomes smaller in bright sunlight.

Behind the pupil is a lens that focuses light. The lens focuses light rays onto the retina at the back of the eye. Receptor cells on the retina send impulses to a nerve bundle called the **optic nerve**. Nerve impulses travel along the optic nerve to the brain. The brain translates the impulses into images you can see. All of this happens faster than you can blink.

Optic nerve
A bundle of nerves that carry impulses from the eye to the brain.

The brain interprets impulses from light energy as pictures.

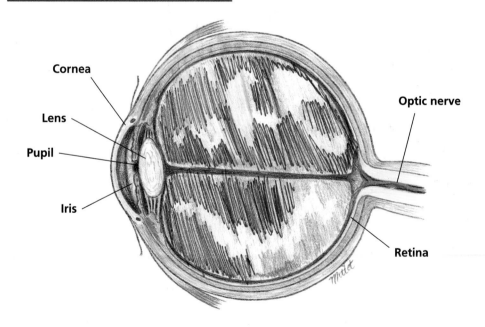

Cornea

Lens

Pupil

Iris

Optic nerve

Retina

The Sense of Hearing

Just as your eyes collect light, your ears collect sound. Review the drawing below as you read about how the ears work. The outer ear acts like a funnel to collect sound waves. The waves travel through the ear canal to the middle ear. The middle ear is made of the **eardrum** and three small bones. The eardrum is a thin tissue that vibrates, or shakes, when sound waves strike it. The sound waves then travel through each of the three bones. The sound waves enter the inner ear. They cause fluid in the **cochlea** to vibrate. The cochlea is a hollow coiled tube that contains fluid and thousands of receptor cells. These cells vibrate when sound waves strike them. The cells send impulses to the **auditory nerve**, which goes to the brain. The brain translates the impulses into sounds you can hear.

The Sense of Touch

The skin receives messages about heat, cold, pressure, and pain. Receptor cells in the skin send nerve impulses to the brain. Then you can tell if something is cold, hot, smooth, or rough. Your fingertips and lips are most sensitive to touch because they have the most receptor cells.

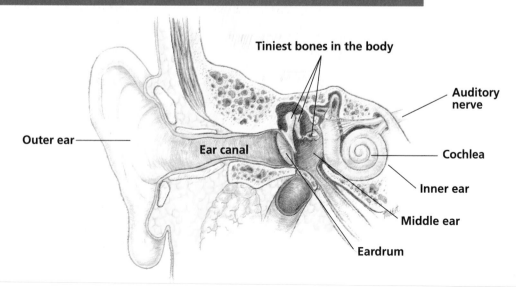

The brain interprets impulses from sound waves as sounds.

Tiniest bones in the body

Auditory nerve

Outer ear

Ear canal

Cochlea

Inner ear

Middle ear

Eardrum

The Senses of Taste and Smell

Taste buds are tiny receptor cells on the tongue that distinguish four basic kinds of tastes. The four tastes are sweet, sour, bitter, and salty. Notice in the drawing that certain parts of the tongue are sensitive to each taste. The taste buds send impulses to the brain. The brain interprets them as tastes.

Much of the sense of taste depends on the sense of smell. Receptor cells in the nose sense smells. If you hold your nose while you chew, much of your sense of taste goes away. Why does this happen? As you chew and swallow, air carrying the smell of the food reaches the nose. When you hold your nose, the air cannot flow freely. The smells never reach the receptor cells.

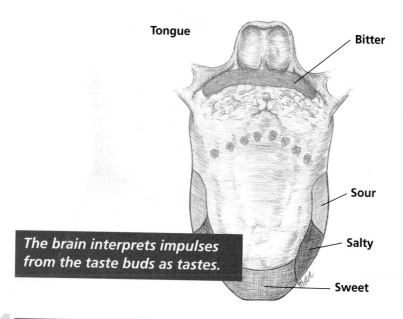

Tongue

Bitter

Sour

Salty

Sweet

The brain interprets impulses from the taste buds as tastes.

Self-Check

1. How is the central nervous system different from the peripheral nervous system?
2. Name the activities that each part of the brain controls.
3. How do impulses travel between neurons?
4. What happens to light energy after it reaches the retina?
5. Describe the path of sound waves moving through the ear.

How Does the Endocrine System Control the Body?

Objectives

After reading this lesson, you should be able to

▶ explain what hormones do.

▶ explain how a feedback loop works.

▶ describe the stress response.

How are the messengers of the endocrine system different from those of the nervous system?

The Endocrine Glands

The endocrine system works closely with the nervous system to control certain body activities. The endocrine system is made of glands. These glands secrete substances called hormones. Hormones are chemical messengers. Glands release hormones into the bloodstream. The hormones then travel all through the body.

What Hormones Do

There are more than 20 different hormones. They affect everything from kidney function to growth and development. Hormones work by attaching to certain cells. They change the function of the cells. Some examples of hormones are aldosterone, insulin, and growth hormone. The adrenal glands secrete aldosterone. This hormone directs the kidney to put more sodium and water back into the bloodstream. This may happen when a person has lost fluids. The pancreas secretes insulin. This hormone changes cells so that glucose can enter them. The pituitary gland secretes growth hormone. This hormone causes bones and muscles to grow.

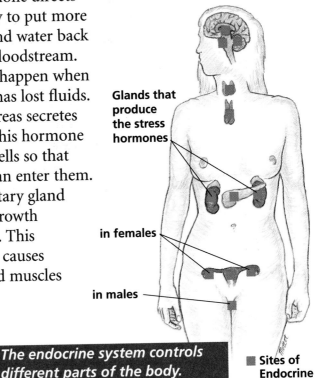

Glands that produce the stress hormones

in females

in males

The endocrine system controls different parts of the body.

■ Sites of Endocrine Glands

The Feedback Loop

Glands must secrete the correct amounts of hormones for the body to work properly. After hormones reach the cells, the cells send a chemical signal back to the gland. That signal tells the gland to continue or to stop secreting the hormone. This process is called a feedback loop.

Hormones and Stress

Some people get upset when they have to take a test. Their palms sweat, their heart rate goes up, and they breathe faster. These are signs of the stress response. When a person feels scared or excited, the adrenal glands secrete a hormone called adrenaline. Adrenaline causes these changes in the body. The stress response can be negative if it continues for a long time. A person can become depressed or ill.

However, the stress response can be positive. Suppose you are running a race. The increase in your heart rate causes more oxygen to be delivered to your muscles. Adrenaline also increases the amount of glucose to your muscles. After the race, your body returns to normal.

Self-Check

1. What is the function of the endocrine system?
2. What are hormones?
3. Name three hormones and how they affect the body.
4. How does the feedback loop work?
5. Give examples that show how the stress response can be positive and how it can be negative.

Red marrow
The spongy material in bones that makes blood cells.

Skeletal system
The network of bones in the body.

The Skeletal System

The 206 bones of the human body make up the **skeletal system**. Bones have several functions. First, bones support the body. They give the body a shape. Bones form a framework that supports the softer tissues of the body. Second, bones protect organs. For example, a rib cage protects the heart and lungs. Vertebrae protect the spinal cord. Vertebrae are the 33 bones that make up the backbone. The pelvis protects reproductive organs. Find these bones in the drawing below.

A third function of bones is to allow movement. Muscles attach to bones and move them. The body has big bones, small bones, flat bones, wide bones, and bones that have unusual shapes. The variety of bones helps a person to move in different ways. Fourth, bones are the place where blood cells are formed. Bones contain spongy material called **red marrow**. Red marrow has special cells that make blood cells. Finally, bones store minerals, such as calcium, phosphorous, and magnesium.

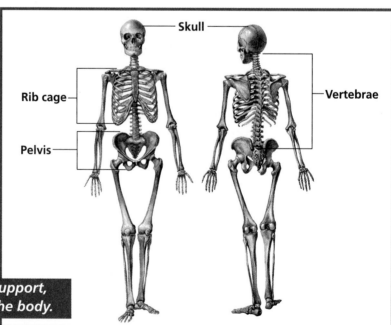

Bones give shape, support, and movement to the body.

Cartilage to Bone

Most bones start out as cartilage. Cartilage is a thick, smooth tissue. It is not as hard as bone. Before birth, the entire skeleton is cartilage. It is gradually replaced by bone. A baby is born with more than 300 bones. Over time, some of the bones join so that a person ends up with 206 bones. However, some parts of the body continue to have cartilage. Feel the end of your nose. It is cartilage and will never become bone. Your outer ear contains cartilage. Inside your body, cartilage surrounds your trachea.

How Bones Change

Bones are organs that are made of tissue. They are always changing. Bones are built up and broken down through life. This is a normal process. For example, enzymes break down bone tissue when the body needs calcium. Calcium is released into the bloodstream. However, if calcium is not replaced properly, a person can develop **osteoporosis**. With this disease, bones become lighter and break easily. It most often affects older people. Regular exercise and a diet higher in calcium can help prevent osteoporosis.

Ligament
A tissue that connects bone to bone.

Osteoporosis
A disease in which bones become lighter and break easily.

Joints

Bones come together at joints. Cartilage covers bones at the joints. This cartilage acts like a cushion. It protects bones from rubbing against one another. At the movable joints, strips of strong tissue called **ligaments** connect bones to each other. Ligaments stretch to allow the bones to move.

There are several kinds of joints. The ball-and-socket joint allows the greatest range of motion. This type of joint is located at the hips and shoulders. It allows you to move your arms and legs forward, backward, side to side, and in a circular motion. Some joints can move only a little, such as your rib and spine joints. A few joints, such as those in your skull, do not move at all.

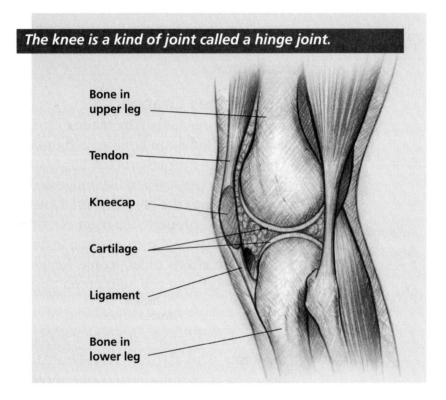

The knee is a kind of joint called a hinge joint.

Bone in upper leg

Tendon

Kneecap

Cartilage

Ligament

Bone in lower leg

The Muscular System

The muscular system consists of the more than 600 muscles in your body. The skeletal and muscular systems work together to produce movement. Tough strips of tissue called tendons attach muscles to bones.

Most muscles work in pairs. When a muscle contracts, or shortens, it pulls on the tendon. The tendon pulls on the attached bone, and the bone moves. A muscle cannot push. Therefore, a different muscle on the opposite side of the bone contracts to return the bone to its starting position.

The drawing below shows an example of muscles working in pairs. When you bend your arm, the biceps muscle contracts. You can feel how the muscle shortens and hardens as it contracts. The biceps pulls on the tendon, which pulls your lower arm toward you. The triceps muscle on the underside of your arm is relaxed. It is long and thin. When you straighten your arm, the triceps contracts. It pulls the lower arm back to its starting position. Now the biceps muscle is relaxed.

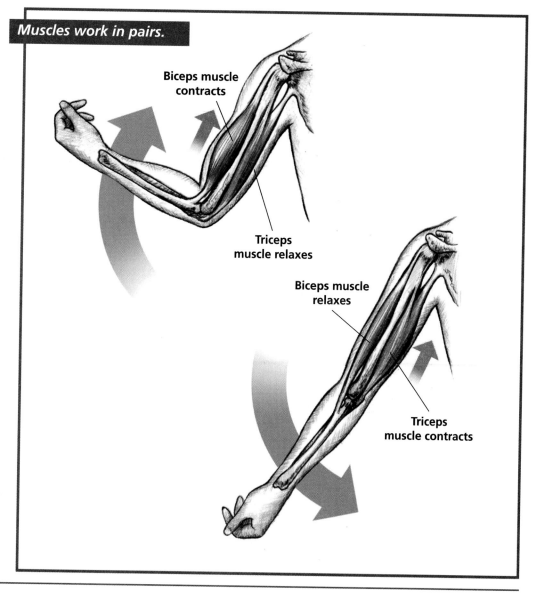

Muscles work in pairs.

Biceps muscle contracts

Triceps muscle relaxes

Biceps muscle relaxes

Triceps muscle contracts

How would your life be different if cardiac muscle was voluntary?

Kinds of Muscle Tissue

The body has three kinds of muscle tissue—skeletal, smooth, and cardiac. Most muscle tissue is skeletal muscle. Skeletal muscles are attached to bones. Skeletal muscles are **voluntary muscles**. That is, you can choose when to use them. The muscles in your arms, legs, and face are voluntary.

The second kind of muscle tissue is smooth muscle. These muscles form layers lining the walls of organs. Smooth muscles are found in the esophagus, stomach, and intestines. These muscles move in wavelike actions to move food through the digestive system. The walls of the blood vessels also are lined with smooth muscles. These muscles contract and relax to maintain blood pressure. Smooth muscles are **involuntary muscles**. You cannot choose when to use them. They react to changes in the body.

The third kind of muscle tissue is cardiac muscle. These muscles make up the heart. They contract regularly to pump blood throughout your body. Cardiac muscles are involuntary.

Self-Check

1. What are five functions of bone?
2. How does bone change during a person's lifetime?
3. What is the difference between ligaments and tendons?
4. How do muscles make bones move?
5. What are the three kinds of muscle tissue?

- During digestion, food changes into a form that can enter cells. The large intestine eliminates undigested food.
- The circulatory system moves materials to and from cells.
- Red blood cells carry oxygen in hemoglobin. White blood cells protect the body from disease. Platelets help blood to clot.
- The respiratory system brings oxygen into your lungs and releases carbon dioxide from your lungs.
- The kidneys filter the blood to get rid of toxic wastes. The filtered wastes form urine.
- The nervous system controls and coordinates body activities. Impulses carry information from one nerve cell to the next.
- The five main sense organs are the eyes, ears, skin, nose, and tongue. Special cells in each of the sense organs gather information for the brain.
- The glands of the endocrine system release hormones into the blood. Hormones help control body activities.
- Bones support and protect the body's soft tissues. Blood cells are made inside some bones. Bones also store minerals.
- Skeletal muscles work in pairs to pull on bones.

Science Words		
	excretory system, 170	plasma, 161
	feces, 157	platelet, 163
alveolus, 166	gallbladder, 156	receptor cell, 174
antibody, 161	hemoglobin, 162	rectum, 157
auditory nerve, 176	involuntary muscle, 184	red marrow, 180
bile, 156	iris, 174	skeletal system, 180
blood pressure, 161	kidney, 170	synapse, 173
bronchiole, 166	ligament, 181	trachea, 166
bronchus, 166	neuron, 173	ureter, 170
cardiac, 158	optic nerve, 175	urethra, 170
chyme, 155	osteoporosis, 181	urine, 170
cochlea, 176	peristalsis, 155	villi, 156
cornea, 174	perspiration, 169	voluntary muscle, 184
eardrum, 176		

Vocabulary Review

Number your paper from 1 to 10. Then choose the word or words from the Word Bank that best complete each sentence. Write the answer on your paper.

WORD BANK

- alveoli
- bile
- chyme
- cochlea
- hemoglobin
- kidneys
- ligament
- neurons
- platelets
- villi

1. The liver produces _____, which breaks down fats.

2. _____ carries oxygen in the blood.

3. Oxygen from outside the body enters tiny air sacs in the lungs called _____.

4. _____ remove wastes from blood and make urine.

5. Food molecules enter the blood through _____ that line the small intestine.

6. The _____ sends impulses to the auditory nerve so that you can hear sounds.

7. Partly digested liquid food called _____ passes from the stomach to the small intestine.

8. Tiny pieces of cells called _____ help blood clot.

9. A(n)_____ connects a bone to another bone.

10. Electrical signals travel along cells called _____.

Concept Review

Number your paper from 1 to 8. Choose the answer that best completes each sentence. Write the letter of the answer on your paper.

1. The retina sends impulses to the _____ nerve.

   a. optic   **b.** auditory   **c.** motor

2. The heart is made of _____ muscle.

   a. smooth   **b.** cardiac   **c.** skeletal

3. You think with your _____.

   a. brain stem   **b.** cerebrum   **c.** cerebellum

4. Skeletal muscles work by _____.

   a. pulling   **b.** pushing   **c.** peristalsis

5. Perspiration leaves the body through the _____.

   a. kidneys   **b.** lungs   **c.** skin

6. You get oxygen into your lungs when you _____.

   a. inhale   **b.** respire   **c.** exhale

7. Most digestion takes place in the _____.

   a. esophagus   **b.** stomach   **c.** small intestine

8. The _____ of the heart forces blood to the rest of the body.

   a. right ventricle **b.** left ventricle   **c.** left atrium

Critical Thinking

Write the answer to each of the following questions.

1. The statement, "All arteries carry blood that is high in oxygen" is incorrect. Why? Write a statement that describes all arteries.

2. Why do hormones travel in the blood?

Test Taking Tip | As you read, try to link a new word to something familiar. This can help remind you of a word's meaning when you see the word on a test.

Chapter

9

Reproduction, Growth, and Development

Reproduction is one of the basic life activities of all organisms. When organisms stop reproducing, their species dies out. Not all organisms reproduce the same way, however. Many people would agree that the photo shows one of the most amazing things in all the universe. It is the development of a new individual in its mother. This individual is only five to six weeks old, yet you can make out many of its features.

ORGANIZE YOUR THOUGHTS

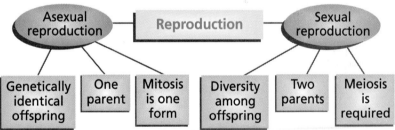

Goals for Learning

▶ To recognize that life comes from other life
▶ To compare and contrast asexual reproduction and sexual reproduction
▶ To describe the processes of reproduction and development in different groups of animals
▶ To trace the steps in human reproduction and development

Objectives

After reading this lesson, you should be able to
- ▶ define *spontaneous generation*.
- ▶ describe how spontaneous generation was proved to be untrue.
- ▶ recognize the importance of DNA in reproduction.
- ▶ explain the importance of diversity in a population.

It may seem obvious that flies come from other flies and frogs come from other frogs. At one time, however, people were not sure where some living things came from.

Spontaneous Generation

Many years ago, some people thought that living things could come from nonliving things. This idea is called **spontaneous generation**. When people saw flies come out of rotten meat, they reasoned that rotten meat produces flies. When they saw frogs hop out of muddy ponds, they thought mud makes frogs.

The diagram shows a famous experiment that helped prove that spontaneous generation does not occur. In the 1600s, an Italian scientist named Francesco Redi put pieces of meat in jars. He covered some of the jars with netting. The netting allowed air, but no adult flies, to get in. Redi left the other jars open. After some time, flies appeared only in the open jars.

Spontaneous generation

The idea that living things can come from nonliving things.

Redi's experiments helped show that spontaneous generation does not occur.

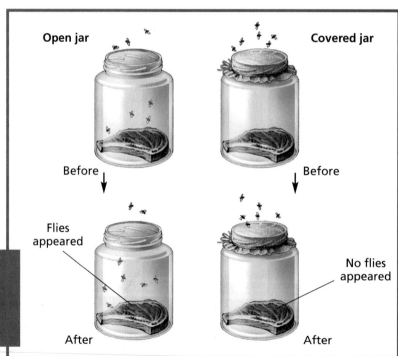

Open jar   Covered jar

Before   Before

Flies appeared   No flies appeared

After   After

Later, scientists discovered that fly eggs laid in meat had produced the flies. Scientists also found frog eggs on the edges of muddy ponds, which explained where the frogs came from. Through many experiments over more than 100 years, spontaneous generation was proved not to be true. Living things come only from other living things.

DNA

As you learned in Chapter 1, all living things are made of cells. Each organism's cells contain the information needed to make another organism just like itself. Cells store this information in the form of a chemical called **DNA**.

DNA stores information in a pattern of chemicals, much as a book stores information in a pattern of letters. The pattern in DNA provides information for making a new cell or a whole new organism. Your DNA contains all the information needed to make a human with all your characteristics, or **traits**.

Each type of organism has its own special, or unique, DNA. All humans have information in their DNA about how to make a human, rather than a rabbit or a frog. Rabbit DNA has information about making a rabbit. A frog has DNA for making a frog.

DNA
The chemical inside cells that stores information about an organism.

Trait
A characteristic of an organism.

DNA and Reproduction

When living things reproduce, they pass exact copies of their DNA to their offspring. In some organisms, such as bacteria, reproduction usually involves just one parent. The parent passes copies of all of its DNA to its offspring. The offspring is identical to the parent because its DNA is identical to the parent's DNA. Most one-celled organisms reproduce this way.

Reproduction in animals and plants usually involves two parents. You may resemble one of your parents more than the other. However, you have traits from both of your parents. That is because your DNA is not an exact copy of just one of your parent's DNA. Your DNA is a combination of both parents' DNA. For that reason, humans, like many other kinds of organisms, produce offspring that are unique.

Diversity
The range of
differences among
the individuals in a
population.

What adaptations
might allow an
animal to live in a
cold environment?

The Advantage of Diversity

Humans and other species that produce unique offspring
are said to have **diversity**. Diversity is the range of
differences found among the members of a population.
You can see diversity in the group of children in the photo.

If a population's surroundings, or environment, change
suddenly, the population's diversity can help it continue to
survive. Suppose a disease sweeps through a population of
deer, killing many of them. If none of the deer is able to
fight, or resist, the disease, then the population will die off.
However, in a diverse population, chances are that a few
deer will be able to resist the disease. As a result, the
population will survive. Resistance to the disease is a kind
of adaptation. Adaptations are traits that allow organisms
to survive in certain environments. Adaptations result
from the information in an organism's DNA.

Humans show a great
deal of diversity.

Self-Check

1. What is spontaneous generation?
2. Explain how Redi's experiment helped prove that
   spontaneous generation does not occur.
3. What is DNA, and what is its function?
4. Why are human offspring unique?
5. What is the advantage of having diversity in a population?

After reading this lesson, you should be able to

▶ recognize the advantages and disadvantages of asexual reproduction.

▶ recognize the advantages and disadvantages of sexual reproduction.

▶ compare mitosis with meiosis.

▶ trace the steps in the fertilization of an egg.

Some bacteria cause diseases in humans. What do you think happens when a single disease-causing bacterium enters the human body?

In Lesson 1, you learned that some organisms need only one parent to reproduce. Other organisms reproduce with two parents. In this lesson, you will learn more about these two types of reproduction.

Asexual Reproduction

Some organisms pass an exact copy of all of their DNA to their offspring. As a result, the offspring are identical to the parent. This form of reproduction is called asexual reproduction. One-celled organisms, such as bacteria and yeasts, usually reproduce asexually. Their cell divides to form two identical cells. Protists, fungi, and some plants and animals can reproduce by means of asexual reproduction too.

Many of the cells that make up your body also undergo asexual reproduction. For example, skin cells, bone cells, and muscle cells reproduce asexually to form new cells. The new cells allow your body to grow, heal, and replace dead cells.

Advantages and Disadvantages of Asexual Reproduction

One advantage of asexual reproduction is that an organism can reproduce alone. It does not have to find a mate. Another advantage is time. One-celled organisms can reproduce quickly. For example, some bacteria divide every 20 minutes under certain conditions.

A disadvantage of asexual reproduction is that the offspring are exact copies of the parent. The offspring lack diversity. Thus, they are likely to respond to changes in the environment in the same way. If a change kills one of the offspring, it will probably kill them all. Thus, asexual reproduction is favorable in environments that do not change much.

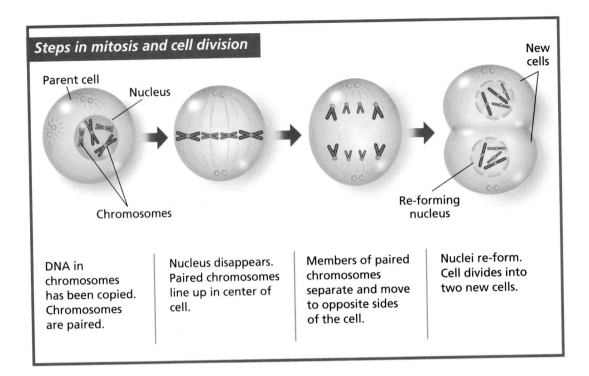

Steps in mitosis and cell division

New cells

Parent cell

Nucleus

Chromosomes

Re-forming nucleus

| DNA in chromosomes has been copied. Chromosomes are paired. | Nucleus disappears. Paired chromosomes line up in center of cell. | Members of paired chromosomes separate and move to opposite sides of the cell. | Nuclei re-form. Cell divides into two new cells. |

Chromosome

A rod-shaped structure that contains DNA and is found in the nucleus of a cell.

Mitosis

The process that results in two cells identical to the parent cell.

Mitosis

In cells that have a nucleus, asexual reproduction occurs in the form of **mitosis** followed by cell division. Mitosis is the dividing of a cell's nucleus. Before a cell undergoes mitosis, it makes a copy of its DNA. The DNA is found in the nucleus in rod-shaped structures called **chromosomes**. When the DNA is copied, the chromosomes form pairs.

The diagram shows the main steps of mitosis and cell division. During mitosis, the nucleus disappears. The pairs of chromosomes line up in the center of the cell. Then, the members of each pair separate and move to opposite ends of the cell. Next, the cell membrane pinches in between the two sets of chromosomes. A nucleus forms around each set. Two identical cells are formed. Each new cell has an exact copy of the chromosomes that were in the parent cell.

Sexual Reproduction

Humans and many other kinds of organisms have two parents. They use a form of reproduction called sexual reproduction. During sexual reproduction, a cell from one parent joins with a cell from the other parent. Most plants and animals reproduce by sexual reproduction.

Disadvantages and Advantages of Sexual Reproduction

A disadvantage of sexual reproduction is that an organism must find a mate to be able to reproduce. Also, sexual reproduction usually takes longer to produce offspring than does asexual reproduction. However, a big advantage of sexual reproduction is that it leads to greater diversity among offspring. That is because the DNA from two different parents is mixed. Each offspring is unique. Its combination of traits is different from the combination of traits of either parent.

Gamete
A sex cell, such as sperm or egg.

Testis
The male sex organ that produces sperm cells. Plural is testes.

Gametes

Sexual reproduction involves both a female parent and a male parent. The female produces egg cells. The male produces sperm cells. Sperm cells and egg cells are called sex cells, or **gametes**. In many animals, **testes** are the male sex organs that produce sperm cells. Ovaries are the female sex organs that produce egg cells.

The gametes of certain species contain one-half the number of chromosomes found in the species' nonsex cells. For example, human sex cells have 23 chromosomes in their nucleus. Human body cells have 46 chromosomes. The sex cells of a dog have 39 chromosomes. A dog's body cells have 78 chromosomes.

The testes produce millions of sperm cells. A sperm cell is about one-thousandth the size of an egg cell. A sperm cell usually has a tail that allows it to move toward an egg. An egg cell contains food for the early stage of the developing offspring.

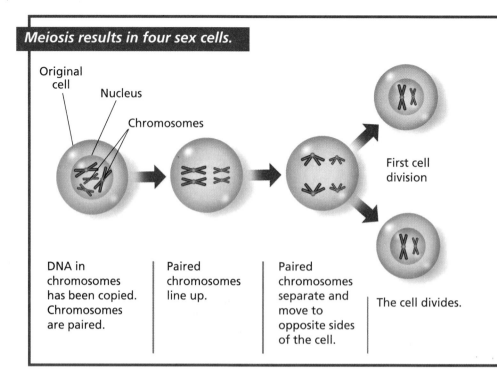

Meiosis results in four sex cells.

Original cell

Nucleus

Chromosomes

First cell division

DNA in chromosomes has been copied. Chromosomes are paired.

Paired chromosomes line up.

Paired chromosomes separate and move to opposite sides of the cell.

The cell divides.

Meiosis

Gametes form by a division of the nucleus called **meiosis**. You can follow the steps of meiosis in the diagram. As in mitosis, meiosis begins after the cell's chromosomes have been copied. During meiosis, the nucleus disappears. The pairs of chromosomes line up in the center of the cell and then separate. A nucleus forms around each set of chromosomes. Next, the cell divides into two new cells. However, in meiosis, unlike mitosis, each new cell divides once again. In this way, one original cell produces four sex cells. Since cell division occurs twice, each sex cell contains one-half the number of chromosomes of the original cell.

Fertilization

Imagine that a female fish has laid her eggs under the water. A male fish swims above the eggs. He releases billions of sperm into the water. The sperm swim through the water toward the eggs. One sperm reaches an egg just ahead of dozens of other sperm. That sperm attaches itself to the outer membrane of the egg. Almost immediately, the egg's membrane changes so that no other sperm can attach.

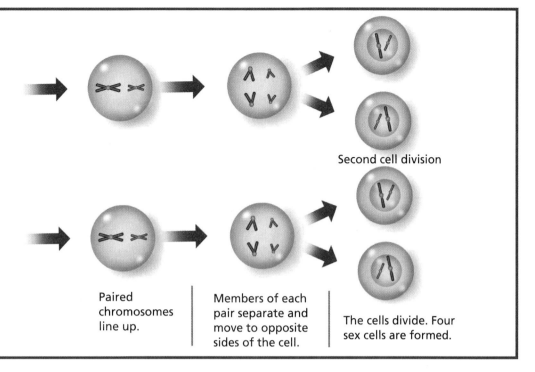

Second cell division

| Paired chromosomes line up. | Members of each pair separate and move to opposite sides of the cell. | The cells divide. Four sex cells are formed. |

External fertilization
The type of fertilization that occurs outside the female's body.

Internal fertilization
The type of fertilization that occurs inside the female's body.

Once a sperm is attached, its nucleus enters the egg. Then the nucleus of the sperm cell and the nucleus of the egg cell join. Fertilization is the process by which a sperm cell and an egg cell join to form one cell. The cell, called a zygote, begins to develop into a new organism. The zygote has a complete set of chromosomes. One-half of the chromosomes came from the sperm cell. The other half came from the egg cell.

The process described above is called **external fertilization** because the egg is fertilized outside the body of the female. Most fish and amphibians use external fertilization. All reptiles, birds, and mammals use **internal fertilization**. In those animals, the male places sperm inside the female's body, where fertilization occurs.

Self-Check

1. What are two advantages of asexual reproduction?
2. What does the process of mitosis result in?
3. What is the main advantage of sexual reproduction?
4. What does the process of meiosis result in?
5. Describe the process of fertilization.

Cell differentiation
The process of cells taking on different jobs in the body.

Embryo
An early stage in the development of an organism.

A new animal begins as a zygote. Recall that a zygote is a single cell that contains a complete set of chromosomes. Usually, the zygote divides to form two identical cells attached to each other. Then those two cells divide. This process is repeated many times, as shown in the picture. Eventually, the zygote divides into millions of cells that make up an **embryo**. An embryo is an early stage in the development of an organism.

Differentiation

An embryo's cells gradually take on different shapes and functions. This process is called **cell differentiation**. In vertebrates, cells at one end of the developing embryo begin to form parts of the head. The cells form the eyes, mouth, gills, and other organs. Inside, the heart, stomach, and other organs develop. Eventually a complete organism forms.

Development

The embryos of many animals, such as fish, reptiles, and birds, develop inside eggs. A fish may lay thousands of eggs. Turtles, birds, and other fish feed on those eggs. Laying large numbers of fish eggs increases the chances that a few eggs will live. This, in turn, increases the chances that the species of fish will survive.

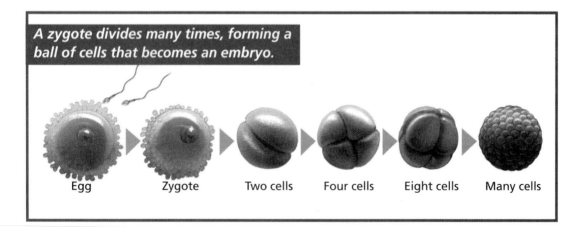

A zygote divides many times, forming a ball of cells that becomes an embryo.

Egg   Zygote   Two cells   Four cells   Eight cells   Many cells

In most fish, when the young hatch from the eggs, they look like the adult fish. Certain insects, such as grasshoppers and praying mantises, also produce young that look like the adults. These young insects are called **nymphs**. However, recall from Chapter 3 that butterflies produce young that are completely different from the adults. The young develop into adults in stages that vary greatly in form. In the pictures, you can see the differences in the developments of a grasshopper and a butterfly.

Nymph

A young insect that resembles the adult.

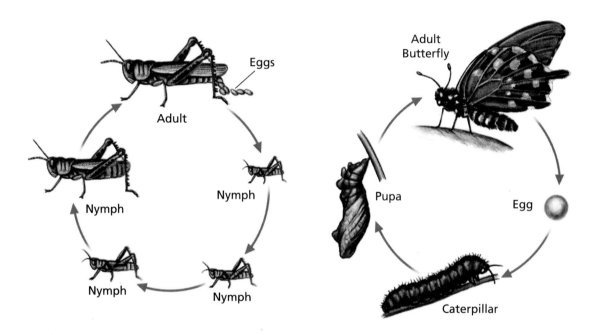

Grasshopper nymphs look like adult grasshoppers but cannot reproduce. Caterpillars look nothing like the butterflies into which they will develop.

Does the development of a human more closely resemble the type of development shown by grasshoppers or by butterflies?

Mammal Offspring

Unlike fish and many other kinds of animals, mammals produce few offspring. Mammal parents often take care of their young for long periods of time. This care protects the young from danger and increases their chances of survival. Thus, fewer offspring are needed to ensure the survival of a mammal species.

Most mammals do not lay eggs. Instead, the eggs develop and are fertilized inside the female's body. Only two kinds of mammals lay eggs: the spiny anteater and the duck-billed platypus. These two mammals live in Australia.

All other mammals carry their young inside their body, at least for some period of time. The female mammal gives birth to the young. **Marsupials** are mammals that give birth to young that are undeveloped. Kangaroos, koalas, and opossums are examples of marsupials. After being born, the young marsupial crawls into its mother's external pouch. There, the young continues to develop. All other mammals that do not lay eggs, including humans, cats, and whales, give birth to young that are more fully developed.

Marsupials complete their development in their mother's pouch.

Food for the Young Mammal

Young mammals may seem small and cuddly to us, but they are giants compared to baby fish. A fish embryo has little food in its egg, so it cannot grow much inside the egg. On the other hand, most mammal embryos, such as human embryos, get food from inside their mother's body. These mammals grow and develop a great deal before they are born.

Most female mammals have a **uterus**. The uterus is an organ that holds and protects a developing embryo. Inside the uterus, the embryo forms protective tissues around itself. Parts of these tissues form a **placenta**. The placenta provides food and oxygen from the mother's body to the developing embryo. When the young mammal is born, it feeds on milk produced by its mother's mammary glands.

The embryos of most marsupials do not obtain food through a placenta. When inside the mother, the embryo obtains food from the fertilized egg for a short time. After the young is born, it feeds on milk from inside the mother's pouch.

Recall that the spiny anteater and the duck-billed platypus are the only mammals that lay eggs. Mammal eggs are much smaller than a hen's egg. That is because the mammal eggs do not contain a large food supply. When the young are born, they feed on milk from their mother's mammary glands.

Placenta
A tissue that provides the embryo with food and oxygen from its mother's body.

Uterus
An organ in most female mammals that holds and protects an embryo.

Mammals produce milk for their young.

Gestation

Different mammals have different **gestation times**, depending on the size of the animal. Gestation time is the period of time from the fertilization of an egg until birth occurs. Gestation times for a variety of mammals are shown in the chart. As you can see, an elephant develops inside its mother for almost two years. But the gestation time of a mouse is only 20 days. In general, the larger the mammal, the longer is its gestation time.

Mammal Gestation Times	
Mammal	**Approximate number of days**
Mouse	20
Rabbit	31
Cat, Dog	63
Monkey	210
Human	275
Cattle	281
Horse	336
Whale	360
Elephant	624

Self-Check

1. How does a zygote become an embryo?
2. Do young butterflies resemble their parents? Explain your answer.
3. What is the advantage of fish laying thousands of eggs at one time?
4. How is the development of a marsupial different from the development of other mammals that give birth to their young?
5. What is gestation time?

Chapter 9

INVESTIGATION

Observing Animal Eggs

Materials

- ✓ spoon
- ✓ preserved frog egg
- ✓ 2 culture dishes
- ✓ water
- ✓ hand lens
- ✓ forceps
- ✓ chicken egg

Purpose

To compare two kinds of animal eggs

Procedure

1. Put the frog egg in a clean culture dish. Cover the egg with water and observe it, using your hand lens.

2. On a sheet of paper, draw a diagram of the frog egg. Show the light part and dark part of the egg in your drawing. The dark part develops into an embryo. The light part provides food for the embryo.

3. Observe the shell of the chicken egg. Then, crack the shell open and pour the contents into a clean culture dish.

4. Examine the white disk on the yolk. This disk is the part that develops into an embryo when the egg is fertilized. The rest of the egg provides food for the embryo. Draw a diagram of the chicken egg. *Safety Alert: Wash your hands after working with the eggs.*

Questions

1. What is the structure and function of the chicken egg's shell?

2. Why do frog eggs have no shell?

Explore Further

Compare the proportion of food in each egg. Suggest an explanation for the difference.

Objectives

After reading this lesson, you should be able to

▶ identify the parts of the male and female reproductive systems in humans.

▶ define *ovulation* and *menstruation*.

▶ describe the main events of pregnancy.

▶ describe changes that occur in males and females during puberty.

Penis
The male organ that delivers sperm to the female body.

Scrotum
The sac that holds the testes.

Vagina
The tubelike canal in the female body through which sperm enter the body.

Like other mammals, humans reproduce sexually. A male parent and a female parent together produce a fertilized egg that develops inside the female's body.

The Male Reproductive System

The picture shows the main reproductive organs of a human male. Recall that the testes produce sperm cells. The testes lie outside the body in a sac called a **scrotum**. Because the scrotum is outside the body, it is about 2°C cooler than the rest of the body. Sperm cells are sensitive to heat. The lower temperature of the scrotum helps the sperm to live.

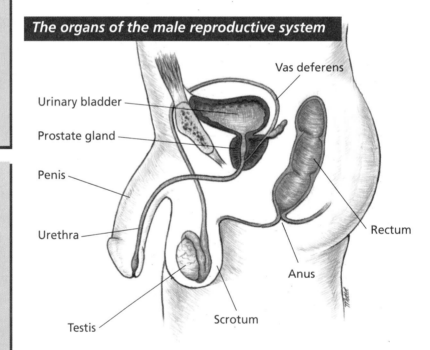

The organs of the male reproductive system

The external male organ, called the **penis**, delivers sperm to the female body. Before this happens, blood flows into the tissues of the penis. The blood causes the penis to lengthen and become rigid, or erect. The erect penis is inserted into a tubelike canal, called a **vagina**, in the female's body.

Sperm cells leave the male body through a tube in the penis called the urethra. The **prostate gland** connects to the urethra. The prostate gland produces fluid that mixes with the sperm cells and carries them through the urethra. The mixture of sperm and fluid is called **semen**. The semen flows through the urethra to the outside of the body. Urine also leaves the body through the urethra. However, urine and semen do not flow through the urethra at the same time.

The Female Reproductive System

You can see the main female reproductive organs in the picture. Females are born with about 400,000 egg cells that are produced and stored in the ovaries. One egg is usually released from one of the ovaries about every 28 days. The release of an egg is called **ovulation**.

After its release, an egg travels through one of the **fallopian tubes**. If sperm are present, a sperm cell may fertilize the egg cell in the fallopian tube. There, the fertilized egg will develop into an embryo, which travels to the uterus. If the egg is not fertilized, it eventually passes out of the female's body.

Fallopian tube
A tube through which eggs pass from an ovary to the uterus.

Ovulation
The process of releasing an egg from an ovary.

Prostate gland
The gland that produces the fluid found in semen.

Semen
A mixture of fluid and sperm cells.

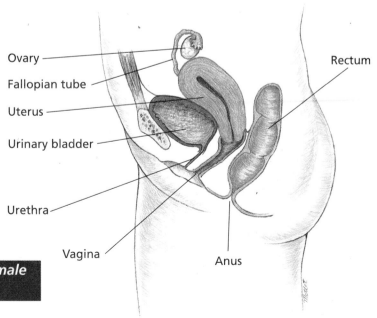

Ovary

Fallopian tube

Uterus

Urinary bladder

Urethra

Vagina

Rectum

Anus

The organs of the female reproductive system

How can a woman tell that she is not pregnant?

Menstruation

Each month, a female's uterus prepares to receive an embryo. The lining of the uterus thickens to form a blood-rich cushion. The lining will hold and nourish the developing embryo. If the egg is not fertilized and no embryo forms, the lining of the uterus breaks down. The unfertilized egg, blood, and pieces of the lining pass out of the female's body through the vagina. This process is called **menstruation**.

Pregnancy

When the male's penis releases semen into the female's vagina, the sperm cells swim to the uterus and fallopian tubes. If a sperm cell fertilizes an egg cell in a fallopian tube, the female begins a period of **pregnancy**. During pregnancy, the fertilized egg develops into a baby.

The picture shows the fertilized egg, or zygote, dividing in the fallopian tube. The zygote becomes an embryo. When the embryo reaches the uterus, it soon attaches to the blood-rich lining of the uterus.

Recall that the embryo forms a placenta. The **umbilical cord**, which contains blood vessels, connects the placenta to the embryo. The embryo's blood flows through blood vessels in the placenta. The mother's blood flows through blood vessels in the lining of the uterus. The two blood supplies usually do not mix. However, they come so close together that food and oxygen pass from the mother's blood to the embryo's blood. The embryo's waste products pass from the embryo's blood to the mother's blood. The embryo's wastes pass out of the mother's body along with her own wastes.

Becoming a Baby

Inside the uterus, the embryo develops rapidly, using the food and oxygen provided by the mother. The embryo takes about nine months to become a fully developed baby.

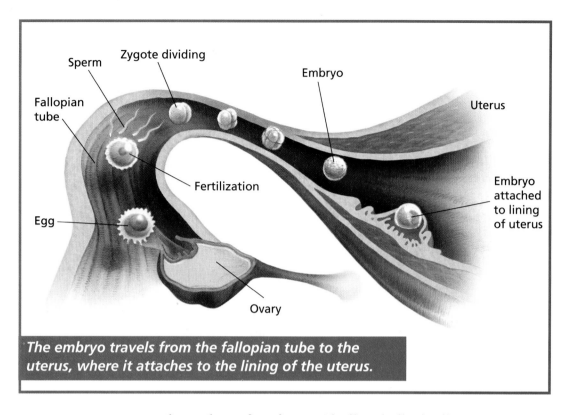

Sperm

Zygote dividing

Embryo

Fallopian tube

Uterus

Fertilization

Egg

Embryo attached to lining of uterus

Ovary

The embryo travels from the fallopian tube to the uterus, where it attaches to the lining of the uterus.

The embryo first forms a hollow ball of cells. Soon, the cells differentiate. The body takes shape, and organs develop. After about three weeks, the embryo's heart begins to beat. Blood vessels form rapidly. The body has a head and has buds for arms and legs. At this point, the embryo is still smaller than a fingernail.

The human embryo at three weeks of development looks similar to the embryo of a fish, chick, or horse. All vertebrates look similar in their early stages of development. A human embryo soon begins to look more like a person.

At about four weeks, tiny hands begin to show fingers. Eyes appear as dark spots. At eight weeks, the embryo is called a **fetus**. It has all the major structures found in an adult. By the time pregnancy is half over, at 4½ months, the fetus may suck its thumb. Sucking is an instinctive behavior that a baby uses to suck milk from its mother's mammary glands.

Fetus

An embryo after eight weeks of development in the uterus.

Did You Know?

After eight weeks of development, a human fetus has all the major structures found in an adult but is only about 5 cm long.

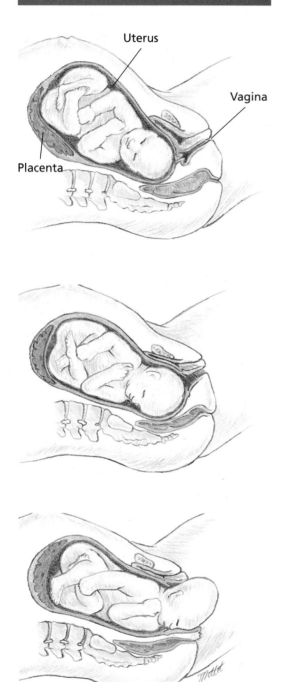

Uterus

Vagina

Placenta

Birth of a Baby

Usually, when the fetus reaches full size, the uterus begins to squeeze together, or contract. At first, the uterus contracts every half hour. Then gradually, it contracts more often. As the uterus contracts, it pushes the baby out of the uterus and through the vagina.

After much work, the mother gives birth to the baby. The mother's body pushes out the placenta soon after the baby is born. The doctor clamps and cuts the umbilical cord. Now the baby can survive outside of the mother's body. The part of the umbilical cord that remains attached to the baby eventually falls off. A person's "belly button," or navel, is where the umbilical cord was once attached.

Parental Care

Compared to a baby horse, which can stand just a few hours after birth, a human baby is born helpless. Human babies are not able to take care of themselves for many years.

Parents spend much time and effort caring for their babies. Some other animals have thousands of offspring at one time and then leave them without care. Humans usually have only one offspring at a time. The care that they give their offspring is one reason for the high survival rate of humans.

Adolescence

Adolescence
The teenage years of a human.

Puberty
The period of rapid growth and physical changes that occurs in males and females during early adolescence.

Humans care for their children through the teen years, called **adolescence**, and often into adulthood. Rapid growth and physical changes take place during **puberty**, which occurs at the beginning of adolescence.

During puberty in males, a boy's voice changes to a low pitch. Hair begins to grow on the face, under the arms, and in the area around the sex organs. The sex organs become more fully developed. During puberty in females, hair also begins to grow under the arms and around the sex organs. The breasts enlarge, and menstruation begins.

Adolescence is also a time when a child learns about becoming an adult. During this time, children take on more responsibilities and learn more about themselves.

Self-Check

1. Describe the path followed by sperm from the testes to the site of fertilization.
2. What happens during ovulation?
3. What is menstruation?
4. How does an embryo get nutrients during pregnancy?
5. What are some changes that occur in males and females during puberty?

SCIENCE
IN YOUR
LIFE

What substances are harmful during pregnancies?

An embryo and a fetus undergo many changes during development. During this time, the unborn baby is sensitive to substances in its environment. The baby's environment is its mother's body.

Any substance that a pregnant woman takes into her body can reach her unborn baby. A woman may take substances into her body by eating, drinking, breathing, and through her skin. Just as food and oxygen can cross the placenta to the baby, so can drugs and other harmful substances.

What is wrong with drinking alcohol or smoking during pregnancy?

Alcohol has a more serious effect on a developing baby than it has on an adult. Even small amounts of alcohol drunk during pregnancy can cause fetal alcohol syndrome (FAS). Babies with FAS have various birth defects, including mental retardation. There is *no* safe amount of alcohol that a woman can drink during pregnancy.

The chemicals in tobacco also may harm an unborn baby. Pregnant women who smoke or are exposed to secondhand smoke are more likely to have babies with asthma, allergies, and other breathing problems.

How do other drugs affect unborn babies?

Pregnant women who take illegal drugs, such as cocaine, are likely to have babies who are addicted to the drugs. The babies also may have birth defects caused by the drugs. Even medicines, such as aspirin and cold medications, can harm a developing baby. It is important to read the information on the package of a medicine before taking it. Also, a woman should always tell her doctor if she is pregnant before taking a prescription drug.

Why is eating a balanced diet during pregnancy important?

To develop properly, an unborn baby needs certain nutrients. Without those nutrients, the baby may be born with physical or mental defects. That is why it is important for a pregnant woman to eat a healthy, balanced diet. Many doctors also recommend that pregnant women take vitamins to ensure that their developing baby gets all the nutrients it needs.

- When organisms reproduce, they pass copies of their DNA to their offspring. The DNA determines the traits of the offspring.

- Asexual reproduction involves one parent and results in offspring identical to the parent.

- In cells that have a nucleus, asexual reproduction occurs by mitosis and cell division. Each new cell receives a copy of the DNA found in the parent cell.

- Sexual reproduction involves two parents and results in offspring that are unique. The offspring have a combination of the DNA found in the parents.

- Sexual reproduction allows for diversity among offspring.

- Sexual reproduction involves meiosis and cell division.

- When a sperm cell and an egg cell unite, a zygote is formed. The zygote develops into a new organism.

- In some types of animals, the female lays eggs that are fertilized outside her body. In mammals, the egg is fertilized inside the female's body.

- In most mammals, offspring develop inside the female's body. The uterus holds and protects the developing fetus.

- The fetus gets food and oxygen from the mother's body.

- After birth, mammal offspring are cared for by their parents.

Science Words

adolescence, 209
cell differentiation, 198
chromosome, 194
diversity, 192
DNA, 191
embryo, 198
external fertilization, 197
fallopian tube, 205
fetus, 207

gamete, 195
gestation time, 202
internal fertilization, 197
marsupial, 200
meiosis, 196
menstruation, 206
mitosis, 194
nymph, 199
ovulation, 205
penis, 204
placenta, 201

pregnancy, 206
prostate gland, 205
puberty, 209
scrotum, 204
semen, 205
spontaneous generation, 190
testis, 195
trait, 191
umbilical cord, 206
uterus, 201
vagina, 204

Vocabulary Review

Number your paper from 1 to 14. Choose the word or words from the Word Bank that best complete each sentence. Write the answer on your paper.

WORD BANK
asexual reproduction
cell differentiation
chromosomes
diversity
fertilization
fetus
gametes
marsupials
meiosis
ovulation
puberty
spontaneous generation
testes
uterus

1. Redi's experiment helped disprove the idea of _____.

2. An embryo's cells take on different jobs in a process called _____.

3. Sperm cells and egg cells are _____.

4. The _____ holds and protects a developing embryo.

5. _____ results in offspring that are identical to their parent.

6. The joining of an egg cell and a sperm cell is _____.

7. The process of _____ results in four sex cells.

8. DNA is found in structures called _____.

9. Sexual reproduction allows for _____ among offspring.

10. Sperm cells are produced in the _____.

11. Unlike most mammals, _____ are born undeveloped.

12. When an ovary releases an egg cell, _____ occurs.

13. After eight weeks of development, a human embryo is called a(n) _____.

14. The period of rapid growth at the beginning of adolescence is _____.

Concept Review

Number your paper from 1 to 4. Then choose the answer that best completes each sentence. Write the letter of the answer on your paper.

1. Offspring resemble their parents because they have copies of their parents' _____ .

    a. DNA   **b.** gametes   **c.** cells

2. The joining of a sperm cell and an egg cell results in a zygote that has _____ the number of chromosomes found in each sex cell.

    a. one-half   **b.** four times   **c.** twice

3. Mammals reproduce by _____.

    a. sexual reproduction and external fertilization
    b. asexual reproduction and internal fertilization
    c. sexual reproduction and internal fertilization

4. A woman _____ when a released egg cell has not been fertilized.

    a. menstruates   **b.** ovulates   **c.** becomes pregnant

Critical Thinking

Write the answer to each of the following questions.

1. How do you think the size of a *newborn* mammal might compare with the size of a *newly hatched* mammal? Explain your answer.

2. Women who use drugs during pregnancy are more likely to give birth to babies with birth defects. Explain why.

Test Taking Tip | Make a labeled drawing to help you remember the correct words of a process or structure.

Chapter

10

Staying Healthy

Look at the people in the photograph. Do you think these people are healthy? What keeps them healthy? One way to stay healthy is to try to avoid illness. Another way is to eat the right kinds of food. Doing these things can make you feel better and look better too. In this chapter, you will learn about illnesses that can spread and ways to prevent them. You will also learn about foods your body needs to stay healthy.

ORGANIZE YOUR THOUGHTS

Goals for Learning

▶ To define the term *infectious disease*

▶ To outline the body's defenses against germs

▶ To describe ways that infectious diseases can be prevented

▶ To identify nutrients the body needs to stay healthy

Objectives

After reading this lesson, you should be able to

▶ explain what an infectious disease is and how it is caused.

▶ list the body's main defenses against pathogens.

▶ describe how infectious diseases can be prevented.

Infectious disease
An illness that can pass from person to person.

Plague
An infectious disease that spreads quickly and kills many people.

If you have ever had a cold or the flu, you've had an infectious disease. An **infectious disease** is an illness that can pass from one person to another. In the past, many kinds of infectious diseases spread through populations. When an infectious disease spreads through a population quickly and kills many people, it is called a **plague**.

In the 1300s, two-thirds of the people in Europe caught the bubonic plague, or Black Death. Bubonic plague causes a person's body to swell in many places. In the 18th century, one out of every three English children came down with smallpox. Those who did not die from the disease were scarred with small pits in their skin. In the 19th century, a cholera plague wiped out thousands of people in the United States. Cholera causes severe problems with a person's digestive system. Even in the 20th century, an infectious disease called polio disabled and killed many children.

Today in the United States and many other parts of the world, these infectious diseases are rarely found. That is because steps have been taken to prevent them. However, new infectious diseases appear all the time. It is important to know what causes infectious diseases and how they spread. That way, people can learn how to prevent them.

In the 1950s, many children who got polio had problems walking and breathing.

Immune system
The body's most important defense against infectious diseases.

Pathogen
A germ.

Phagocyte
A white blood cell that surrounds and destroys pathogens.

Virus
A type of germ that is not living.

Pathogens

Germs, or **pathogens**, cause infectious diseases. Most pathogens are so small that they can be seen only with a microscope. Pathogens include protists, fungi, bacteria, and **viruses** that cause diseases. You learned about protists, fungi, and bacteria in Chapter 5. Unlike these pathogens, viruses are not living.

Pathogens are found in garbage, on unwashed dishes, and on the pages of this book. They are everywhere. Animals, wind, water, and other things carry pathogens from place to place.

The Body's Defenses

If pathogens are everywhere, why aren't you sick all the time? You stay healthy because your body has ways to protect itself, called defenses. The body's first line of defense prevents pathogens from entering it. Your skin, nose, and throat all work to keep pathogens out of your body.

Your skin forms a protective covering over your body. The oil and sweat on your skin kills pathogens. Your nose and throat have a sticky lining and tiny hairs that trap pathogens. When you sneeze or blow your nose, you get rid of many pathogens.

What happens if some pathogens do get into your body? Your stomach makes an acid that kills most of the pathogens that you swallow. White blood cells called **phagocytes** surround pathogens and destroy them, as shown in the picture. Your **immune system** also fights pathogens inside your body. The immune system is your body's most important defense against infectious diseases.

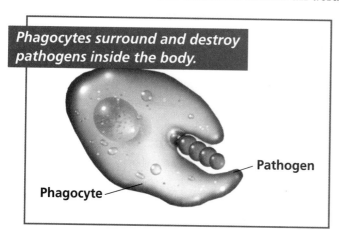

Phagocytes surround and destroy pathogens inside the body.

Phagocyte

Pathogen

Immunity

Your immune system includes white blood cells called **lymphocytes.** When a pathogen enters your body, the lymphocytes make **antibodies** to fight that pathogen. The picture shows that antibodies fight specific pathogens by binding with them.

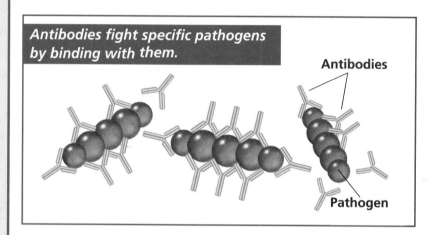

Antibodies fight specific pathogens by binding with them.

Antibodies

Pathogen

Antibodies help you get over a disease caused by a specific pathogen. In addition, the antibodies help prevent future attacks by that pathogen. That is because they remain in your body after the disease is gone. When this happens, your body is said to have **immunity** against the disease. If the pathogen that causes the disease enters your body again, it probably won't make you sick. Your body is prepared to fight the pathogen.

Vaccines

You might have heard someone say, "I'll never get mumps because I got a mumps shot." This person probably has immunity to mumps. Mumps is a childhood disease that causes fever and swelling under the jaw. When you get a "shot," your body makes antibodies against a specific pathogen. The shot is called a **vaccine**. It has a material that causes your body to make the antibodies. Getting a vaccine is another way you can develop immunity to a disease.

In 1796, an English doctor named Edward Jenner made the first vaccine. At that time, people realized that once you had smallpox, you would never get the disease again. In other words, you were immune to the disease. Jenner noticed that people who had had cowpox did not get smallpox. Cowpox is a disease that causes sores on the hands. However, cowpox is not dangerous to people.

Jenner tried using material from a cowpox sore as a vaccine against smallpox. He put the cowpox material on the scratched arm of a young boy. The boy became sick with cowpox, but then he became well. Next, Jenner gave the boy smallpox pathogens. The boy did not get smallpox. The cowpox material had given the boy immunity against smallpox.

Which diseases are you immune to? Ask your parents or your doctor which vaccines you have received.

Today, because of Jenner's vaccine, smallpox has been wiped out throughout the world. Vaccines have also made people immune to chicken pox, measles, polio, and other infectious diseases. Because specific pathogens cause certain diseases, a different vaccine must be made for each disease.

People get vaccines to protect themselves from many different infectious diseases.

Sanitation

When you want a drink of water, you just turn on the faucet. The water usually is clean and safe to drink. In the past, this was not always the case. People drank water that was piped in from rivers that had sewage. Sometimes people drank water from town pumps that contained many pathogens. These situations caused plagues. Thousands of people got sick and died from drinking water that was not clean.

Years ago, people did not know about pathogens. They did not realize that pathogens in water or food could harm them. Even doctors did not know that pathogens could pass from one patient to another.

Sanitation

The practice of keeping things clean to prevent infectious diseases.

Today, we know that pathogens cause many diseases. **Sanitation** is the practice of keeping things clean to prevent infectious diseases. For example, restaurants and supermarkets follow sanitation practices to keep foods safe to eat. Water treatment plants test water supplies for pathogens. Chemicals may be added to the water to kill pathogens. Hospitals sanitize linens and equipment so that diseases do not spread among the patients. Sanitation is also part of what you do every day. You practice sanitation when you wash dirty dishes, take out the garbage, and do the laundry. Washing your hands regularly is one of the best ways you can practice sanitation.

Self-Check

1. What are infectious diseases?
2. What is the body's first line of defense against pathogens?
3. How do antibodies fight pathogens?
4. How do vaccines prevent diseases?
5. Why is sanitation important?

Nutrition
The types and amounts of foods a person eats.

People often say, "Good nutrition is important if you want to stay healthy." **Nutrition** is the types and amounts of foods a person eats. Good nutrition involves eating the foods that your body needs to live and grow. In this lesson, you will learn how to make sure you have good nutrition.

Nutrients

Nutrients are the parts of food that the body can use. Your body's cells use nutrients for energy, growth, and other life activities. Your cells work properly when they get the nutrients they need. There are six kinds of nutrients that your body should get every day. These are carbohydrates, fats, proteins, water, vitamins, and minerals.

Your cells use each kind of nutrient in a different way. Carbohydrates are sugars and starches. They are your body's main fuel. That's why you have so much energy after you eat starchy foods, such as pasta, rice, or potatoes. Fats and oils also store energy. Although proteins can give your body energy, they are not the best nutrients to use for energy. Cells use proteins mostly to repair themselves and to reproduce, or make copies of themselves. The photos show foods that are rich in carbohydrates, fats and oils, or proteins.

These foods are rich in carbohydrates, fats and oils, or proteins.

Proteins

Carbohydrates

Fats and oils

Your body needs a great deal of water. Water makes up about 70 percent of your body. Your cells use water for many of their activities. However, your body loses a great deal of water each day. You lose water when you sweat. You breathe out water in the form of a gas called water vapor. You also lose water when your body releases wastes. You need to replace all the water that your body loses. For that reason, drink at least eight glasses of water every day.

Vitamins and Minerals

Unlike carbohydrates, proteins, and fats, vitamins and minerals do not give your body energy. However, vitamins and minerals are important to good health. They help the body use other nutrients and carry out life activities. The body needs small amounts of many different kinds of vitamins and minerals.

The vitamin chart on the next page lists some of the jobs of different vitamins. It also tells you which foods contain each vitamin. Tiny amounts of vitamins are found in foods. Because different foods contain different vitamins, it's important to eat various kinds of foods every day. That way, you can be sure to get all the vitamins your body needs.

Your body can store some vitamins, such as vitamin A. Other vitamins, such as vitamin C, pass through your body if they are not used. This means that you have to eat foods that contain vitamin C every day.

The foods we eat contain many different minerals. Calcium and phosphorus are important minerals for strong bones and teeth. Sodium and potassium help cells send messages to one another. Like vitamins, minerals are found in very small amounts in foods. Milk and cheese are two foods that have calcium and phosphorus. You can get potassium from bananas and meat. Salty foods, such as ham and crackers, have had sodium added to them. You should eat various kinds of foods every day to make sure you get all the minerals you need.

Vitamin Chart

Vitamin	Job in the body	Foods that have this vitamin
Vitamin A	Keeps the skin, hair, and eyes healthy	Milk, egg yolk, liver, carrots, spinach
B vitamins		
Niacin	Protects the skin and nerves	Meat, cereal, whole wheat, milk, fish, legumes
Thiamin	Protects the nervous system; aids digestion	Pork, whole grains, green beans, peanut butter
Riboflavin	Protects the body from disease	Milk, eggs, bread, meat (especially liver), green vegetables
Vitamin C	Helps form bones and teeth and fights infectious diseases	Citrus fruits, tomatoes, potatoes
Vitamin D	Helps form strong bones and teeth	Milk, fish oils
Vitamin E	Helps prevent cell damage	Vegetable oils, margarine
Vitamin K	Helps blood clot	Cabbage, spinach, soybeans, oats, egg yolks

What have you eaten so far today? How does that compare with the suggestions in the Food Guide Pyramid?

Food Guide Pyramid
A guide for good nutrition.

The Food Guide Pyramid

Your body needs many different kinds of nutrients in different amounts. How do you know if you are getting all the nutrients your body needs? One simple guide to good nutrition is the **Food Guide Pyramid**, which is shown below. The Food Guide Pyramid can help you choose the right foods. It can also help you eat the right amounts of different foods. That way, you are more likely to get the nutrients you need every day.

The Food Guide Pyramid can help you make sure you are getting good nutrition.

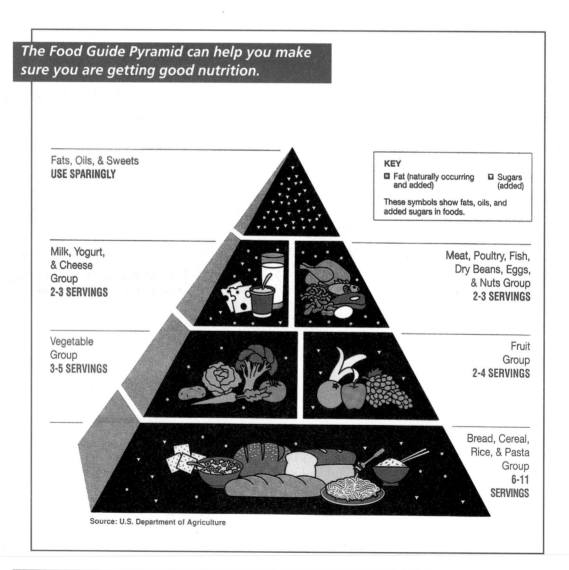

Fats, Oils, & Sweets
USE SPARINGLY

KEY
▢ Fat (naturally occurring and added)   ▢ Sugars (added)
These symbols show fats, oils, and added sugars in foods.

Milk, Yogurt, & Cheese Group
2-3 SERVINGS

Meat, Poultry, Fish, Dry Beans, Eggs, & Nuts Group
2-3 SERVINGS

Vegetable Group
3-5 SERVINGS

Fruit Group
2-4 SERVINGS

Bread, Cereal, Rice, & Pasta Group
6-11 SERVINGS

Source: U.S. Department of Agriculture

Serving Sizes

The Food Guide Pyramid gives the number of servings of each kind of food you should eat every day. How much food is one serving? In general, one serving is about the amount of a food you can hold in the palm of your hand. Below are some examples of what makes up one serving for different foods.

Eating the right foods is not enough. You also need to eat them in the right amounts.

Grains
- 1 slice of bread
- ½ cup of rice or pasta
- ½ cup of cooked cereal

Vegetables
- ½ cup of vegetables
- ½ cup of vegetable juice

Meat, beans, eggs, nuts
- 1 egg
- 2 tablespoons of peanut butter
- 2–3 oz. of meat
- ½ cup of cooked beans

Fruits
- 1 apple, banana, or orange
- ½ cup of fruit
- ¾ cup of fruit juice

Milk, yogurt, cheese
- 1 cup of milk
- 1 cup of yogurt
- 1.5 oz. of cheese

Self-Check

1. What are nutrients?
2. Which nutrients give your body energy?
3. How much water does your body need each day?
4. List three vitamins that your body needs and the jobs they perform in the body.
5. What is the Food Guide Pyramid?

Chapter 10

INVESTIGATION

Reading Food Labels

Materials

✓ paper
✓ pencil
✓ 8 food labels

Purpose
To determine the kinds and amounts of nutrients in different packaged foods

Procedure
1. Collect food labels from eight different packaged foods. You might choose different kinds of the same food, such as different brands of cereal. That way, you can compare different brands.

2. Copy the table below on your paper.

Food	Serving size	Carbohydrates (in grams)	Proteins (in grams)	Fats (in grams)	Vitamins and minerals (percentage)
1.					
2.					
3.					
4.					
5.					
6.					
7.					
8.					

3. Choose a food label. Write the name of the packaged food in your table.

4. Look for the size of a serving of that food. Write this information in your table.

5. Look for the kinds and amounts of carbohydrates, proteins, and fats in one serving size. Notice that they are given in grams and in percentages. In your table, write the number of grams of each nutrient found in one serving.

6. Are any vitamins or minerals in the food? Add to your table the names and percentages of any vitamins and minerals listed on the food label.

7. Repeat steps 3–6 for each food label you collected.

Questions

1. Compare the data in your table. Which food has the most carbohydrates?

2. Which food has the most proteins?

3. Which food has the most fats?

4. Which food has the most vitamins and minerals?

5. Compare the serving sizes of the foods. Which food has the smallest serving size? Which has the largest serving size?

Explore Further

1. Look at all the data you collected. Which food do you think is the healthiest? Give reasons for your choice.

2. Does the information in your table change your ideas about eating certain foods? Why or why not?

SCIENCE
IN YOUR
LIFE

How can eating fat be bad for you?

Your body needs fat to stay healthy. But eating too much fat can lead to health problems.

What's wrong with eating a lot of fat?

There are two main kinds of fats: saturated fats and unsaturated fats. Saturated fats are usually solid at room temperature. Foods that are high in saturated fat usually come from animals and often contain a fatty material called cholesterol. Unsaturated fats are usually liquid at room temperature. They are usually found in plant foods.

Eating too much saturated fat and cholesterol can cause your blood vessels to become clogged with fatty materials. This condition can lead to heart disease, heart attack, stroke, and other diseases.

Fats also have more calories than other nutrients do. Eating foods that are high in calories can cause a person to gain weight. Thus, eating too much fat can make a person overweight. Being overweight puts a person at risk for diabetes, stroke, heart disease, and other health problems.

How do you know if a food has fat in it?

You could read the food label to see exactly how much fat a food contains. But what if you are eating something that doesn't have a food label? Perhaps you want to know how much fat is in a hamburger or in a milk shake. You could look up the foods in a book at the library. *Food Values of Portions Commonly Used* is one such book. There also are software packages available. These will help you figure out the amount of fat (and other nutrients) in different foods.

One simple way to compare the amounts of fat in different foods is to use brown paper, like that used to make grocery sacks. You just rub the food on a square of clean brown paper. Then, let the paper dry. If the food contains fat, the paper will still have a wet-looking stain on it the next day. The darker and larger the stain, the more fat the food contains. You might want to try this paper test on some foods you eat regularly.

- Infectious diseases can spread from one person to another. Pathogens cause infectious diseases.
- Most pathogens are so small that they can be seen only with a microscope.
- The body's first line of defense against pathogens includes the skin, nose, and throat.
- When pathogens enter the body, phagocytes may surround the pathogens and destroy them. Stomach acid kills pathogens that are swallowed.
- The immune system is the body's most important defense against pathogens. Lymphocytes of the immune system make antibodies that fight specific pathogens.
- Suppose the body has antibodies that fight a specific pathogen. The person is unlikely to become ill the next time that pathogen enters the body. This condition is called immunity.
- A vaccine causes a person's body to make antibodies against the pathogen that causes the disease.
- Nutrients are the parts of food that the body can use. Nutrients are necessary for cell repair, growth, and other life activities.
- The body needs six nutrients: proteins, carbohydrates, fats, water, vitamins, and minerals.
- Carbohydrates, proteins, and fats and oils give the body energy. Cells use water for many of their life activities.
- Vitamins and minerals help the body use other nutrients and carry out life activities.
- The Food Guide Pyramid suggests the kinds and amounts of foods needed for good nutrition.

Science Words

antibody, 218	pathogen, 217
Food Guide Pyramid, 224	phagocyte, 217
immune system, 217	plague, 216
immunity, 218	sanitation, 220
infectious disease, 216	vaccine, 218
lymphocyte, 218	virus, 217
nutrition, 221	

Vocabulary Review

Number your paper from 1 to 12. Then choose the word or words from the Word Bank that best complete each sentence. Write the answer on your paper.

WORD BANK

antibodies

Food Guide Pyramid

immune system

immunity

infectious diseases

nutrition

pathogens

plague

sanitation

vaccines

viruses

water

1. When antibodies remain in your body after the disease is gone, you have _____ against that disease.

2. The _____ can help you determine how much and what kinds of foods to eat.

3. _____ can spread from person to person.

4. You need to replace all the _____ that your body loses each day.

5. _____ cause the body to produce antibodies against specific pathogens.

6. Unlike bacteria, _____ are not living organisms.

7. _____ cause infectious diseases.

8. Keeping drinking water clean is an example of _____.

9. Your body makes _____ to fight pathogens.

10. The type and amount of food you eat is _____

11. An infectious disease that spreads quickly through a population and kills many people is a(n) _____.

12. Your _____ is your body's first line of defense against disease.

Concept Review

Number your paper from 1 to 6. Then choose the answer that best completes each sentence. Write the letter of the answer on your paper.

1. Your body's first line of defense against pathogens is your _____.
   a. skin **b.** stomach **c.** antibodies

2. White blood cells called _____ surround and destroy pathogens.
   a. antibodies **b.** viruses **c.** phagocytes

3. White blood cells called _____ produce antibodies to fight disease.
   a. phagocytes **b.** lymphocytes **c.** protists

4. Cells use _____ to repair themselves and to reproduce.
   a. carbohydrates **b.** proteins **c.** fats

5. Water, minerals, and _____ do not give the body energy.
   a. proteins **b.** fats **c.** vitamins

6. The greatest amount of your daily food should come from the _____ group.
   a. bread, cereal, rice, and pasta
   b. vegetable **c.** milk, yogurt, and cheese

Critical Thinking

1. Give one reason why early doctors and scientists did not realize that pathogens cause infectious diseases.

2. Do you have good nutrition? Explain your answer using the Food Guide Pyramid.

Test Taking Tip | If you know you will have to define certain terms on a test, write each term on a separate card. Then, write the definition of each term on the other side of the card. Use the cards to test yourself, or work with a partner.

Chapter

11

Genetics

Have you noticed that members of the same family often look alike? Have you ever been told that you look like someone in your family? Most of your physical characteristics, from the color of your eyes to the length of your legs, are due to your parents. The same is true of all organisms, whether they are rosebushes or spiders or frogs. In this chapter, you will learn how parents pass their characteristics to their offspring.

ORGANIZE YOUR THOUGHTS

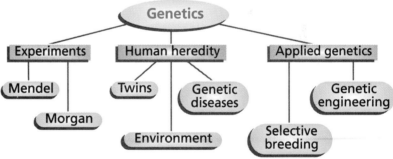

Goals for Learning

▶ To explain how genes pass traits from parents to offspring

▶ To describe the role of chromosomes in heredity

▶ To identify patterns of heredity in humans

▶ To explain how scientists are able to use the principles of genetics to affect the traits of organisms

233

Genetics
The study of heredity.

Heredity
The passing of traits from parents to offspring.

P generation
The pure plants that Mendel produced by self-pollination.

Self-pollination
The movement of pollen from the male sex organs to the female sex organs of flowers on the same plant.

Family members have many of the same characteristics, or traits. The passing of traits from parents to their children is called **heredity**. All organisms pass information about traits to their children, or offspring. That is why bluebirds produce bluebird chicks, and lions produce lion cubs.

Mendel's Studies

Genetics is the study of heredity. More than 100 years ago, a scientist named Gregor Mendel made important discoveries about heredity. Mendel took seeds from tall pea plants and planted them. Most of the plants that grew from the seeds were tall. However, some of the plants were short. Mendel wondered why the short pea plants were unlike their tall parents.

Mendel decided to study pea plants and their seeds. He began by trying to grow plants that would produce only tall plants from their seeds. The flowers of pea plants have both male sex organs and female sex organs. Mendel moved pollen from the male sex organs to the female sex organs on the same plant. In this way, he carried out **self-pollination** of each plant. After self-pollination occurred, each flower produced seeds. Mendel planted the seeds, and then self-pollinated the plants that grew from those seeds. He did this again and again. Finally, Mendel had seeds that would produce only tall pea plants. These were "pure tall" seeds.

Using the same method of self-pollination, Mendel grew plants that were pure for the trait of shortness. He called the "pure tall" and the "pure short" plants the **P generation**. *P* stands for parent generation. To understand what a generation is, think of your grandparents as one generation. Your parents are part of a second generation, and you are part of a third generation.

The F₁ Generation

Mendel wondered what type of offspring two *different* pure parent plants would produce. He used the method of **cross-pollination** to find out. Mendel moved the pollen from pure tall pea plants to the female sex organs of pure short pea plants. He also placed pollen from pure short plants on the female sex organs of pure tall plants.

When the cross-pollinated flowers produced seeds, Mendel took the seeds and planted them. He called these plants the **F₁ generation**. The *F* stands for filial, which means son or daughter. The *1* stands for the first filial generation.

Mendel's studies of pea plants had three main steps.

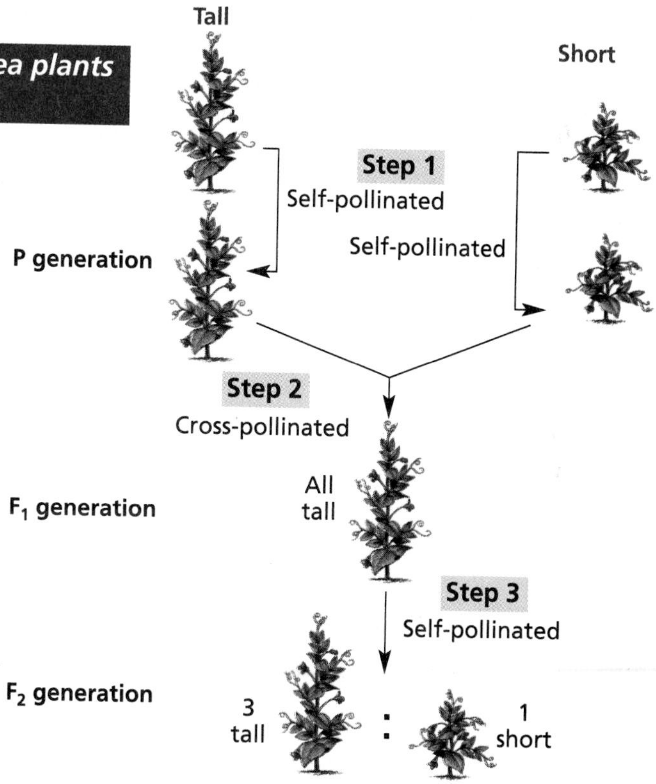

Tall
Short

Step 1
Self-pollinated

Self-pollinated

P generation

Step 2
Cross-pollinated

F₁ generation
All tall

Step 3
Self-pollinated

F₂ generation
3 tall : 1 short

The diagram above shows the results of Mendel's studies. To his surprise, Mendel found that all the F₁ generation plants were tall. Mendel crossed hundreds of pure short and pure tall pea plants. He observed the offspring plants carefully. Each time, the results were similar. All the offspring were tall. What had happened to shortness? Why had this trait disappeared?

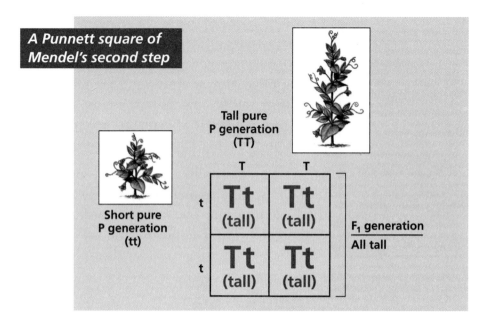

A Punnett square of Mendel's second step

Tall pure
P generation
(TT)

Short pure
P generation
(tt)

	T	T
t	**Tt** (tall)	**Tt** (tall)
t	**Tt** (tall)	**Tt** (tall)

F₁ generation
All tall

Punnett Squares

A model called a **Punnett square** can be used to explain crosses like those Mendel did. The Punnett square above shows Mendel's cross of pure tall pea plants with pure short pea plants. *TT* stands for a pure tall parent plant. *tt* stands for a pure short parent plant. The capital *T* represents the gene for tallness. The lowercase *t* represents the gene for shortness. A **gene** is the information that a parent passes to its offspring for a trait. Therefore, a pea plant receives, or inherits, two genes for height. One gene is inherited from each parent.

Notice that although all of the F₁ pea plants were tall, they also had the gene for shortness. A gene that is hidden when it is combined with another gene is called a **recessive gene**. The gene that shows up is called a **dominant gene**. A capital letter is used to represent a dominant gene. A lowercase letter is used to represent a recessive gene.

In the case of pea plants, the gene for tallness is dominant. The gene for shortness is recessive. That explains why all the pea plants in the F₁ generation were tall.

F₂ generation
The plants that resulted when Mendel self-pollinated plants from the F₁ generation.

Genotype
An organism's combination of genes for a trait.

Phenotype
An organism's appearance as a result of its combination of genes.

What is the genotype of a short pea plant?

Genotypes and Phenotypes

An organism's combination of genes for a trait is called its **genotype**. For example, the genotype of the F₁ pea plants was Tt. What an organism looks like as a result of its genes is its **phenotype**. The phenotype of the F₁ pea plants was "tall." An organism has both a genotype and a phenotype for all its traits.

The F₂ Generation

Mendel produced yet another generation of pea plants by self-pollinating the F₁ generation plants. He called this third group of plants the F₂ generation. Mendel found that short pea plants reappeared in the **F₂ generation**. In fact, in the F₂ generation, about ¾ of the plants were tall, and about ¼ were short. Mendel repeated his experiments many times. He got similar results each time. The F₂ generation always included short pea plants.

The Punnett square below explains Mendel's results. Short plants reappeared in the F₂ generation because they inherited two recessive genes for shortness, one from each tall parent. The recessive genes were hidden in the tall parent plants.

The F₂ generation pea plants showed two different phenotypes: tall and short. However, notice in the Punnett square that the F₂ generation had three different genotypes. All the short plants had the genotype tt. But the tall plants had either the genotype TT or the genotype Tt.

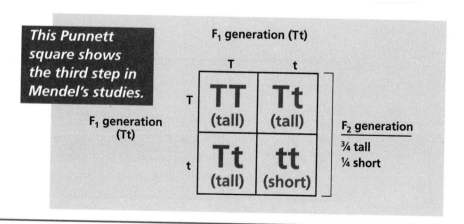

This Punnett square shows the third step in Mendel's studies.

F₁ generation (Tt)

F₁ generation (Tt)

	T	t
T	TT (tall)	Tt (tall)
t	Tt (tall)	tt (short)

F₂ generation
¾ tall
¼ short

Mendel's Conclusions

Mendel also studied other traits of pea plants. Each trait was inherited the same way as plant height. For example, Mendel obtained only round seeds when he crossed plants pure for round seeds with plants pure for wrinkled seeds. He obtained only green pea pods when he crossed plants pure for green pea pods with those pure for yellow ones.

Mendel concluded that there was information in a plant that caused it to have certain traits. He called this information **factors**. He reasoned that since traits came in pairs, the factors did too. Mendel also thought that one factor of the pair was more powerful than the other factor. The more powerful factor hid the appearance of the weaker factor. Today, we know that Mendel's factors are genes. Dominant genes hide the appearance of recessive genes.

Mendel also thought that the paired factors separated during sexual reproduction. That way, the offspring received half the factors from one parent and half from the other parent. In the next lesson, you will learn how genes are inherited during sexual reproduction.

Genes determine whether a pea plant is short or tall. Genes also determine your traits. Genes determine whether your eyes are brown or blue. They determine whether you get freckles when you go in the sun. In all organisms, genes carry the information about traits from parents to their offspring.

Factors
The name that Mendel gave to information about traits that parents pass to offspring.

Self-Check

1. What is heredity?
2. Describe the three steps in Mendel's studies of pea plants.
3. Contrast the terms *dominant gene* and *recessive gene*.
4. What is the difference between genotype and phenotype?
5. Draw a Punnett square to represent Mendel's cross between pure tall plants and pure short plants.

What is your genotype?

Many traits in pea plants are inherited according to the patterns that Mendel observed. You can record your phenotype for three human traits that are inherited according to those patterns. Then, you can determine your genotype for each trait.

1. On a sheet of paper, make a chart like the one below.

Trait	Your phenotype	Dominant or recessive?	Possible genotype
Type of hairline			
Presence or absence of middigital hair			
Type of earlobes			

2. Fill in your chart as you observe your phenotype for each trait. First, look in the mirror and pull your hair back from your hairline. Is your hairline straight? Or does the hairline come to a point in the middle of your forehead? If it comes to a point, then you have a widow's peak. A widow's peak is determined by a dominant gene.

3. Look at your fingers. Each finger has three segments. Do your fingers have hairs in the middle segment? If you have even one hair in the middle segment, you have middigital hair. Middigital hair is determined by a dominant gene.

4. Do the tips of your earlobes hang free? Or are they completely attached to the side of your head? Attached earlobes are determined by a recessive gene.

5. Based on the information you have recorded in your chart, fill in your genotype in the last column. Use capital letters to represent dominant genes. Use lowercase letters to represent recessive genes.

Objectives

After reading this lesson, you should be able to

► explain what a chromosome is.

► compare mitosis with meiosis.

► explain how sex is determined in humans.

► explain what a sex-linked trait is.

Chromosomes are rod-shaped bodies located in the nucleus of a cell. Chromosomes are made of proteins and a chemical called DNA. Sections of DNA make up an organism's genes, which determine all the traits of an organism. A chromosome may contain hundreds of genes.

Mitosis and Cell Division

From your study of one-celled organisms, you know that amebas reproduce by splitting in half. Before doing so, the ameba's chromosomes make a copy of themselves. Then, the ameba's nuclear membrane dissolves. The two sets of chromosomes separate and a nucleus forms around each set. The division of the nucleus into two new nuclei is called mitosis.

Following mitosis, the entire cell divides. When the ameba becomes two amebas, each new ameba gets one nucleus with a complete set of chromosomes. Each set of chromosomes is identical to the parent ameba's chromosomes. Thus, each new ameba is identical to the parent ameba.

Just as amebas go through mitosis and cell division, so do the cells that make up the human body. The photo shows a human cell dividing. Body cells divide by mitosis and cell division as the body grows and repairs itself. However, to reproduce itself, the body uses a different kind of process.

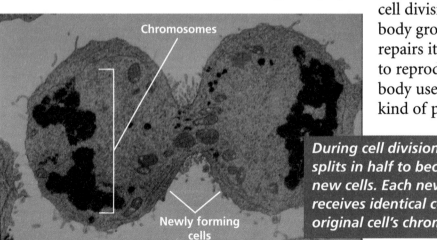

Chromosomes

Newly forming cells

During cell division, one cell splits in half to become two new cells. Each new cell receives identical copies of the original cell's chromosomes.

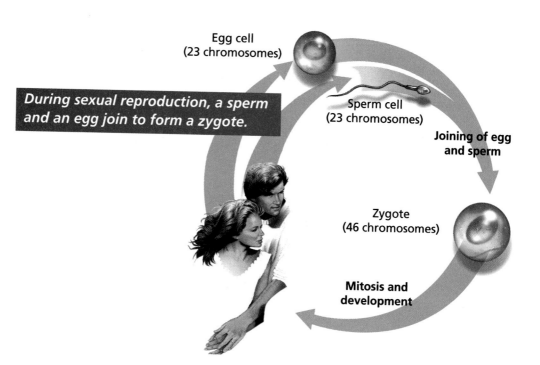

Egg cell
(23 chromosomes)

Sperm cell
(23 chromosomes)

During sexual reproduction, a sperm and an egg join to form a zygote.

Joining of egg
and sperm

Zygote
(46 chromosomes)

Mitosis and
development

Sexual Reproduction

Humans and most other many-celled organisms reproduce sexually. In sexual reproduction, two cells called gametes join to form one complete cell. Males produce gametes called sperm cells. Females produce gametes called egg cells. Each gamete has only one-half of the chromosomes found in the organism's body cells. When gametes join, they form a cell that has a complete set of chromosomes.

Most humans have 46 chromosomes in their body cells. Notice in the diagram above that human sperm cells have only 23 chromosomes. Human egg cells also have only 23 chromosomes. When humans reproduce, a sperm and an egg join to form a cell called a zygote. A zygote has 46 chromosomes and eventually develops into an adult.

Together, the 46 human chromosomes carry 50,000 to 100,000 genes. The mix of chromosomes from both parents during sexual reproduction produces an offspring that is different from either parent.

Meiosis

As you know, mitosis results in new cells that have a complete set of chromosomes. Gametes form by a different kind of process. They form by a division of the nucleus called meiosis.

The diagram below compares the process of meiosis with that of mitosis. As in mitosis, meiosis begins with the copying of the chromosomes in a parent cell. Then, the cell divides into two new cells. However, in meiosis, each new cell divides again. Thus, one parent cell results in four new sex cells. Each sex cell contains one-half the number of chromosomes of the parent cell.

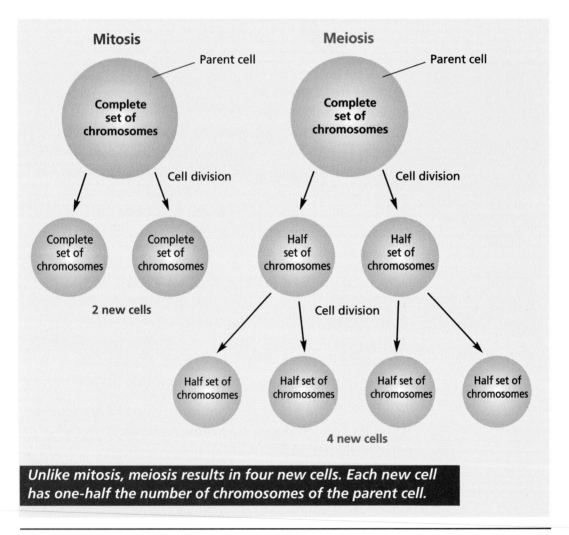

Unlike mitosis, meiosis results in four new cells. Each new cell has one-half the number of chromosomes of the parent cell.

Sex chromosome
A chromosome that determines the sex of an organism.

Sex Chromosomes

As you know, humans have 46 chromosomes. The chromosomes consist of 23 pairs. Each chromosome that makes up a pair comes from a different parent. For 22 of the pairs, the two chromosomes look much alike. However, the chromosomes that make up the 23rd pair look different from each other. These two chromosomes are called **sex chromosomes** because they determine a person's sex. There are two kinds of human sex chromosomes: an X chromosome and a Y chromosome.

A human female has two X chromosomes. A human male has one X chromosome and one Y chromosome. Parents pass one of their sex chromosomes to their offspring. A male can pass an X chromosome or a Y chromosome to its offspring. A female can pass only an X chromosome.

The Punnett square below shows how human sex chromosomes determine the sex of an offspring. An offspring that inherits an X chromosome from both parents is a female (XX). An offspring that inherits an X chromosome from its mother and a Y chromosome from its father is a male (XY). Notice that the chance of producing a female offspring is 50 percent. The chance of producing a male offspring is also 50 percent.

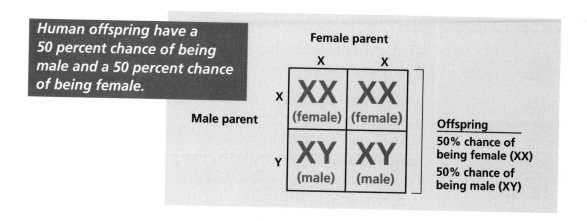

Human offspring have a 50 percent chance of being male and a 50 percent chance of being female.

Female parent

Male parent

	X	X
X	XX (female)	XX (female)
Y	XY (male)	XY (male)

Offspring
50% chance of being female (XX)
50% chance of being male (XY)

Experiments With Fruit Flies

Recall that Mendel used pea plants in his study of heredity. About 50 years later, another scientist, Thomas Morgan, used fruit flies to learn about chromosomes and genes. Fruit flies are useful to study for a number of reasons. Their cells have only four pairs of chromosomes. The chromosomes are large and easy to see under a microscope. Fruit flies reproduce quickly. In addition, it is easy to tell the male fruit fly from the female.

Sex-Linked Traits

Fruit flies usually have red eyes. However, Morgan noticed that one of the male fruit flies had white eyes. Morgan mated the white-eyed male with a red-eyed female. He called the offspring the F_1 generation. All the offspring in the F_1 generation had red eyes. Morgan concluded that the gene for red eyes was dominant in fruit flies.

Next, Morgan mated the flies from the F_1 generation to produce an F_2 generation. This time, some of the offspring had red eyes and some had white eyes. However, all the white-eyed flies were males. None of the females had white eyes. Morgan concluded that white eye color in fruit flies is linked to the sex of the fly. Traits that are linked to the sex of an organism are said to be **sex-linked traits**.

Sex-linked trait
A trait that is determined by an organism's sex chromosomes.

As in humans, a female fruit fly has two X chromosomes. A male has one X chromosome and one Y chromosome. Morgan found that the gene for eye color in fruit flies is on the X chromosome. There is no gene for eye color on the Y chromosome. That explains why eye color in fruit flies is a sex-linked trait.

The Punnett squares on the next page show Morgan's experiments. Notice that only the X chromosome carries a gene for eye color. The genotypes $X^R X^R$ and $X^R X^r$ represent a red-eyed female fly. The genotype $X^R Y$ represents a red-eyed male. White-eyed males have the genotype $X^r Y$.

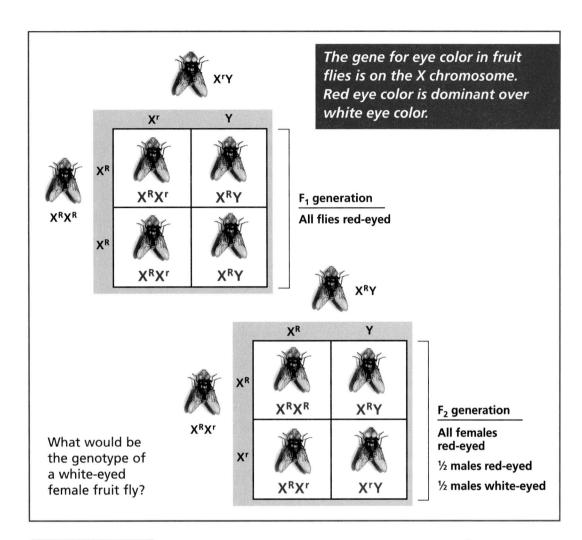

The gene for eye color in fruit flies is on the X chromosome. Red eye color is dominant over white eye color.

X^rY

X^RX^R

	X^r	Y
X^R	X^RX^r	X^RY
X^R	X^RX^r	X^RY

F₁ generation

All flies red-eyed

X^RY

X^RX^r

	X^R	Y
X^R	X^RX^R	X^RY
X^r	X^RX^r	X^rY

F₂ generation

All females red-eyed

½ males red-eyed

½ males white-eyed

What would be the genotype of a white-eyed female fruit fly?

Carrier
An organism that carries a gene but does not show the effects of the gene.

Notice that a female fly with the genotype X^RX^r has red eyes even though it carries a gene for white eyes. An organism that carries a gene but does not show the gene's effects is called a **carrier**.

Self-Check

1. What are chromosomes?
2. Describe mitosis.
3. Describe meiosis.
4. What are the sex chromosomes of a human female? What are the sex chromosomes of a human male?
5. Why is eye color a sex-linked trait in fruit flies?

Objectives

After reading this lesson, you should be able to

▶ explain some ways that scientists study heredity in humans.

▶ describe DNA and how it replicates.

▶ explain what a mutation is.

▶ give examples of genetic diseases.

Fraternal twins
Twins that do not have identical genes.

Identical twins
Twins that have identical genes.

Identical twins have identical genes. Fraternal twins do not.

Human genetics is the study of how humans inherit traits. Human genetics is more complicated than the genetics of fruit flies for a number of reasons. First, humans have more chromosomes than fruit flies do. Second, humans do not reproduce as quickly as flies. And third, humans cannot be used in laboratory experiments. Scientists study heredity in humans by studying identical twins. They also look at families to learn how genetic diseases are passed from one generation to the next.

Different Kinds of Twins

There are two types of twins: **identical twins** and **fraternal twins**. As you can see below, they form in different ways. Identical twins form from the same zygote and therefore have identical genes. First, a sperm cell joins with an egg cell to form a zygote. Then, the zygote divides into two cells that separate completely. Each cell develops into an offspring, resulting in identical twins.

Fraternal twins do not have identical genes. They are just like other brothers and sisters. Fraternal twins form from two different zygotes. The zygotes develop into offspring with different sets of genes.

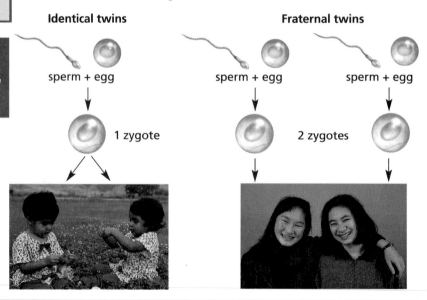

Identical twins — sperm + egg → 1 zygote

Fraternal twins — sperm + egg, sperm + egg → 2 zygotes

Heredity and Environment

You are born with certain genes. That is your heredity. Your genes determine your skin color, eye color, body shape, and other characteristics. But, your **environment** also may affect your characteristics. Your family, the air you breathe, and everything else in your surroundings make up your environment. To find out how environment affects a person's characteristics, scientists study identical twins who have been separated since birth. Both twins have the same genes, but they grew up in different environments. Scientists look for differences in the characteristics of the twins. If they find any different characteristics, they know the environment caused those differences.

The Influence of Environment

Food, sunlight, air, and other parts of the environment can affect a person's characteristics. For example, a person who doesn't have good nutrition may not grow tall, even though he has a gene for tallness. A person who avoids sunlight may not form freckles, even though she has a gene for freckles. The environment also affects a developing baby. Studies show that babies born to women who smoke cigarettes weigh less than babies born to women who are nonsmokers.

The environment can directly affect a person's genes. For example, X rays and some types of chemicals cause changes in genes. These changes are called **mutations**. Mutations can cause problems in humans and other organisms. How do mutations occur? Before you can understand mutations better, you need to know more about DNA.

DNA

DNA in chromosomes is the material that contains an organism's genes. DNA passes the genes from one cell to another during cell division. All the information needed to carry out life activities is in DNA. All the information that makes a duck a duck is in the duck's DNA. All the information that makes you a human is in your DNA.

You can see below that DNA is a large molecule shaped like a twisted ladder. The rungs of the ladder are made of four different kinds of molecules called **bases**. The letters *T, A, C,* and *G* are used as abbreviations for the names of the four bases. The order of the bases in the DNA molecules of a cell provides a code for all the information that the cell needs to live.

The DNA molecules of different organisms have different orders of bases. The greater the difference between the organisms, the greater is the difference in the order of their bases. Thus, the order of bases in a frog's DNA is very different from the order of bases in your DNA. The difference in the order of bases between your DNA and your friend's DNA is not as great.

Recall that a gene is a section of a DNA molecule. A gene is made up of a certain order of bases. Different genes have a different order of bases. This difference allows genes to provide different kinds of information. For example, the order of bases in a gene for hair color determines whether the hair will be black, red, or blonde.

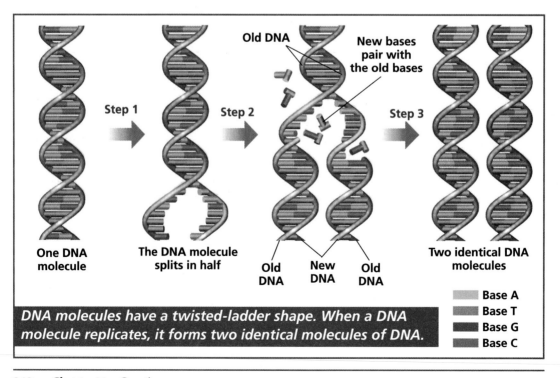

DNA molecules have a twisted-ladder shape. When a DNA molecule replicates, it forms two identical molecules of DNA.

An important feature of DNA is that it can **replicate**, or copy itself. A DNA molecule is held together at its rungs. Notice in the drawing that each rung is made of a pair of bases. The bases pair in certain ways. Base A pairs with base T. Base C pairs with base G. When DNA replicates, it first splits down the middle of its rungs. The paired bases separate. Then, new bases pair with the separated bases on each half of the DNA molecule. The result is two identical copies of the original DNA molecule.

DNA replication occurs every time a cell divides normally. The new cells receive copies of the DNA molecules. In this way, genetic information is passed on from cell to cell.

What might happen if a person's DNA is not copied exactly?

Mutations

Sometimes there is a change in the order of bases in a DNA molecule. This change is called a mutation. Recall that parts of the environment, such as X rays and chemicals, can cause mutations.

Mutations cause changes in genes. Since genes determine traits, mutations may affect the traits of an organism. For example, white eye color in fruit flies is the result of a mutation. Mutations may be harmful or helpful to organisms or may have no effect at all.

Genetic Diseases

A **genetic disease** is a disease that results from the genes a person inherits. Recessive genes cause most genetic diseases. That means a person must inherit the recessive gene for the disease from both parents to have the disease. Dominant genes cause other genetic diseases. Genetic diseases result from mutations.

A recessive gene causes a form of **diabetes**. The gene prevents the body from making insulin. Insulin is a protein that controls the amount of sugar in the bloodstream. People who have diabetes have too much sugar in their blood. They must take insulin, either by mouth or by injection, to lower the amount of blood sugar.

Diabetes
A genetic disease in which a person has too much sugar in the blood.

Genetic disease
A disease that is caused by a mutated gene.

Replicate
To make a copy of itself.

A recessive gene also causes **sickle-cell anemia**. You can see in the photos that the disease causes a person's red blood cells to have a sickle shape. The sickle cells clog blood vessels. People with sickle-cell anemia have weakness and an irregular heart beat.

Sickle-cell anemia is a genetic disease. It causes a person's red blood cells to have a sickle shape.

Normal red blood cells

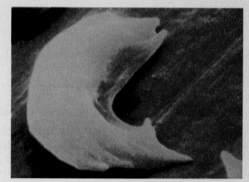

Sickled red blood cells

Gene pool
The genes found within a population.

Inbreeding
Sexual reproduction between organisms within a small gene pool.

Sickle-cell anemia
A genetic disease in which a person's red blood cells have a sickle shape.

Inbreeding

With the billions of people who live in the world, there is a great variety of human genes. A **gene pool** is all the genes that are found within a certain population. The larger the population is, the larger is the gene pool. In a large population, a person who is a carrier of a genetic disease is unlikely to marry someone who also is a carrier. Their children will probably not have the disease. However, people living in a small population often marry each other. Their gene pool is small. After several generations, there is a greater likelihood of couples having children with genetic diseases. The same is true when people marry close relatives. Sexual reproduction among people who are part of a small gene pool is called **inbreeding**.

Inbreeding caused a disease called **hemophilia** to occur frequently within the royal families of Europe. In hemophilia, a gene that causes blood to clump, or clot, is not normal. As a result, the blood does not have a protein it needs to clot. People who have hemophilia bleed a great deal when they are just slightly injured. They need to receive the protein from normal blood to help their blood clot.

Hemophilia is sometimes called the "Royal Disease." People from royal families generally married other people from royal families, including cousins. The royal gene pool was very small. This increased the likelihood of hemophilia showing up in the family members.

Human Sex-Linked Traits

In the last lesson, you learned that eye color in fruit flies is sex-linked. A number of human traits also are sex-linked. For example, the gene for color blindness is a recessive gene found on the X chromosome. People who are color-blind have trouble telling certain colors apart. For a female to be color-blind, she must inherit two genes for color blindness, one on each X chromosome. However, a male who inherits a single gene for color blindness on his X chromosome is color-blind. For that reason, color blindness is more common in males than in females. Hemophilia and muscular dystrophy are two other sex-linked traits found in humans. They are both caused by a recessive gene found on the X chromosome. Therefore, they are also more common in males than in females.

Self-Check

1. What is the difference between identical twins and fraternal twins?
2. Give an example of how both heredity and environment may affect a certain human characteristic.
3. What is DNA?
4. What is a mutation?
5. Define the term *genetic disease* and give an example of a genetic disease.

Chapter 11

INVESTIGATION

Tracing a Genetic Disease

Materials

✓ paper
✓ pencil

Purpose
To trace a genetic disease by using a family history and a diagram called a pedigree

Procedure
1. The diagram below is called a pedigree. Pedigrees are used to trace traits from generation to generation. This pedigree shows the inheritance of a trait called albinism. A person who is an albino lacks coloring. As a result, the person has milky-white skin and hair.

2. Compare each set of parents in the pedigree with their children. Based on the pedigree, determine whether a recessive gene or a dominant gene causes albinism. (*Hint:* If a recessive gene causes albinism, then two normal parents are able to produce a child with albinism. If a dominant gene causes albinism, then every albino child will have at least one albino parent.)

Pedigree Key

☐ Normal male
○ Normal female
■ Albino male
● Albino female

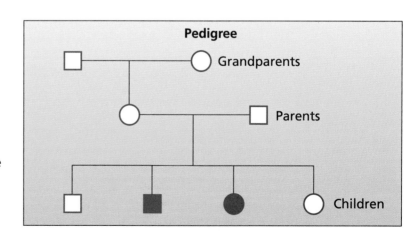

3. Read the following family history.

   Huntington's disease is a genetic disorder that affects the nervous system. John has Huntington's disease, but his sister, Nancy, does not. John's father also had Huntington's disease, but his mother did not. John's father's mother (John's grandmother) had Huntington's disease. John's father's father (John's grandfather) did not.

4. On a sheet of paper, draw a pedigree to show the history of Huntington's disease in John's family. Make a pedigree key similar to the one shown on page 252.

Questions

1. Based on the pedigree shown on page 252, is albinism caused by a recessive gene or by a dominant gene? Explain.

2. Look at the pedigree you drew in step 4. How many generations does your pedigree show?

3. Does the pedigree you drew show a genetic disease that is caused by a recessive gene or by a dominant gene? How do you know?

4. From which parent did John inherit Huntington's disease?

5. Do you think that Nancy is a carrier for Huntington's disease? Why or why not?

Explore Further

1. Based on your answer to question 3 above, give John's genotype for Huntington's disease. Explain your answer.

2. Assume that John marries a woman who does not have Huntington's disease. Draw a Punnett square to show the chance that a child of theirs will inherit the disease.

Objectives

After reading this lesson, you should be able to

▶ define *applied genetics*.

▶ give examples of selective breeding.

▶ explain how genetic engineering has been used to improve the lives of humans.

Applied genetics
The process of using knowledge of genetics to affect heredity.

Selective breeding
The process of breeding plants and animals so that certain traits repeatedly show up in future generations.

Farmers use breeding techniques to grow hardier and better-tasting crops. Animal breeders use breeding techniques to make prizewinning horses. Scientists transfer genes from one organism to another. These all are examples of people affecting the traits that organisms inherit. When people use their knowledge of genetics to affect heredity, they are practicing **applied genetics**.

Useful Mutations

A mutation may sound like a bad thing, but it has caused many helpful changes in organisms. For example, a mutation that results in an animal with white fur would be helpful to that animal in a snowy region. Animals with white fur would probably survive longer and have more offspring than those with dark fur. That is because the white fur would blend in with the snow. Eventually, there would be more white-furred animals than dark-furred animals in the snowy region. Over long periods of time, mutations may lead to changes in populations. This is one way that new species are formed.

Selective Breeding

Farmers and scientists use their knowledge of genetics to produce new varieties of plants and animals. The method of selecting useful mutations and breeding organisms so that the mutation shows up again is called **selective breeding**. For example, at one time, a mutation for short legs arose in a sheep. Short legs may not seem to be a desirable trait in sheep. However, short legs prevent sheep from jumping over fences. Farmers bred the short-legged sheep and its offspring until a new breed of short-legged sheep was produced.

Farmers have used selective breeding to produce cows that give large amounts of milk and chickens that lay larger eggs. Selective breeding has also resulted in pink grapefruits and navel oranges.

Breeding Racehorses

Selective breeding is used to produce great racehorses. The horse named Secretariat won the three most important horse races in the United States. To breed a winner, Secretariat's owner selected parents with desirable genes. Secretariat's father was known for fathering horses that won short races. From his mother's side, Secretariat inherited strength and the ability to go long distances. The result was an oversized horse with excellent speed and a stride of about 25 feet. Breeders select horses that have a good temperament, as well. An animal's genes also affect its behavior.

What are some kinds of traits that breeders have selected in different breeds of dogs?

Breeders use selective breeding methods to produce winning racehorses, like Secretariat.

Genetic Engineering

In the 1970s, scientists began introducing new genes into organisms. This process is called **genetic engineering**. At first, scientists transferred genes from one species of bacterium to another species of bacterium. Today, scientists are able to transfer genes between entirely different organisms. For example, scientists have transferred human genes into bacteria. The human genes function in the bacteria as they do in human cells. When scientists transferred the gene for human insulin into bacteria, the bacteria produced human insulin. The insulin has been used to treat people with diabetes.

Scientists have also used genetic engineering to improve crop plants. For example, they have transferred a bacterial gene into plants that makes the plants resistant to insect attacks.

Some scientists would like to use genetic engineering to cure genetic diseases. So far, they have not been able to permanently replace disease-causing genes in humans with normal ones. However, scientists have found ways to temporarily introduce normal genes into people who have certain genetic diseases. As a result, the people are free of the diseases for a while.

Genetic engineering
The process of transferring genes from one organism to another.

Self-Check

1. What is applied genetics?
2. Give an example of a mutation that is helpful to an organism.
3. What is selective breeding?
4. Define the term *genetic engineering*.
5. Describe one way that scientists have used genetic engineering to help humans.

- Heredity is the passing of traits from parents to their offspring.
- Gregor Mendel, while working with pea plants, discovered that traits in organisms are due to paired factors.
- Mendel's factors are now called genes. Genes are located on chromosomes, which are found in the nucleus of a cell.
- Chromosomes are able to make copies of themselves. During mitosis and cell division, each new cell gets an exact copy of the parent cell's chromosomes.
- Meiosis is the process by which sex cells form. Each sex cell contains one-half the number of chromosomes in the parent cell.
- There are two kinds of human sex chromosomes: an X chromosome and a Y chromosome. A human female has two X chromosomes. A human male has one X chromosome and one Y chromosome.
- Chromosomes contain DNA. The order of bases in DNA provides a code for information about all the traits of an organism.
- Mutations are changes in DNA. Harmful mutations cause genetic diseases, such as diabetes and hemophilia.
- In selective breeding, the helpful results of mutations produce better varieties of plants and animals.
- The transfer of genes from one organism to another is called genetic engineering.

Science Words		
applied genetics, 254	fraternal twins, 246	mutation, 247
base, 248	gene, 236	P generation, 234
carrier, 245	gene pool, 250	phenotype, 237
cross-pollination, 235	genetic disease, 249	Punnett square, 236
diabetes, 249	genetic engineering, 256	recessive gene, 236
dominant gene, 236	genetics, 234	replicate, 249
environment, 247	genotype, 237	selective breeding, 254
F_1 generation, 235	hemophilia, 251	self-pollination, 234
F_2 generation, 237	heredity, 234	sex chromosome, 243
factors, 238	identical twins, 246	sex-linked trait, 244
	inbreeding, 250	sickle-cell anemia, 250

Vocabulary Review

Number your paper from 1 to 10. Choose the word or words from the Word Bank that best complete each sentence. Write the answer on your paper.

WORD BANK

dominant

environment

genetic
  engineering

genotype

heredity

mutations

P generation

Punnett square

recessive

sex-linked

1. The pure breeding parent pea plants that Mendel studied were called the _____.

2. _____ is an organism's combination of genes for a trait.

3. A gene that is hidden when combined with another gene is said to be _____.

4. The passing of traits from parents to offspring is _____.

5. _____ genes are usually represented by capital letters.

6. The crossing of two organisms' traits can be shown in a model called a _____.

7. Everything in your surroundings make up your _____.

8. Changes in an organism's DNA are _____.

9. A gene located on a sex chromosome is said to be _____.

10. The process of moving genes from one organism to another is called _____.

Concept Review

Number your paper from 1 to 8. Then choose the answer that best completes each sentence. Write the letter of the answer on your paper.

1. After _____ and cell division, each new cell has the same number of chromosomes as the parent cell.
   a. meiosis   **b.** mitosis   **c.** reproduction

2. When Mendel crossed pure tall pea plants with pure short pea plants, all the offspring were tall because the gene for tallness is _____ .
   a. recessive   **b.** dominant   **c.** a factor

3. _____ twins have identical genes.
   a. Identical   **b.** Fraternal   **c.** Human

4. Parents pass traits to their offspring through their _____.
   a. body cells   **b.** phenotypes   **c.** genes

5. _____ is a genetic disease in which a person has too much sugar in the bloodstream.
   a. Diabetes   **b.** Hemophilia   **c.** Insulin

6. Mating dogs that have desirable traits is an example of _____.
   a. genetic engineering   **b.** selective breeding
   c. a mutation

7. A human female passes one _____ chromosome to her offspring.
   a. Y   **b.** sex-linked   **c.** X

8. Before a cell can divide normally, its DNA molecules have to _____ .
   a. produce bases   **b.** replicate   **c.** mutate

Critical Thinking

Write the answer to each of the following questions.

1. When Mendel studied flower color in pea plants, the F_1 generation had only purple flowers. The F_2 generation had three purple flowers for every white flower. Which gene do you think is probably dominant: the gene for purple flowers or the gene for white flowers?

2. In humans, does the mother or the father of an offspring determine the sex of the offspring? Explain.

Test Taking Tip | If you have to choose the correct beginning to a sentence, combine the last part of the sentence with each available choice. Then choose the beginning that best fits the sentence.

Chapter

12

Ecology

Living things depend on one another and on the nonliving things in the world around them. The beavers in the photograph depend on plants for food. They also use air, water, soil, and energy from the sun to help them meet their needs. In this chapter, you will learn how organisms depend on one another as they live together in groups. You will also learn how organisms use the nonliving things in their environment to help them survive.

ORGANIZE YOUR THOUGHTS

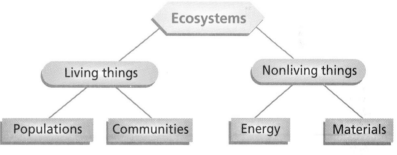

Goals for Learning

▶ To identify ways in which living things interact with one another and with nonliving things

▶ To describe feeding relationships among the organisms in a community

▶ To explain how energy flows through ecosystems

▶ To identify materials that cycle through ecosystems

How Do Living Things and Nonliving Things Interact?

Organisms act upon, or **interact** with, one another and with nonliving things in their environment. For example, you interact with the air when you inhale oxygen and exhale carbon dioxide. You interact with plants when you eat fruits and vegetables. **Ecology** is the study of the interactions among living things and the nonliving things in their environment.

Levels of Organization

Organisms interact at different levels. For example, organisms of the same species interact with one another. Organisms of different species also interact. The diagram shows the organization of living things into different levels. The higher the level, the more interactions there are.

Ecology
The study of the interactions among living things and the nonliving things in their environment.

Interact
To act upon or influence something.

Life on Earth is organized into levels. The higher the level, the more interactions there are.

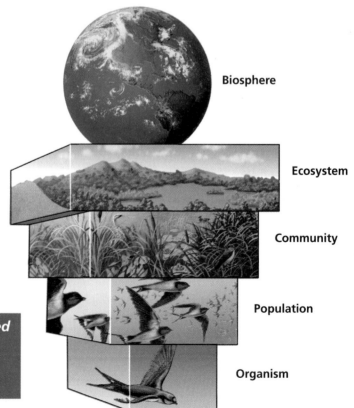

Biosphere

Ecosystem

Community

Population

Organism

Notice that the lowest level of organization is the individual organism. The place where an organism lives is its **habitat**. Each organism is adapted to live in its habitat. For example, tuna use their fins to swim through the ocean. A spider monkey uses its long tail to hang from trees.

Populations

The next level of organization is a **population**. A group of organisms of the same species that live in the same area form a population. The grizzly bears in Yellowstone National Park make up a population. All the people in the United States make up the country's human population.

The individual members of a population interact with one another. For example, the males and females in a population interact when they mate. The individuals also interact when they compete for food, water, and space.

Communities

A **community** is the third level of organization of living things. Populations of different species that live in the same area make up a community. Bears, rabbits, pine trees, and grass are different populations of organisms, but they all may live together in the same forest community.

The populations in a community interact with one another in many ways. In a forest, large trees determine how much light gets through to the shrubs and grass on the forest floor. The trees also provide shelter and food for animals, such as squirrels. Some of the nuts that squirrels bury grow to become new trees. A hawk may eat squirrels and use a tree as a nest.

Ecosystems

All the interactions among the populations of a community and the nonliving things in their environment make up an **ecosystem**. Organisms interact with nonliving things when they breathe air, drink water, or grow from the soil. Ecosystems occur on land, in water, and in air. The interactions that occur in a fish tank make up an ecosystem. So do the interactions in an ocean.

Changes in Ecosystems

As the community of organisms and the nonliving things of an ecosystem interact, they may cause changes. These changes may result in the community changing into a different type of community. For example, a pond community may change into a forest community. The changes that occur in a community over time are called **succession**.

The illustration shows the succession of a pond community into a forest community. Notice that small organisms and few plants live in a young pond. The bottom of the pond has little soil. When these organisms die, their bodies sink to the bottom and decay. The dead matter helps to form a layer of soil on the bottom of the pond. Soil is also washed into the pond from the surrounding land. Soon, larger plants are able to grow from the soil in the pond. Larger animals that feed on those plants move into the pond. Over the years, the pond fills up with even more soil. Grasses and other small land plants begin to grow on the dry edges of the pond. Small land animals, such as mice and rabbits, move into the area. Changes continue. The pond completely fills in. Bushes shade out the grass. Then trees overgrow the bushes. Squirrels and deer move into the area. Eventually, the area that was once a pond becomes a forest.

A pond community changes into a forest community by the process of succession.

Eventually, a community reaches a point at which it changes little over time. A community that is stable is called a **climax community**. A climax community, such as an oak–hickory forest, may stay nearly the same for hundreds of years. A climax community usually has a great diversity of organisms. However, a volcano, forest fire, or earthquake can destroy large parts of a climax community within a short time. When that happens, the community goes through succession once again.

Effects of Pollution on Ecosystems

People produce a variety of wastes and waste products that affect ecosystems. **Pollution** is anything added to the environment that is harmful to living organisms. Pollution is most often caused by human activities. For example, the burning of coal, oil, or gasoline releases a colorless, poisonous gas called sulfur dioxide. This gas poisons organisms that breathe it. Sulfur dioxide in the air also makes rainwater more acidic. This **acid rain** decreases the growth of plants and harms their leaves. Acid rain that falls into lakes and streams can harm or kill organisms living in the water.

Other types of pollution affect lakes and other bodies of water as well. Topsoil that is washed off the land because of construction and bad farming practices fills up streams and lakes. Fertilizer that washes off the land into bodies of water pollutes the water with chemicals. Chemicals that factories dump into lakes and streams kill plants and animals in the water. This affects birds and other animals that depend on the water animals and plants for food.

Biomes

Some ecosystems are found over large geographic areas. These ecosystems are called **biomes**. Some biomes, such as deserts, pine forests, and grasslands, are on land. Water biomes include oceans, lakes, and rivers.

Biome
An ecosystem found over a large geographic area.

Tropical rain forests may have more species of organisms than are found in all other land biomes combined. Why do you think this is so?

Tundra

The photos show two completely different biomes. They are a tundra and a tropical rain forest. Different biomes are found in different climates. Temperature, sunlight, and rainfall are all part of a biome's climate. For example, tropical rain forests get plenty of rainfall and are hot. Tundras are found in areas that are dry and cold. A desert is the driest of all biomes. Some deserts get as little as 2 cm of rain in a year.

Tropical rain forest

Biosphere
The part of Earth where living things can exist.

Resource
A thing that an organism uses to live.

The types of organisms found in a particular biome depend on the **resources** available to the organisms. Resources are things that organisms use to live. Resources include water, air, sunlight, and soil. Fish are not found in a desert biome because a desert has little water. Most cactuses do not grow in a tropical rain forest because the soil in the forest is too wet.

The Biosphere

Look back at the diagram on page 262. Notice that the highest level of organization of life is the **biosphere**. The desert biome, the ocean biome, and all the other biomes on Earth together form the biosphere. The biosphere is the part of Earth where life can exist.

Think of Earth as an orange or an onion. The biosphere is like the peel of the orange or the skin of the onion. It is the thin layer on a large sphere. The biosphere includes the organisms living on Earth's surface, in water, underground, and in the air. The biosphere also includes nonliving things, such as water, minerals, and air.

The biosphere is a tiny part of Earth. This thin surface layer can easily be damaged. Thus, humans need to be aware of how they can protect the biosphere. One way is to avoid polluting it. The survival of living things depends on the conditions of the nonliving parts of the biosphere.

Self-Check

1. What is the difference between a population and a community?
2. What kinds of interactions make up an ecosystem?
3. Describe how a pond community changes into a forest community.
4. How does acid rain affect plants and animals?
5. Define *biome* and list three or more examples of biomes.

INVESTIGATION

Testing the pH of Rain

Materials

- ✓ 3 small trash cans
- ✓ 3 new plastic trash bags
- ✓ pH paper
- ✓ pH scale
- ✓ distilled water

Purpose

To find out if the rain in your area is acid rain

Procedure

1. Copy the data table below on a sheet of paper.

Date	pH of sample 1	pH of sample 2	pH of sample 3	Average pH of samples
pH of distilled water:				

2. On a rainy day, place open plastic bags inside the trash cans.

3. If there is no thunder and lightning, place the containers outside in the rain. Make sure that the containers collect rainwater that has not touched anything on the way down, such as a roof or the leaves of a tree.

4. When a small amount of rainwater has been collected, touch the edge of the pH paper to the rainwater in one of the containers.

5. Notice the change in color of the pH paper. Compare the color of the pH paper to the colors on the pH scale. The matching color on the scale indicates the pH of the sample of rainwater. In your data table under sample 1, record the pH value of the rainwater.

6. Repeat steps 4 and 5 for the other two samples of rainwater. Record the pH of the samples in the correct columns.

7. If the pH values that you recorded for the three samples are not the same, compute the average pH of the samples. To do this, add all of the pH values and divide by 3. Record this number in the last column in your table.

8. Use the pH paper to determine the pH of distilled water. Record the pH in your data table.

9. Repeat this Investigation on one or two more rainy days. Record in your data table the dates on which you collected the rainwater.

Questions

1. How does the pH of distilled water compare with the pH of the rainwater you tested?

2. When water has a pH lower than 7, it is acidic. Normal rain is always slightly acidic and has a pH between 4.9 and 6.5. When rain has a pH of less than 4.9, it is called acid rain. Were any of the samples of rainwater you tested acid rain?

3. Recall from Lesson 1 how acid rain forms. Is acid rain more likely to fall in cities or in rural areas? Explain.

4. Was the pH of the rainwater the same every day you collected samples? What are some reasons the pH of rainwater could vary from day to day?

Explore Further

Test the pH of the water in a local pond, lake, or stream. *Safety Alert: Wear protective gloves when you collect the water samples.* Is the pH of the body of water the same as that of rainwater? Why might the values be different?

A water plant captures the energy from sunlight. It uses the energy to make sugars and other molecules. A small fish eats the plant. A bigger fish eats the small fish. A bird eats the big fish. This feeding order is called a **food chain**. Almost all food chains begin with plants or other organisms that capture the energy of the sun.

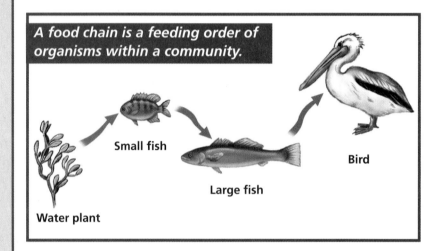

A food chain is a feeding order of organisms within a community.

Small fish

Bird

Large fish

Water plant

Consumer

An organism that feeds on other organisms.

Food chain

The feeding order of organisms in a community.

Producer

An organism that makes its own food.

Producers

Plants, some protists, and some bacteria make their own food. Organisms that make, or produce, their own food are called **producers**. Every food chain begins with a producer. Most producers use the energy of sunlight to make food by the process of photosynthesis.

Consumers

Organisms that cannot make their own food must get food from outside their bodies. These organisms get their food from other organisms. **Consumers** are organisms that feed on, or consume, other organisms. All animals and fungi and some protists and bacteria are consumers.

Omnivore
A consumer that eats both plants and animals.

Pyramid of numbers
A diagram that compares the sizes of populations at different levels of a food chain.

Are you an herbivore, a carnivore, or an omnivore?

Consumers may eat plants or other consumers. Consumers, such as rabbits, that eat only plants are called herbivores. Consumers, such as lions, that eat only animals are carnivores. Some consumers, such as bears, are **omnivores**. They eat both plants and animals.

The consumers in a food chain are classified into different feeding levels, called orders, depending on what they consume. First-order consumers eat plants. Rabbits are first-order consumers. Second-order consumers eat animals that eat plants. A snake eats rabbits. Thus, a snake is a second-order consumer. A hawk that eats the snake is a third-order consumer.

Numbers of Producers and Consumers

The African plains are covered with billions of grass plants. Herds of antelope feed on the grasses. However, the number of antelope is far less than the number of grass plants. In the same area, there may only be a few dozen lions. Lions need a wide range in which to hunt antelope and other animals.

You might think of a food chain as a pyramid with the highest-level consumers at the top. Notice in the **pyramid of numbers** that a food chain begins with a large number of producers. There are more producers in a community than there are first-order consumers feeding on the producers. The sizes of the populations decrease at each higher level of a food chain.

The pyramid of numbers compares population sizes at different levels of a food chain.

Food Webs

Few consumers eat only one kind of food. The American crow is an example of a bird that eats a wide range of foods. It eats grains, seeds, berries, insects, dead animals, and the eggs of other birds. Eating a variety of foods helps to ensure that the consumer has a sufficient food supply.

The frogs in a pond eat a variety of foods, including insects and worms. The frogs in turn may be eaten by snakes or birds. Thus, frogs are part of more than one food chain. The diagram shows some food chains in a pond community. Trace the different food chains. Notice that the food chains are linked to one another at certain points. Together, the food chains form a **food web**.

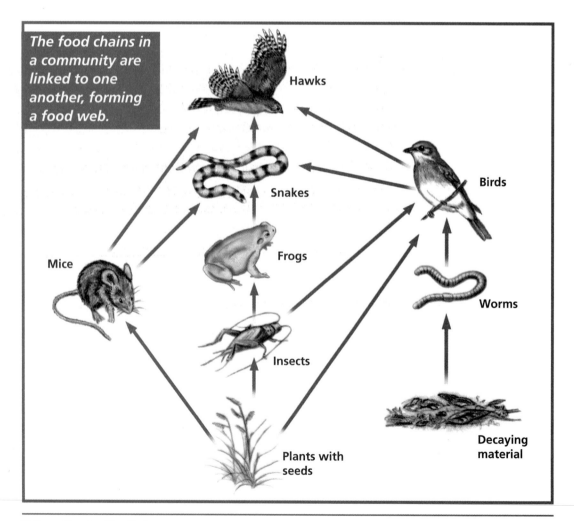

The food chains in a community are linked to one another, forming a food web.

Hawks

Snakes

Birds

Mice

Frogs

Worms

Insects

Plants with seeds

Decaying material

Decomposers

Suppose that a high-level consumer, such as a lion, dies but is not eaten by another animal. Does the food chain stop there? No, because decomposers continue the food chain by feeding on the dead animal. Recall that decomposers are certain bacteria, fungi, and protists that feed on dead organisms. Decomposers feed on dead organisms at each level of a food chain. They feed on producers and consumers.

Decomposers get food by breaking down complex chemicals in dead organisms into simple chemicals. The simple chemicals become part of the soil. Plants take in these chemicals through their roots and use them to grow.

Self-Check

1. What is the difference between a producer and a consumer?
2. Define the terms *herbivore, carnivore,* and *omnivore.*
3. Diagram a food chain that includes three levels of consumers. Which level of consumers has the smallest population size?
4. What is the relationship between food chains and food webs?
5. What is the role of decomposers in a community?

SCIENCE IN YOUR LIFE

What kind of consumer are you?

Like all consumers, you cannot make your own food. You must eat, or consume, food. Are you a first-order, second-order, or third-order consumer? When you eat plants or parts of plants, you are a first-order consumer. For example, if you eat an apple or a peanut, you are a first-order consumer.

When you eat the meat or products of animals that feed on plants, you are a second-order consumer. For example, if you eat a hamburger or drink milk, you are a second-order consumer. Milk and hamburger come from cows, which feed on plants. When you eat the meat or products of animals that feed on other animals, you are a third-order consumer. If you eat swordfish or lobster for dinner, you are a third-order consumer.

You probably eat many different kinds of food. Depending on what you eat, you are part of different food chains. The picture shows the food chains that you are a part of when you eat a chicken sandwich. Trace the different food chains. What kind of consumer are you when you eat a chicken sandwich?

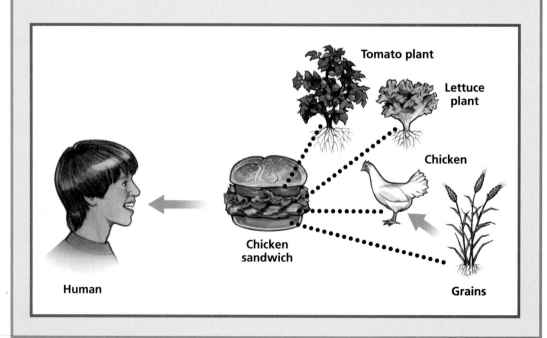

Tomato plant

Lettuce plant

Chicken

Chicken sandwich

Human

Grains

How Does Energy Flow Through Ecosystems?

Objectives

After reading this lesson, you should be able to

▶ explain why organisms need energy.

▶ describe how energy flows through a food chain.

▶ compare the amount of energy available at different levels of a food chain.

▶ explain how the amount of available energy affects the sizes of populations.

Plants use energy from the sun to make food. You get energy from the food you eat. What is energy? Energy is the ability to do work, to move things, or to change things. Energy comes in many forms. For example, light and heat from the sun are energy. Electricity also is energy. Batteries store chemical energy. A moving bicycle has mechanical energy.

You and all organisms need energy to live. Your muscles use energy to contract. Your heart uses a lot of energy to pump blood. Your brain uses energy when you think. Your cells use energy when they make new molecules.

Like the boy in the photo, you probably get tired when you work hard. You might even say that you have "run out of energy" to describe how you feel. You take a break and eat some lunch to "get your energy back." Food contains energy.

Food gives us the energy we need to do work.

Energy in Food

Recall from Chapter 7 that plants absorb energy from the sun. A plant's chlorophyll and other pigments absorb some of the light energy. By the process of photosynthesis, the plant uses the absorbed energy to make sugar molecules. Photosynthesis is a series of chemical reactions. During these reactions, light energy is changed into chemical energy. The chemical energy is stored in the sugar molecules.

Plants use the sugar to make other food molecules, such as starches, fats, and proteins. All these nutrients store chemical energy. When plants need energy, they release the energy stored in the nutrients. Plants need energy to grow, reproduce, make new molecules, and perform other life processes. To use the energy stored in nutrients, plant cells break down the molecules into simpler molecules. As the molecules are broken down, they release the stored energy.

Plants also use the nutrients they make to produce tissues in their leaves, roots, and stems. The nutrients' chemical energy is stored in the tissues. When you eat potatoes, asparagus, or other plant parts, you are taking in the plants' stored chemical energy.

Flow of Energy Through Food Chains

Animals and other consumers are unable to make their own food. They must eat plants or other organisms for food. As organisms feed on one another, the energy stored in the organisms moves from one level of the food chain to the next.

The flow of energy in a food chain begins with the producers, such as plants. As you know, plants absorb the sun's energy to make food. They use some of the energy in the food for life processes. As plants use this energy, some is changed to heat. The heat becomes part of the environment. The rest of the energy is stored as chemical energy in the plants' tissues.

The energy stored in plants is passed on to the organisms that eat the plants. These first-order consumers use some of the food energy and lose some energy as heat. The rest of the energy is stored as chemical energy in the nutrients in their body.

The energy stored in the first-order consumers is passed on to the second-order consumers. Then, energy stored in the second-order consumers is passed on to the third-order consumers. At each level of the food chain, some energy is used for life processes, some is lost as heat, and the rest is stored in the organisms.

Energy Pyramid

The **energy pyramid** below compares the amounts of energy available to the populations at different levels of a food chain. The most energy is available to the producers. They get energy directly from the sun. Less energy is available to the insects, the first-order consumers that feed on the producers. That is because the producers have used some of the sun's energy for their own needs. Also, some of the energy was lost as heat. Only the energy that is stored in the producers is passed on to the insects.

> **Energy pyramid**
> *A diagram that compares the amounts of energy available to the populations at different levels of a food chain.*

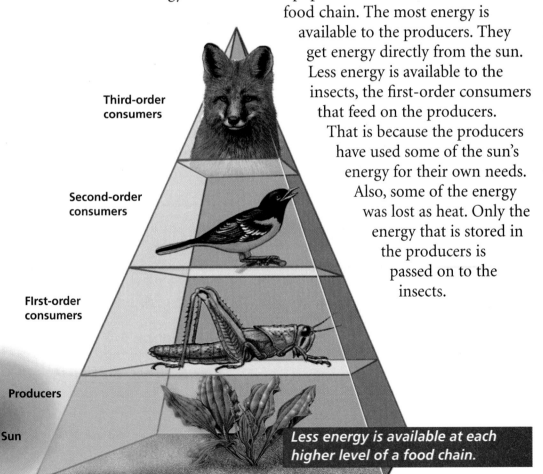

Third-order consumers

Second-order consumers

First-order consumers

Producers

Sun

Less energy is available at each higher level of a food chain.

The insects use some of the energy they take in for their own needs. Again, some energy is lost as heat. Thus, the amount of energy available to the birds, the second-order consumers, is less than the amount of energy available to the insects. Notice that the amount of available energy decreases at each higher level of a food chain. The foxes have the least amount of energy available. They are at the highest level of the food chain.

The amounts of energy available to the different populations of a food chain affect the sizes of the populations. Look back to the pyramid of numbers shown on page 271. Recall that the size of the population decreases at each higher level of a food chain. That is because less energy is available to the population at each higher level.

Importance of the Sun

How do you get energy from the sun when you eat chicken for dinner?

Without the sun, there would be no life on Earth. All plants and animals and most other organisms depend on energy from the sun. Energy flows from the sun to producers, and then to consumers. Communities lose energy as it flows through food chains. The sun continuously replaces the lost energy.

Self-Check

1. Why do organisms need energy?
2. Which organisms in a community get energy directly from the sun?
3. How does energy flow through a food chain?
4. Explain why less energy is available at each higher level of a food chain.
5. How does the amount of energy available to a population affect the size of the population?

How Do Materials Cycle Through Ecosystems?

Objectives

After reading this lesson, you should be able to

▶ describe how water cycles through ecosystems.

▶ explain the roles of photosynthesis and cellular respiration in the carbon, oxygen, and water cycles.

▶ describe how nitrogen cycles through ecosystems.

▶ explain how cycles in ecosystems are linked to one another.

The planet Earth is sometimes compared to a spaceship. Like a spaceship, Earth is isolated in space. All the materials we use to build homes, to make tools, and to eat come from the biosphere. If a material is in short supply, there is no way to get more of it. Materials in the biosphere must be used over and over again. For example, chemicals continuously cycle between organisms and the nonliving parts of Earth. Some chemicals important for life are water, carbon, oxygen, and nitrogen.

The Water Cycle

The diagram shows the water cycle between the living and nonliving parts of an ecosystem. The most noticeable water in ecosystems is the liquid water in lakes, rivers, and oceans. In addition, **groundwater** exists beneath the surface of the land.

Groundwater
The water under Earth's surface.

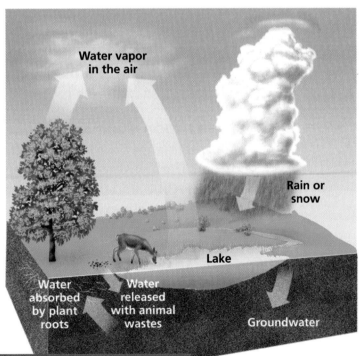

Water vapor in the air

Rain or snow

Lake

Water absorbed by plant roots

Water released with animal wastes

Groundwater

Water continuously cycles through ecosystems.

How might a molecule of water that was once in the ocean be a part of the milk you drank this morning?

What happens when a puddle of water dries up? As the puddle dries, the liquid water changes into a gas, or **evaporates**. This gaseous water is called water vapor. Water from oceans, lakes, and rivers evaporates and becomes part of the air. Water vapor comes from other places too. Organisms produce water when they get energy from food during the process of cellular respiration. Plants release water vapor through their leaves. Animals release water vapor with their breath. They also release liquid water with their wastes.

Water vapor is always in the air, but you cannot see it. Have you ever noticed that the outside of a glass of ice water becomes wet? Water vapor from the air **condenses**, or changes into a liquid, on the outside of the glass. The ice water cools the air next to the glass, causing the water vapor to condense.

Water vapor in the air may cool and condense into water droplets in a cloud. When enough water gathers in the cloud, rain or snow may fall. That water may be used by organisms. Organisms need water for various life processes. For example, plants need water to make food during photosynthesis. Plants take in water from the soil through their roots. Animals may drink water from ponds or streams. Animals also get water from the food they eat.

The Carbon Cycle

All living things are made up of chemicals that include carbon. Carbohydrates, fats, and proteins contain carbon. Carbon is also found in the nonliving parts of the environment. For example, carbon dioxide gas is in the air and in bodies of water. Carbon is found in fossil fuels, such as coal and oil.

The diagram on the next page shows how carbon cycles through an ecosystem. Plants and other organisms that undergo photosynthesis take in carbon dioxide and use it to make food. Animals take in carbon-containing chemicals when they eat plants or other animals.

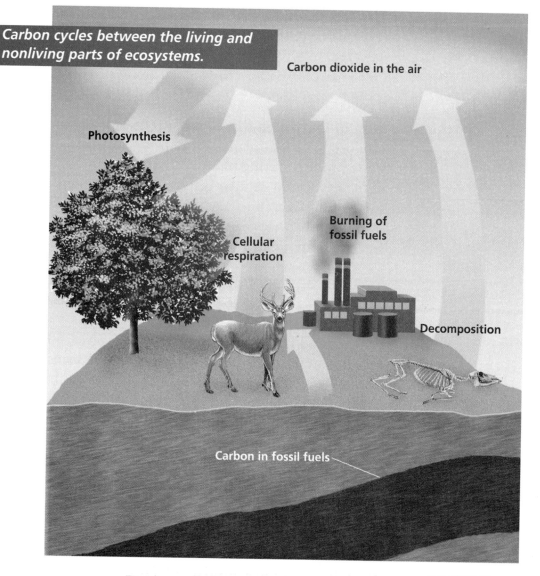

Carbon cycles between the living and nonliving parts of ecosystems.

Carbon dioxide in the air

Photosynthesis

Cellular respiration

Burning of fossil fuels

Decomposition

Carbon in fossil fuels

During cellular respiration, plants, animals, and other organisms produce carbon dioxide. Plants release carbon dioxide through their leaves and other plant parts. Animals release carbon dioxide when they exhale. Decomposers release carbon dioxide as they break down dead organisms. The carbon dioxide that is released by organisms may become part of the air or a body of water. People also produce carbon dioxide when they burn fossil fuels. In these ways, carbon continues to cycle through ecosystems.

The Oxygen Cycle

Oxygen is a gas that is essential to almost every form of life. Oxygen is found in air and in bodies of water. Organisms use oxygen for cellular respiration. The oxygen is used to release energy that is stored in food.

Most of the oxygen that organisms use comes from producers, such as plants. Producers release oxygen as a waste product during photosynthesis. Producers use some of the oxygen for cellular respiration. Consumers take in some of the oxygen and use it themselves. Thus, oxygen continuously cycles between producers and consumers in an ecosystem.

The Nitrogen Cycle

Nitrogen is a gas that makes up about 78 percent of the air. Many chemicals important to living things, such as proteins and DNA, contain nitrogen. However, the nitrogen in the air is not in a form that organisms can use. Certain bacteria are able to change nitrogen gas into a chemical, called ammonia, that plants can use. These bacteria live in the soil and in the roots of some plants. The process by which the bacteria change nitrogen gas into ammonia is called **nitrogen fixation**.

Nitrogen fixation
The process by which certain bacteria change nitrogen gas from the air into ammonia.

The diagram of the nitrogen cycle on the next page shows that plants take in the ammonia through their roots. Some of the ammonia, however, is changed by certain bacteria into chemicals called nitrates. Plants use both ammonia and nitrates to make proteins and other chemicals they need.

Not all of the nitrates are used by plants. Notice in the diagram that bacteria change some of the nitrates back into nitrogen gas. The return of nitrogen gas to the air allows the nitrogen cycle to continue.

Animals get the nitrogen they need by feeding on plants or on animals that eat plants. When organisms die, decomposers change the nitrogen-containing chemicals in the organisms into ammonia. The ammonia may then be used by plants or may be changed into nitrates by bacteria.

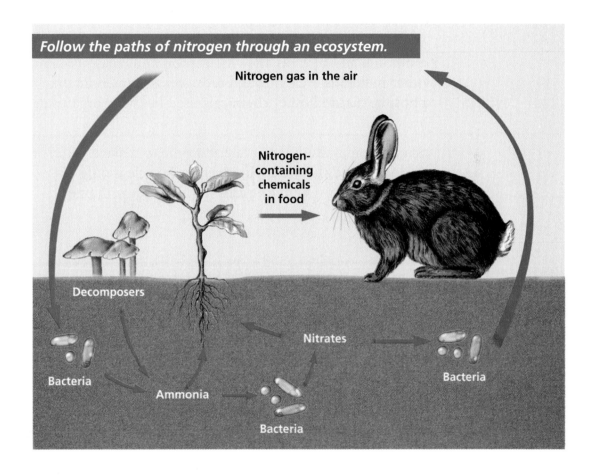

Follow the paths of nitrogen through an ecosystem.

Nitrogen gas in the air

Nitrogen-containing chemicals in food

Decomposers

Bacteria

Ammonia

Bacteria

Nitrates

Bacteria

System of Cycles

The different cycles in an ecosystem are linked to one another. For example, the carbon cycle, oxygen cycle, and water cycle are linked by photosynthesis and cellular respiration. Plants take in carbon dioxide and water for photosynthesis, and release oxygen. Animals, plants, and other organisms use the oxygen for cellular respiration and release carbon dioxide and water.

When plants make nitrogen-containing chemicals from ammonia and nitrates, they use carbon and oxygen. Many other materials cycle through ecosystems. Iron, calcium, phosphorus, and other chemicals used by living organisms are cycled.

Scientists may study one cycle at a time to make it easier to understand the cycle. However, each cycle is only a small part of a system of cycles that interact with one another.

Self-Check

1. Describe how water may move from a plant to a cloud and back to a plant.
2. Why is carbon important to living things?
3. How are photosynthesis and cellular respiration part of the carbon cycle?
4. How are photosynthesis and cellular respiration part of the oxygen cycle?
5. How is nitrogen gas from the air changed into a form that plants can use?

- A population is a group of organisms of the same species that live in the same area.

- A community is a group of different populations that live in the same area.

- Communities may change over time by a process called succession.

- All the interactions among the populations of a community and the nonliving things in their environment make up an ecosystem. Ecology is the study of these interactions.

- The feeding order of organisms is called a food chain. Every food chain begins with producers, which can make their own food. Consumers must take in food.

- All the food chains in a community that are linked to one another make up a food web.

- Energy flows through food chains. The amount of available energy decreases at each higher level of a food chain.

- Materials, such as water, carbon, oxygen, and nitrogen, cycle through ecosystems.

- Water evaporates and condenses as it cycles between organisms and the environment.

- During photosynthesis, organisms take in carbon dioxide and water and release oxygen. During cellular respiration, organisms take in oxygen and release carbon dioxide and water.

- In the nitrogen cycle, certain bacteria change nitrogen gas from the air into nitrogen-containing chemicals that plants can use. Other bacteria change nitrogen-containing chemicals back to nitrogen gas.

Science Words		
acid rain, 265	ecology, 262	nitrogen fixation, 282
biome, 266	ecosystem, 263	omnivore, 271
biosphere, 267	energy pyramid, 277	pollution, 265
climax community, 265	evaporate, 280	population, 263
community, 263	food chain, 270	producer, 270
condense, 280	food web, 272	pyramid of numbers, 271
consumer, 270	groundwater, 279	resource, 267
	habitat, 263	succession, 264
	interact, 262	

Vocabulary Review

Number your paper from 1 to 14. Then choose the word or words from the Word Bank that best complete each sentence. Write your answer on your paper.

WORD BANK
biomes
biosphere
climax community
consumers
ecology
ecosystems
food chains
habitat
nitrogen fixation
omnivores
pollution
population
producers
succession

1. _____ absorb the energy of the sun.
2. The study of how living things interact with one another and with nonliving things in their environment is _____.
3. Consumers that eat both plants and animals are _____.
4. Deserts, grasslands, and oceans are all examples of _____.
5. Anything added to the environment that is harmful to living things is _____.
6. The place where an organism lives is its _____.
7. All the biomes on Earth together form the _____.
8. _____ feed on other organisms.
9. All the _____ in a community that are linked to one another make up a food web.
10. _____ consist of all the interactions among populations and the nonliving things in their environment.
11. The process by which a community changes over time is called _____.
12. A community that changes very little over time is called a(n) _____.
13. All the deer of the same species living in a forest make up a(n) _____.
14. Certain bacteria change nitrogen gas from the air into ammonia by the process of _____.

Concept Review

Number your paper from 1 to 4. Then choose the answer that best completes each sentence. Write the letter of the answer on your paper.

1. More energy is available to second-order consumers in food chains than is available to _____.

   a. first-order consumers   **b.** producers
   c. third-order consumers

2. Photosynthesis and cellular respiration help to cycle _____ through ecosystems.

   a. carbon, oxygen, and water   **b.** only carbon
   c. nitrogen

3. Decomposers feed on _____.

   a. only consumers   **b.** only producers
   c. both producers and consumers

4. Plants store _____ energy in their tissues.

   a. chemical   **b.** heat   **c.** light

Critical Thinking

Write the answer to each of the following questions.

1. What would Earth be like if there were no decomposers?

2. Identify the producers and the first-order, second-order, and third-order consumers in the food web shown here. Remember that organisms may be part of more than one food chain.

Test Taking Tip   When taking a test, first answer all the questions that have short answers. Then, divide the remaining time among the questions that require longer answers.

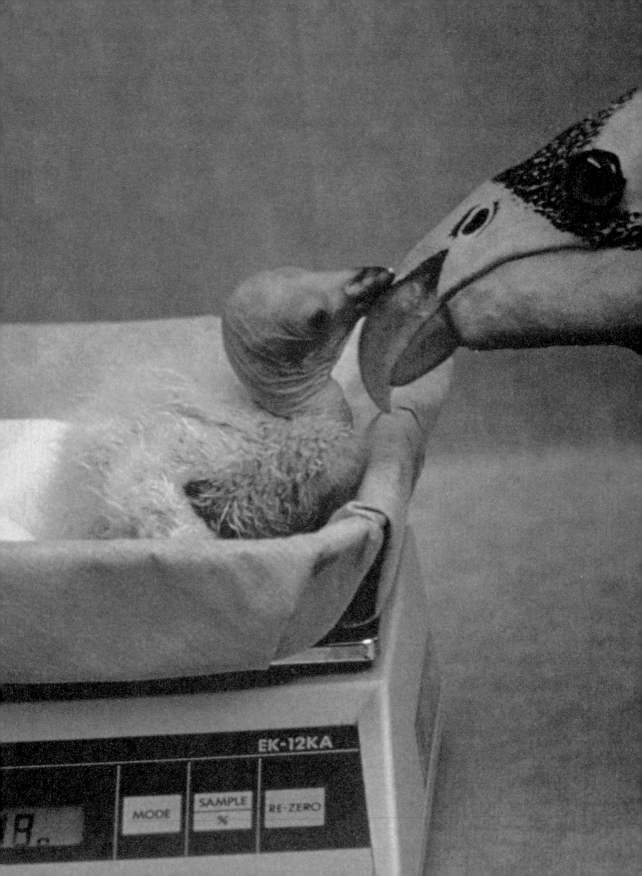

Chapter 13

The Behavior of Organisms

Why is a puppet feeding the California condor chick? An adult condor is not available to feed the chick. Scientists use a condor puppet so that the chick learns what its mother looks like. Learned behavior is one way that animals behave, or act. The behaviors of all animals, including humans, help them to survive.

ORGANIZE YOUR THOUGHTS

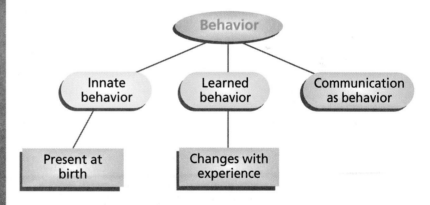

Goals for Learning

▶ To recognize that behaviors are responses to stimuli
▶ To identify behavior as innate or learned
▶ To identify ways that animals communicate
▶ To recognize that behaviors help organisms survive

Behavior
The way an organism acts.

Innate behavior
A behavior that is present at birth.

Instinct
A pattern of innate behaviors.

Stimulus
Anything to which an organism reacts.

Behavior is the way an organism acts. When organisms behave, they are reacting to something. Anything to which an organism reacts is called a **stimulus**. There are two main types of behavior, innate and learned.

A behavior that is present at birth is called an **innate behavior**. The behavior is inherited. It does not have to be learned. An animal usually performs the behavior correctly on the first try. Ask a classmate to pass a hand close to your eyes. Chances are you will blink. Blinking is a reflex that protects the eyes from harmful objects. A reflex is an innate behavior.

Unlike a reflex, an **instinct** is a pattern of behavior. Many parts of the body work together to produce actions in a certain order. For example, the eyes, nerves, and brain of a deer help the deer to see a wolf. The brain, nerves, and muscles work together to cause the deer to stand still. The wolf may not see the deer in the trees. The deer did not learn this behavior. It is innate. Innate behaviors help animals to survive.

Nest-Building Behavior

Nest building is one example of an instinct. Each species of bird builds its own kind of nest. They build nests of all sizes and in different places. They use materials they find in their habitats. A habitat is the part of an ecosystem where each species lives.

Woodpeckers drill a hole in the side of a tree to make a nest. The nest helps protect their eggs and young.

Suppose you train your dog to shake hands. Is that an innate behavior? Explain your answer.

Gulls use seaweed and plants to build a large nest on the ground. Terns make a hole in the sand where they lay their eggs. Nests provide safe places for eggs and young birds. The instinct of nest building helps their species survive.

Flying Behavior

You may have heard that birds learn to fly. Birds do improve their flight skills as they grow older. However, flying is an innate behavior. In one experiment, young birds were prevented from flapping their wings. The birds grew to the age when they normally would fly. The birds were released. They were able to fly on their first try. They had never practiced. The birds did not need to learn how to fly. Their bodies had developed to the point where they could fly. This shows that flying is innate.

Courtship Behavior

Courtship behaviors are behaviors to attract and get a mate. Animals must make sure they mate with the same species. Bluejays must mate with bluejays. Swallowtail butterflies must mate with swallowtail butterflies. Two different species may be able to produce offspring. However, the offspring will not be able to produce more offspring. Courtship behaviors help the species to continue. Each species behaves in certain ways to attract a mate. One animal starts the courtship behavior. The other animal responds in a certain way. These behaviors help the animals recognize their species.

Courtship behavior
Behavior that helps attract and get a mate.

Courtship behaviors are different for different animals. Birds may attract a mate with a certain song. Some birds, such as peacocks, show off their feathers to get a mate. Frogs have special mating sounds. Think of several species of birds and frogs that live in the same field or pond. Each species needs a way to identify its kind. Special songs or sounds help animals recognize their kind.

Territorial Behavior

A territory is an area that is defended by an animal. Usually the animal defends the territory from other animals of the same species. Behaviors that claim and defend an area are called **territorial behaviors**. These behaviors help animals survive. All animals need a place to find food, shelter, and a mate. The survival of a species is tied to its ability to reproduce. In their territories, animals can court, mate, produce offspring, and raise their young.

Territorial behavior
Behavior that defends an area.

Birds often claim their territories with their songs. The mockingbird finds the tallest trees on which to sing its territorial song. In neighboring territories, other male mockingbirds sing to claim their own space. Animals may mark an area with their scent. The scent warns others that the area is claimed.

An animal that claims a territory may be challenged to give it up. Other animals may try to fight the animal. The animal that already has the territory usually wins. The animal fights harder to keep the territory. It also may be older and more experienced in defending the area.

Behavior in Spiders and Bees

A young spider knows at birth how to build a web. The ability to weave a web is inherited. The parents do not take care of newly hatched young. The young do not have time to learn how to weave a web. They need the web to trap prey. Without this instinct, young spiders would not survive long. The same is true for bees. Bees are born with the ability to build a hive and find food. They also know how to care for the queen bee and protect the hive.

These plants are leaning toward the sunlight. This response is called phototropism.

Did You Know?

Other organisms respond to the time of day just as plants do. Your pulse rate, blood pressure, and temperature change with the time of day.

Phototropism
The response of a plant to light.

Responses of Plants

Plants do not behave in the same ways as animals. However, they do respond to their environment. Plants respond to light, gravity, water, temperature, and other factors. Parts of plants turn toward light. Roots grow downward. Flowers and leaves open and close according to the time of day.

Response to Light

The response of plants to light is called **phototropism**. *Photo* means "light", and *tropic* means "turning". Geraniums placed near a window will lean toward the sunlight. Suppose an indoor plant is turned around so that it faces away from a window. In just hours, the leaves turn toward the light. This happens because of chemical changes inside the plant. The cells on the leaves opposite the light get longer. This causes the plant to bend toward the light. Sunflowers in a field will follow the sun from sunrise to sunset. Phototropism helps a plant survive by getting sunlight to make food.

Response to Gravity

If you plant seeds, the roots grow downward and the sprouts grow upward. What would happen if you planted the seeds sideways or upside down? The seedling still would grow in the same way. This is a response to gravity called **gravitropism**. The stem grows upward to get sunlight. The root grows downward to get nutrients and water from the soil.

Response to Touch

Picture an insect landing on the Venus's-flytrap in the picture. The pressure of the insect stimulates sensitive hairs that line the surface of the leaves. The leaves close and capture the insect. All this happens within seconds of the fly touching the leaf. The response of the Venus's-flytrap to touch helps this plant to get food.

Another touch response occurs in mimosa plants. The leaflets of the mimosa plant usually are spread apart. When it is windy, the leaflets move closer together. The closing of its leaves helps prevent evaporation. This behavior helps the mimosa to conserve water. It could also protect the plant from animals. Thorns on the stems stand out when the leaves fold.

Sensitive hairs line the leaves of the Venus's-flytrap. When an insect touches them, the leaves close together and trap the insect.

Response to touch helps some plants to grow. Morning glories coil around an object that they touch. Vines wrap around tree trunks, fences, and posts. They grow in response to the object they are touching. These plants need support to grow upright. This helps them get more sunlight.

Other Plant Responses

Have you ever seen a plant that raises its leaves during the day and lowers them at night? These are called sleep movements. They are an example of plant responses to light. Other plant responses to time follow the seasons. Flowers bloom at certain times of the year. Some trees lose their leaves in autumn. These are examples of plant responses to length of daylight and temperature.

Self-Check

1. What is innate behavior?
2. Why are courtship behaviors important?
3. How do territorial behaviors help an animal to survive?
4. How do plant responses help them to survive?
5. Do plants have behaviors? Explain your answer.

What Is Learned Behavior?

Objectives

After reading this lesson, you should be able to

- ▶ tell the difference between innate and learned behaviors.

- ▶ define and give an example of each of the different types of learned behaviors.

- ▶ explain how learned behavior helps animals survive.

Imprinting
Learning in which an animal bonds with the first object it sees.

Learned behavior
Behavior that results from experience.

In Lesson 1, you learned about innate behaviors. Unlike innate behavior, **learned behaviors** are not present at birth. They are behaviors that are the result of experience. Learned behaviors can change over the lifetime of an organism. Five types of learned behaviors are imprinting, observational learning, trial-and-error, conditioning, and insight.

Imprinting

Baby geese bond with the first object they see. This behavior is called **imprinting**. In nature, the first object is the mother goose. A scientist named Karl Lorenz removed goose eggs from their nest. He hatched them in a lab. The baby geese saw Lorenz first. They learned that Lorenz was their "mother" and followed him wherever he went.

Young geese will follow their "first sight" leader. It can be the mother goose, a person, or even a ticking clock. Lorenz found that once imprinting is set, it does not change. His geese followed him everywhere. They even preferred him to their mother or other geese.

In nature, imprinting helps animals survive. It keeps young geese in the family circle. The young stay close to the mother, who protects and feeds them.

Did You Know?

Salmon travel from the stream where they were hatched to the ocean. After many years, they may return to their stream to mate. The journey may be long. How do they know the location of the stream? Newly hatched salmon use a form of imprinting in which odors are stored in their memory. They use this information to find their way back.

Have you ever watched someone train a pet? How were their actions like or different from those used by Skinner?

Observational Learning

Birdsongs are both innate and learned. The behavior is innate because birds are born knowing how to sing. A bird that is raised alone will sing. However, the song is different from songs by the same species. Birds must learn their songs by hearing other adult birds sing. This type of behavior is called **observational learning**. An animal learns by watching or listening to another animal.

Trial-and-Error Learning

B. F. Skinner, an American scientist, studied behavior in rats. He designed a box with a lever inside. A food pellet dropped into the box when the lever was pressed. At first, rats pressed the lever by accident as they moved. Soon they learned that pressing the lever resulted in food. This type of learning is called **trial-and-error learning**. Animals connect a behavior with a reward or punishment. In this case, the food pellet was the reward.

This type of learning is used to train pets and performing animals. In nature, trial-and-error learning helps animals survive. Animals learn which foods taste good or bad. They learn where to find food.

In this Skinner box, a rat presses a lever and is rewarded with water.

Conditioning

The keeper of an aquarium feeds the fish twice a day. At feeding time, the keeper taps lightly on the glass. The fish swim to the corner near the keeper. Every day, the actions are the same. The keeper taps before sprinkling the food. The fish have learned that they will get food when the keeper taps on the glass.

What if the keeper approached the aquarium but did not tap the glass? The fish would not move to the corner. They have learned to connect the tap with food. The tap is the first stimulus. The food is the second stimulus. This type of behavior is called conditioning. **Conditioning** is a type of learning in which an animal connects one stimulus with another stimulus.

The work of Ivan Pavlov is a famous example of conditioning. Pavlov was a Russian scientist who studied digestion and feeding behavior in dogs. Dogs naturally make saliva at the sight and smell of meat. Pavlov showed the dogs meat. He collected and measured their saliva. Then he began ringing a bell before he gave the dogs meat. After a while, he discovered that the dogs made saliva when he rang the bell. He did not have to show the meat. The dogs had learned to connect the bell with food. The dogs' response was conditioned.

Insight

Imagine a chimpanzee in a room with a banana hanging from the ceiling. Boxes are scattered about the room. The chimpanzee stacks the boxes. It climbs on them to reach the banana. The chimpanzee has never done this before. It gets the banana on the first try. However, this behavior is not innate. The chimpanzee was not born knowing how to get a banana from a ceiling. It solved the problem by using previous experience. For example, the chimpanzee might have climbed rocks or seen an animal climb in the past. Based on this and other experiences, the chimpanzee solved this problem. This type of learning is called **insight**.

Conditioning
Learning in which an animal connects one stimulus with another stimulus.

Insight
The ability to solve a new problem based on experience.

This raven solved the problem of getting the food on the string. It pulled on the string with one foot. It held the pulled string with the other foot.

Insight learning is the highest type of learning. Insight is most common in primates, especially humans. However, other animals also show insight.

The Importance of Learning

Learning helps animals to survive when the environment changes. They can change their behavior. They can depend on memory to help them. Squirrels remember where they have stashed food. Birds in a park learn that people will feed them. Scientists develop ways to grow more food for more people.

Innate behaviors are seen more in simpler animals, such as invertebrates. A cockroach does not have time to decide whether to run when a light is turned on. Bees do not have time to train other bees how to make a hive. Learned behaviors are not necessary. For such animals, innate behavior helps them to survive in their environments.

Self-Check

1. How is learned behavior different from innate behavior?
2. Why is imprinting a learned behavior?
3. Explain how some birds learn their songs.
4. What is conditioning?
5. Animals use insight to do something correctly on the first try. Why is this not instinct?

INVESTIGATION

Observing Learning Patterns

Materials

- ✓ large sheet of unlined paper
- ✓ pencil
- ✓ drinking straws
- ✓ safety goggles
- ✓ scissors
- ✓ transparent tape
- ✓ blindfold
- ✓ stopwatch or watch with a second hand

Purpose

To compare the learning rates for completing a maze

Procedure

1. Look at the maze below. You will build a maze but make it different from the one shown. As you work on your maze, do not show it to anyone else.

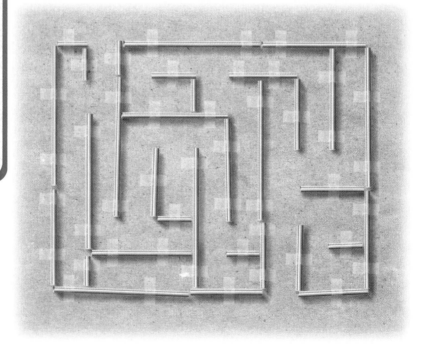

2. Draw an outline of your maze on a sheet of unlined paper. Make sure your maze has a start and a finish. Make only one path between the start and the finish.

3. Cut and tape straws to make the walls. Place the straws lengthwise over the lines you drew. Leave openings for the start and finish. *Caution:* Wear safety goggles. Cut in a direction away from your body. Keep scissors and straws away from your eyes.

4. Blindfold your partner. Place his or her finger at the start of your maze. Have your partner try to find the finish. Your partner must not cross any straws or lift his or her finger.

5. Time how long it takes your partner to finish. Record the time in seconds on your chart.

6. Have your partner complete your maze five times. Have other classmates try your maze five times. Record all the times in your chart.

Partner's Name	Try 1 (time in seconds)	Try 2 (time in seconds)	Try 3 (time in seconds)	Try 4 (time in seconds)	Try 5 (time in seconds)

Questions

1. Compare the times for each partner's first try with his or her last try. Do you see a pattern?

2. Explain why the times may have changed across the tries.

Explore Further

1. Have each partner retry your maze five more times. Record the times in a chart. Then, graph the times for each partner's tries.

2. Did your partner's times increase or decrease?

Objectives

After reading this lesson, you should be able to

- ▶ define *communication*.
- ▶ identify different channels of communication.
- ▶ give examples of different kinds of animal communication.
- ▶ explain how human language helps humans survive.

Channel
A way of communicating.

Communication
Sending and receiving information.

When a frog croaks, it is communicating. When a mockingbird sings, it is communicating. When a bee dances, it is communicating. When you speak or nod your head, you are communicating. In this lesson, you will learn about different ways that animals communicate.

What Is Communication?

Communication is sending information. You may think only of language and speech when you think of communication. However, there are many other ways, or **channels**, to communicate. Animals use actions, such as showing their teeth. They also use smells, electricity, and sounds.

Communication has a purpose. Frogs croak to find a mate. Mockingbirds sing to protect their territory. Bees dance to show the location of food. You nod your head to mean "yes" or you speak to welcome a friend. Nodding also is a type of behavior.

Chemical Signals

Some animals use odors to send information. These are chemical signals. They are common among mammals and insects. Dogs and cats mark their territory with urine. Female silkworm moths give off a chemical that attracts males. The chemical can travel several kilometers.

Here are the patterns of two honeybee dances. These dances tell bees where to find food.

Direction of food

Round dance

Waggle dance

Some ants release an alarm scent when other ants invade their territory. The scent calls other ants to help defend the area. You have probably seen a trail of ants. They are following a path that other ants made with chemicals. The path leads to food.

Visual Signals

Visual signals are signals that other organisms can see. Honeybees perform a dance to send information about food. The dance pattern shows other bees the direction and distance of flowers from their hive. If food is close to the hive, a bee might dance in circles.

Birds use many visual signals. Baby birds open their mouths to be fed. Male birds get into fighting postures with other males. They gain or keep their place as head of the flock by such behavior. Many male birds show off their beautiful feathers to attract a mate.

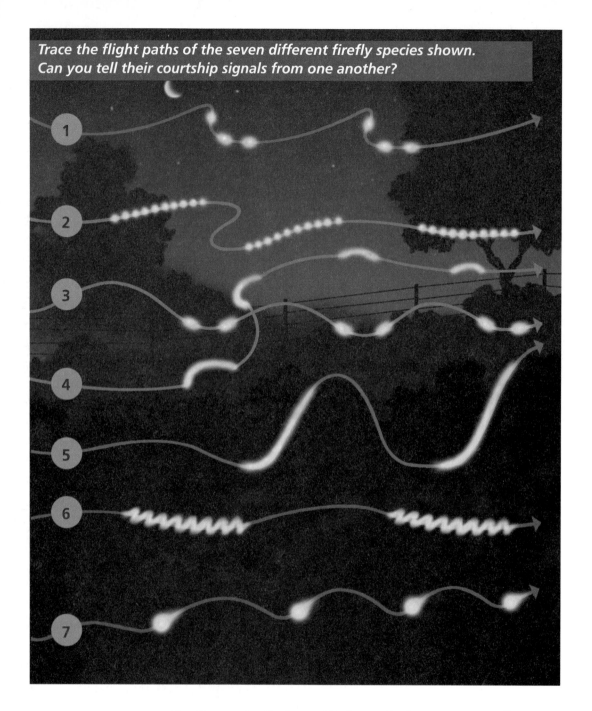

Trace the flight paths of the seven different firefly species shown. Can you tell their courtship signals from one another?

Fireflies make flashes of light to find a mate. Usually, a male firefly makes a certain pattern of flashes as he flies. A female flashes back in response. Different species of fireflies use different patterns of flashes.

Sound Signals

Many animals produce sounds to attract mates and keep their territory. Birds sing. Crickets rub their forewings together. Frogs belt out mating calls. Female mosquitoes buzz. Female elephants send out a sound that can be heard only by male elephants.

Human Language

Human language is the most highly developed communication. Humans can speak, write, and use sign language. More than three thousand different human languages have been studied. Humans are able to speak more than one language at a time.

Languages allow us to talk about things that happened in the past or that will happen in the future. They also allow us to talk about ideas or about things that are not present.

Human language is a behavior that helps humans survive. Humans can put ideas into words. They can tell other humans how they changed their behavior when the environment changed. They can pass their knowledge from one generation to the next. New generations are helped by knowing what has worked. They use this knowledge to solve new problems.

Self-Check

1. Why do animals communicate?
2. List three types of channels that animals use to communicate.
3. How do bees communicate about food with other bees?
4. Give two examples of how animals use chemical signals.
5. How does language help humans to survive?

SCIENCE
IN YOUR
LIFE

Can nonhuman primates learn human language?

Researchers have tried for years to teach human language to chimpanzees and gorillas. They started by trying to teach American Sign Language because chimps can easily move their hands. The first experiment began in the 1960s with a chimp named Washoe. Although Washoe learned as many as 30 signs, she was never able to make new sentences. She imitated her teachers. Other chimps have been trained to connect meaning with plastic chips or other symbols. Scientists have used computers to try to teach human language to chimpanzees and bonobos, a relative of chimpanzees.

Language experts agree that, like Washoe, other nonhuman primates simply learn to imitate their trainers. In some studies, the nonhuman primates can connect symbols with objects or behaviors. However, they are not able to produce new sentences using the rules of language. Humans as young as two years old can make up new sentences. Some scientists continue to try to teach nonhuman primates human language. They insist that they are making some progress.

Dr. Herb Terrace worked with Washoe and other chimps for more than ten years. He now says that trying to teach nonhuman primates human language is fruitless. He believes that scientists should be asking different questions. "How do chimpanzees think without language, how do they remember without language? Those are much more important questions than trying to reproduce a few tidbits of language from a chimpanzee trying to get rewards," he says.

- Behavior is the way an organism acts. The two main types of behavior are innate behavior and learned behavior. Behaviors help animals to survive.

- Innate behavior is behavior that is present at birth. It is inherited. An instinct is a pattern of innate behavior.

- Nest building, courtship behaviors, and flying are innate behaviors in birds. Web weaving is innate in spiders. In bees, building and protecting a hive are innate behaviors.

- Plants do not behave the way animals do. They do respond to their environment. They respond to light, gravity, touch, and other factors.

- Behavior that can change with experience is called learned behavior.

- Some types of learning are observational learning, imprinting, trial-and-error learning, conditioning, and insight.

- Communication is sending information. Animals communicate through chemical signals, sounds, and visual signals.

- Communication has a purpose. Animals attract mates, defend territory, and give the location of food.

- Humans can communicate by using language. In this way, people can store information and pass it from one generation to the next. People use this information to help solve new problems.

Science Words		
behavior, 290	insight, 298
channel, 302	instinct, 290
communication, 302	learned behavior, 296
conditioning, 298	observational learning, 297
courtship behavior, 291	phototropism, 293
gravitropism, 294	stimulus, 290
imprinting, 296	territorial behavior, 292
innate behavior, 290	trial-and-error learning, 297

Vocabulary Review

Number your paper from 1 to 12. Choose the word or words from the Word Bank that best complete each sentence. Write the answer on your paper.

WORD BANK
behavior
channel
communication
conditioning
gravitropism
innate
insight
instinct
learned
phototropism
stimulus
trial-and-error

1. The way an organism acts is its _____.
2. Inherited behavior is _____ behavior.
3. _____ behavior changes over an organism's lifetime.
4. Sending and receiving information is called _____.
5. An innate behavior that follows a pattern is called a(n) _____.
6. A plant's response to light is called _____.
7. Roots growing downward is a(n) _____.
8. Anything that causes an organism to react is called a(n) _____.
9. Most animals are trained using _____ learning.
10. When an animal solves a new problem based on experience, this is called _____.
11. A response to one stimulus that is connected with another stimulus is called _____.
12. A visual signal is an example of a(n) _____ that an organism may use to communicate.

Concept Review

Number your paper from 1 to 6. Then choose the word or words that best complete each sentence. Write the letter of the answer on your paper.

1. Fighting is an example of _____ behavior.
   a. courtship   b. territorial   c. observational

2. A vine that wraps around a post is an example of
_____.

   a. phototropism   **b.** gravitropism   **c.** imprinting

3. Learning that keeps geese close to their mother is called
_____.

   a. insight   **b.** conditioning   **c.** imprinting

4. A dog that was stung has learned by _____ to leave bees alone.

   a. trial-and-error   **b.** conditioning   **c.** insight

5. Flying is _____ behavior in birds.

   a. observational   **b.** innate   **c.** trial-and-error

6. Chemical signals can be _____.

   a. odors   **b.** sounds   **c.** bee dances

Critical Thinking

1. Certain electric female fish give off an electric pulse during breeding season. Males of the same species respond with their own electric signals. What kind of behavior is this? Which channel is being used?

2. The famous biologist John Maynard Smith once said, "The one thing that really separates us from other animals is our ability to talk." Does the information in this chapter support this statement? Explain your answer.

Test Taking Tip | If a word is new to you, try to break it into parts. Then, identify the parts of the word you know to help you understand the word's meaning.

Chapter

14

Evolution

L ook at the remains of the dinosaur skeleton in the photograph. As you know, dinosaurs once roamed Earth, but they no longer exist. Scientists study the remains of organisms to learn about life that existed in the past. They also piece together evidence from the past to learn how life on Earth has changed over time. In this chapter, you will learn how species change over time and about the processes that cause these changes.

ORGANIZE YOUR THOUGHTS

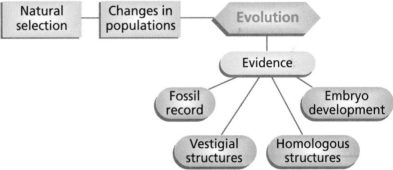

Goals for Learning

▶ To recognize patterns of change in populations over time

▶ To give examples of evidence that supports evolution

▶ To explain the theory of evolution by natural selection

▶ To describe the fossils of early human ancestors

Objectives

After reading this lesson, you should be able to

► define *evolution*.

► relate genes and mutations to the process of evolution.

► describe how new species can form.

Evolution
The changes in a population over time.

You have probably noticed that there are many different kinds of organisms alive today. Many of these organisms are quite different in their structure and behavior from organisms that lived in the past. For example, modern reptiles are smaller than dinosaurs and other ancient reptiles. Modern reptiles also eat different foods. The diversity of organisms today and in the past is the result of a process called **evolution**, or change over time.

Organisms, Populations, and Change

An organism changes as it grows and develops. However, these changes are not evolution. Individual organisms do not evolve. Evolution is the changes that occur in a population of organisms over time. As you learned in Chapter 12, a population is made up of individuals of the same species that live in the same place. A species is made up of individuals of the same kind that are able to interbreed and reproduce. What species make up the population shown in the picture?

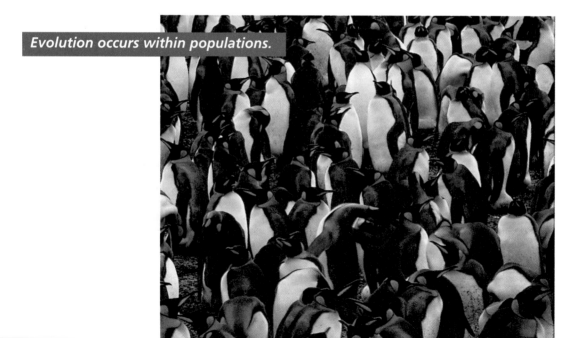

Evolution occurs within populations.

If you start exercising and develop large muscles, has your body evolved in the scientific sense of the word? Why or why not?

Most populations of organisms exist over long periods of time. A population exists much longer than any individual in the population. For example, as individual penguins die and leave the population, other penguins are born into it. The population of penguins continues even though individuals die.

The process of evolution takes place over many generations. For example, it may take millions of years for a population of short-necked animals to change, or evolve, into a population of long-necked animals. Evolution involves changes in populations over extremely long periods of time. Evolution has occurred on Earth over many millions of years.

Changes in Genes

As you know, genes determine the traits of all living things. Thus, genes determine the characteristics of a population. Evolution involves changes in a population's gene pool. As you learned in Chapter 11, radiation and chemicals in the environment can cause genes to change. Genes also change if they are copied incorrectly during DNA replication.

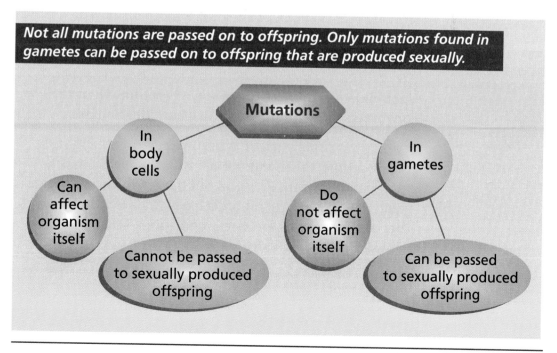

Not all mutations are passed on to offspring. Only mutations found in gametes can be passed on to offspring that are produced sexually.

Recall that a change in a gene is a mutation. Notice in the diagram on page 313 that mutations may occur in two different kinds of cells. Some mutations occur in an organism's body cells. These mutations can cause cancers and other changes in the organism. In organisms that reproduce sexually, body-cell mutations are not passed on to the offspring. For this reason, body-cell mutations are not involved in the evolution of most plants and animals.

Mutations can also occur in an organism's gametes. If the genes in an organism's gametes change, these mutations usually do not affect the organism itself. However, the mutations are passed on to the organism's offspring. The mutations can affect the traits of the offspring and of future generations.

Lethal mutation
A mutation that results in the death of an organism.

Effects of Mutations Over Time

Often, mutations cause harmful changes in traits. A **lethal mutation** is one that results in an organism's death. Organisms that inherit a lethal mutation usually do not live long enough to reproduce. As a result, the mutation is not passed on to offspring.

Sometimes a mutation results in a trait that improves an organism's chances for survival. An organism that survives is more likely to reproduce. The favorable mutation is then passed on to the offspring. As the mutation is passed on to future generations, it becomes more and more common within the population. Over time, all of the members of the population may have the mutation.

Mutations usually occur at a slow rate in populations. For example, the mutation rate in one generation of a population of fruit flies is about 0.93. This means that less than one fly per generation is likely to have a mutation. Because mutations are rare, populations usually evolve slowly.

Changes in a Population's Environment

If a population's environment changes, members of the population that have certain traits may be more likely to survive. For example, if the environment turns cold, an animal with white fur may be more likely to survive. The white fur helps to hide the animal against the white background of snow.

Organisms that survive and reproduce pass their genes on to following generations of the population. In this way, traits that help animals survive in the environment become more common within the population. Over time, the population evolves.

Environmental changes can affect populations in other ways. A change in the environment may split a population into two isolated groups. For example, a barrier, such as a large river or canyon, may form and divide a population in two. The single population becomes two populations that have no contact with each other. This is called **geographic isolation**. Over time, different mutations may occur in each isolated population. As a result, the populations have different gene pools. Eventually, the populations may evolve into different species. Look at the squirrels below. They live on opposite sides of the Grand Canyon. Scientists think the differences between the squirrels are the result of geographic isolation as the canyon formed over millions of years.

Geographic isolation

The separation of a population into two populations that have no contact with each other, caused by a change in the environment.

Kaibab squirrels on the north side of the Grand Canyon are isolated from the Abert's squirrels on the south side.

A population may also become divided into groups when members of the population move out of the area. For example, individuals from a population may travel from a mainland to a neighboring island. On the island, they interbreed and reproduce for generations. Over time, the population's genes change. If enough change occurs, the island population may evolve into a different species.

Large changes in the gene pool of a population can lead to the formation of new species. The chart lists some of the different ways new species evolve.

Formation of New Species

- Groups become physically separated.
- Groups move to different habitats.
- Groups reproduce at different times.
- Groups are not attracted to one another.
- Mating results in infertile offspring.
- Differences in body structures prevent mating.

Self-Check

1. What is evolution?
2. Do individual organisms evolve? Explain your answer.
3. In organisms that reproduce sexually, through what type of cells are mutations passed to offspring?
4. Relate mutations to a population's ability to evolve.
5. Describe one way in which a population might become two species.

Objectives

After reading this lesson, you should be able to
▶ explain how some fossils form.
▶ give examples of information learned from fossils.
▶ discuss how scientists determine the age of fossils.

Cast
A type of fossil that is formed when a mold in rock is filled with minerals that harden.

Fossil
The remains or traces of an organism that lived in the past.

Mold
A type of fossil that is formed when a dead organism decays and leaves an empty space in rock.

Sediment
The bits of rock and mud that settle to the bottom of a body of water.

Fossils are the remains or traces of organisms that lived in the past. Fossils are found in rock, in tree sap, and in other materials. The word *fossil* comes from the Latin word *fossilis*, which means "dug up." People have dug up different kinds of fossils all over the world.

Types of Fossils

The dinosaur skeleton on page 310 is a fossil. When an organism dies, its soft parts, such as skin and hair, usually decay rapidly. But its hard parts, such as bones and teeth, may remain as fossils for millions of years.

Sometimes when organisms die, they become buried in mud and bits of rock, called **sediment**, at the bottom of bodies of water. Over time, layers of sediment harden into rock. When the trapped remains of the organisms decay, they leave a type of fossil called a **mold**. The mold is an empty space inside the rock. Minerals and other particles dissolved in water may fill the mold and harden into a **cast**. The cast resembles the organism that formed the mold. What organism is shown in the cast in the picture on page 318?

Organisms may become trapped in certain materials in which their bodies do not decay. For example, insects have been found trapped in hardened tree sap. Large mammals have been found frozen in ice.

The preserved solid wastes of animals also have been found. These fossils tell the types of food eaten by animals in the past. Animal tracks and imprints of plants in rock are other types of fossils.

When did dinosaurs
first appear in the
fossil record? When
did dinosaurs
appear to die out
according to the
fossil record?

The Fossil Record

Paleontologists, or scientists who study life in the past,
look for and study fossils. Their findings have formed a
fossil record that tells about the organisms that have lived
on Earth. The fossil record also shows how organisms
have changed over time.

*Trilobites lived at the bottom of
oceans about 500,000 years ago.*

The history of life on Earth is a long one, going back
about 3.5 billion years. Using fossils, paleontologists have
put together the **geologic time scale** shown on the next
page. The geologic time scale is a chart that divides Earth's
history into different time periods. It shows the kinds of
organisms that first appeared during each time period.

The Geologic Time Scale

| Era | Period | Epoch | Years Before the Present (approximate) | | Life Forms | Physical Events |
			Began	Ended		
Cenozoic	Quaternary	Recent	11,000		Humans dominant	West Coast uplift continues in U.S.; Great Lakes form
		Pleistocene	2,000,000	11,000	Primitive humans appear	Ice age
	Tertiary	Pliocene	7,000,000	2,000,000	Modern horse, camel, elephant develop	North America joined to South America
		Miocene	23,000,000	7,000,000	Grasses, grazing animals thrive	North America joined to Asia; Columbia Plateau
		Oligocene	38,000,000	23,000,000	Mammals progress; elephants in Africa	Himalayas start forming, Alps continue rising
		Eocene	53,000,000	38,000,000	Ancestors of modern horse, other mammals	Coal forming in western U.S.
		Paleocene	65,000,000	53,000,000	Many new mammals appear	Uplift in western U.S. continues; Alps rising
Mesozoic	Cretaceous		136,000,000	65,000,000	Dinosaurs die out; flowering plants	Uplift of Rockies and Colorado Plateau begins
	Jurassic		195,000,000	136,000,000	First birds appear; giant dinosaurs	Rise of Sierra Nevadas and Coast Ranges
	Triassic		230,000,000	195,000,000	First dinosaurs and mammals appear	Palisades of Hudson River form
Paleozoic	Permian		280,000,000	230,000,000	Trilobites die out	Ice age in South America; deserts in western U.S.
	Pennsylvanian		310,000,000	280,000,000	First reptiles, giant insects; ferns, conifers	Coal-forming swamps in North America and Europe
	Mississippian		345,000,000	310,000,000		
	Devonian		395,000,000	345,000,000	First amphibians appear	Mountain building in New England
	Silurian		435,000,000	395,000,000	First land animals (spiders, scorpions)	Deserts in eastern U.S.
	Ordovician		500,000,000	435,000,000	First vertebrates (fish)	Half of North America submerged
	Cambrian		570,000,000	500,000,000	Trilobites, snails; seaweed	Extensive deposition of sediments in inland seas
Precambrian			4,600,000,000	570,000,000	First jellyfish, bacteria, algae	Great volcanic activity, lava flows, metamorphism of rocks. Evolution of crust, mantle, core

Dating Fossils

The geologic time scale is based, in part, on the ages of fossils. Scientists can determine the relative ages of fossils by comparing their locations in rock. Relative age means whether a fossil is older or younger than another fossil. Fossils in lower layers of rock are older than fossils in upper layers of rock if the layers are undisturbed. That is because the lower rock layers were formed first.

Scientists can also determine the actual ages of fossils. Actual age tells the number of years ago the fossil formed. Scientists use **radioactive minerals** to date fossils. Radioactive minerals give off energy as they change to another substance over time. For example, uranium-238 changes to lead very slowly. The rate of change of uranium-238 to lead is like a clock ticking off time. The "radioactive clock" is measured in a unit called a **half-life**. A half-life is the amount of time it takes for one-half of a sample of radioactive mineral to change into another substance. For example, the half-life of uranium-238 is 4.5 billion years. That means every 4.5 billion years, one-half of a given sample of uranium-238 becomes lead.

To determine the ages of fossils, scientists compare the amount of uranium-238 to the amount of lead in the rocks in which the fossils are found. Carbon-14, thorium-230, and potassium-40 are other radioactive minerals that scientists use to date fossils.

Extinctions

The fossil record shows that different species of organisms lived and then disappeared during Earth's history. When a species disappears, it is said to be **extinct**. As species become extinct, new species appear.

During certain periods of Earth's history, large numbers of species became extinct. These **mass extinctions** were probably caused by major changes in the environment, such as the cooling of the climate. For example, dinosaurs and some other reptiles became extinct about 65 million years ago.

Fossils and Evolution

Fossils show how groups of organisms have changed over time. The diagram shows the evolution of the horse as indicated by the fossil record. You can see that about 50 million years ago, the earliest horses had four toes on each front foot. These horses were less than 48 centimeters high, about the size of a dog. As the horse evolved, it became larger. Its four toes became a single hoof.

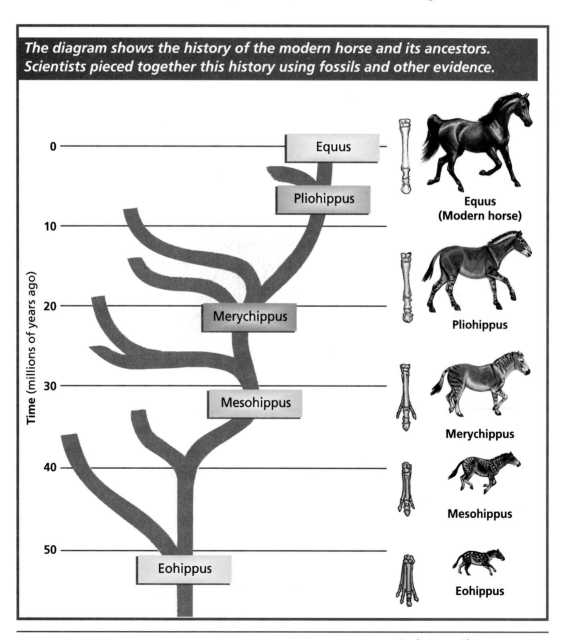

The diagram shows the history of the modern horse and its ancestors. Scientists pieced together this history using fossils and other evidence.

Fossils and Living Organisms

Paleontologists learn more about fossil organisms by comparing them to organisms that are alive today. They look for similarities in body structures, such as teeth and bones. Paleontologists also compare the organisms' environments.

The study of fossils has helped paleontologists discover the relationships among different groups of organisms. For example, the fossil record indicates that certain fishes evolved into amphibians. Some reptiles evolved into mammals. Other reptiles evolved into birds. The photo shows a fossil of an extinct organism called *Archaeopteryx*. The organism lived about 140 million years ago. *Archaeopteryx* had features of both reptiles and birds. Like a bird, *Archaeopteryx* had wings, feathers, and a beak. Like a reptile, it had a tail and teeth.

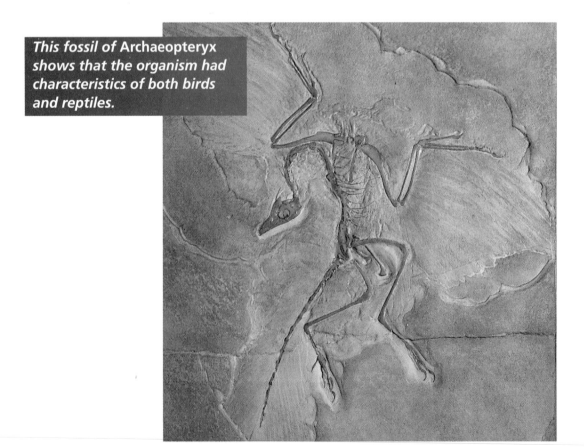

This fossil of Archaeopteryx shows that the organism had characteristics of both birds and reptiles.

Hunting for Fossils Today

Paleontologists continue to search for and analyze fossils. New fossils are found all the time. As fossils are discovered, scientists try to fit the information they provide into the history of life on Earth.

New techniques are helping scientists learn more information from fossils. Scientists are now able to compare the DNA of modern organisms. They can also compare the DNA of modern organisms with the DNA found in fossils. For example, in 1994, a scientist named Mary Schweitzer found DNA in a dinosaur bone. By comparing the DNA of organisms, scientists can study changes that occurred in genes over time. This can help scientists piece together the history of life on Earth.

More and more evidence is becoming available to show the relationships between organisms that are alive today and those that appear in the fossil record. These relationships are used to explain how evolution occurs. In Lesson 3, you will learn more about the process of evolution.

Self-Check

1. What are fossils?
2. Name two kinds of fossils.
3. What does the fossil record show about the evolution of the horse?
4. What is radioactive dating?
5. How might studying DNA help scientists piece together the history of life on Earth?

Making Molds

Purpose
To make molds of plant and animal remains

Materials
- ✓ seashell
- ✓ leaf with thick veins and a petiole
- ✓ petroleum jelly
- ✓ disposable gloves
- ✓ safety goggles
- ✓ plaster mixture
- ✓ small containers, such as aluminum pie pans or disposable plastic bowls

Procedure
1. Copy the data table below on your paper.

	Observations
Mold of shell	
Mold of leaf	

2. Choose a shell and a leaf from the collection provided by your teacher. *Safety Alert: The sharp edges of shells can cut your skin. Handle them carefully.*

3. Choose a disposable container that fits the shape and size of one of the specimens. *Safety Alert: Wear goggles and disposable gloves when handling the wet plaster mixture. Keep the plaster mixture away from your face and mouth.* Fill the container with the plaster mixture.

4. Choose the side of the specimen that you would like to make a mold of. Cover this side with a thin layer of petroleum jelly. Then, set the specimen on top of the plaster mixture with the side you want to make a mold of facing down.

5. Press the specimen into the plaster mixture. Do not push the specimen below the surface of the mixture.

6. Set the container in a place where it will not be disturbed. Allow the plaster mixture to harden.

7. Repeat steps 3–6, using the other specimen you selected.

8. After the plaster mixtures have hardened, carefully remove the shell and leaf. Record your observations of the two molds.

Questions

1. How is each specimen similar to its mold?

2. How is each specimen different from its mold?

3. Based on your observations in this Investigation, what kinds of remains would make the best fossil molds?

Explore Further

Cover each mold with a thin layer of petroleum jelly. Then use more plaster to make casts.

SCIENCE IN YOUR LIFE

How long is 4.6 billion years?

Many scientists think that Earth is about 4.6 billion years old. That is a long time compared to the time spans we deal with every day. One way to understand how long 4.6 billion years is would be to make a model of the geologic time scale.

You will need to gather colored pencils, a meterstick, tape, scissors, and sheets of unlined paper. Then, follow the steps below.

1. Using the meterstick and scissors, tape the sheets of paper together end-to-end until you reach 4.6 meters. One meter will represent 1 billion years in your model.

2. Find an area of the floor where you can spread out the sheets of paper. Then, tape the paper to the floor. This will be your model.

3. Mark one end of your model "Origin of the Earth." Mark the opposite end of your model "Today."

4. Refer to the geologic time scale on page 319. Using the chart below, map each event in the geologic time scale on your model.

5. Where is the year of your birth on the time scale? Is it possible to find it?

Length	Number of Years
1 meter =	1 billion years
10 centimeters =	100 million years
1 centimeter =	10 million years
1 millimeter =	1 million years

Objectives

After reading this lesson, you should be able to

▶ define the term *scientific theory.*

▶ state the two theories that come from Darwin's work.

▶ give two types of evidence that support the theory of evolution.

Scientific theory
A generally accepted and well-tested scientific explanation.

What is the difference between a hypothesis and a scientific theory? Give an example of each.

Thousands of years ago, the early Greeks believed that the diversity of organisms on Earth resulted from evolution. However, it was not until the mid-1800s that people could explain how evolution occurs. These ideas came from two British scientists, Charles Darwin and Alfred Wallace. In this lesson, you will learn about the current theory of evolution.

Scientific Theory

In science, the term *theory* is used in a way that is different from its use in common language. In everyday language, you might say that you have a theory about why a friend did not go to a party. That is, you might have a hunch. But in science, the term *theory* indicates more than a hunch or a guess. A **scientific theory** is an explanation that has undergone many tests. Many different kinds of evidence support a scientific theory. For an explanation to be a scientific theory, no evidence can contradict the explanation.

The theory of evolution is not the only theory in science. For example, the cell theory states that all living things are made of cells. The germ theory states that germs cause disease. Theories explain the basic ideas of science. As scientists find new evidence, they compare the evidence to the theory. If the evidence contradicts the theory, the theory is changed.

Darwin's Travels and Observations

Charles Darwin spent five years traveling around the world, from 1831 to 1836. During his travels, Darwin studied fossils from rock formations that were known to be very old. He compared those fossils with fossils from younger rock formations. Darwin found similar organisms in the different rock formations. He noted that the similar organisms had undergone change. Darwin was trying to answer the question "Do species ever change?" The fossil evidence showed that species did change over time.

Darwin also collected and made sketches of plants and animals during his travels. The map shows the route that Darwin took aboard the ship H.M.S. *Beagle*. Based on his observations and collections, Darwin came up with ideas of how evolution occurs. Darwin shared his ideas with other scientists but did not publish them right away.

Later, from 1848 to 1852, Alfred Wallace traveled in South America and the East Indies. As he collected information about organisms, he also formed an explanation of how evolution occurs. Wallace's explanation was similar to Darwin's. When Darwin learned of this, he hurried to write his ideas in a book. The book, *The Origin of Species,* was published in 1859. Darwin became famous for his ideas about evolution.

Hypothesis
A testable explanation of a question or problem. Plural is hypotheses.

Darwin's Theories

When Darwin first proposed his ideas about evolution, the ideas were hypotheses. A **hypothesis** is a testable explanation of a question or problem. Darwin's

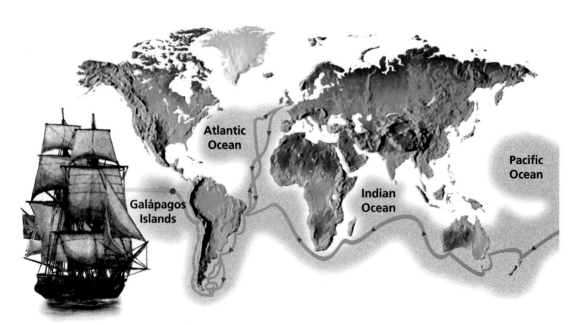

This map shows the route that Darwin took as he traveled around the world.

hypotheses have been tested. Many kinds of evidence have been found to support them. Today, Darwin's hypotheses about evolution are stated as two theories.

The first theory is called **descent with modification**. It says that more recent species found in the fossil record are changed descendants of earlier species. In other words, present organisms are related to past organisms. In fact, all organisms have descended from one or a few original life forms. Descent with modification basically says that evolution occurs in nature.

The second theory is called **natural selection**. This theory explains how evolution occurs. Recall from Lesson 1 that environmental conditions influence which organisms in a population survive. According to the theory of natural selection, organisms that are best suited to the environment are more likely to survive and reproduce. Those organisms will pass on their genes to their offspring. In this way, the organisms in a population with traits that are best suited to the environment increase in number. The population adapts to its environment as it gains genes that are suited to the environment. This process results in the evolution of a new species over a long period of time.

The following four points summarize Darwin's theory of natural selection to explain how evolution occurs.

1. Organisms tend to produce more offspring than can survive. For example, fish lay thousands of eggs, but only a few live to be adult fish.

2. Individuals in a population have slight variations. For example, fish in a population may differ slightly in color, length, fin size, or speed.

3. Individuals struggle to survive. Individuals that have variations best suited to the environment are more likely to survive.

4. Survivors pass on their genes to their offspring. Gradually, the population changes.

Example of Descent With Modification

Darwin observed descent with modification when he visited the Galápagos Islands off the coast of South America. He was amazed by the variety of living things he saw. Darwin found a variety of birds called finches. He observed 14 different species of island finches. The finches differed in the shapes and sizes of their beaks.

Notice in the pictures that the differences in the beaks were related to differences in the birds' diets. For example, large, thick beaks were used to crack seeds. Long, pointed beaks were used to eat insects.

Darwin noted that the island finches resembled the finch species on the nearby coast of South America. He reasoned that the island species were probably descended from the mainland species. Isolated by the water barrier for a long time, the finch populations on the different islands had undergone different genetic changes. These genetic changes resulted in the evolution of the 14 finch species.

The beaks of different finch species on the Galápagos Islands are adapted for eating different kinds of foods.

Medium ground finch (eats seeds)   Warbler finch (eats insects)

Example of Natural Selection

Natural selection affects all populations of organisms. An example is the natural selection of snakes that have a specialized upper tooth. Young snakes use the tooth to cut their way out of their shell. Snakes that are able to leave their shell with ease are more likely to survive and reproduce. The presence and use of the specialized tooth give the young snakes an **adaptive advantage**. The environment selects individuals in a population that have an adaptive advantage. Young snakes that do not have the specialized tooth do not live to reproduce. Their genes are lost from the population.

Evidence of Evolution

If populations really do change slowly over time, then there should be evidence of the change. As you know, the fossil record shows recent species that are slightly different from earlier species. This is one line of evidence that supports the theory of evolution.

Other evidence is that the embryos of some kinds of organisms go through similar stages of development. For example, an early human embryo has a tail and gill pouches, just as an early fish embryo has. Similarities in the development of vertebrate embryos are an indication that all vertebrates descended from a common ancestor.

Another indication that certain organisms are related to one another is the presence of **vestigial structures**. A vestigial structure is a body part that appears to be useless to an organism. For example, in humans, there is no known function for the tailbone at the tip of the spine. The tailbone in humans is a vestigial structure. It is thought to be a "leftover" structure that once had an important function in human ancestors who had tails.

The similar front limbs of these vertebrates are homologous structures.

Penguin

Alligator

Bat

Human

Homologous structures
Body parts that are similar in related organisms.

Look at the front limbs of the vertebrates in the diagram. Notice how similar they are. The limbs are **homologous structures**. Homologous structures are body parts that are similar in related organisms. Homologous structures are thought to have first appeared in an ancestor that is common to all the organisms that have the homologous structures. Thus, vertebrates probably share a common ancestor that had front limbs like those you see above.

Self-Check

1. Distinguish between the meaning of the term *scientific theory* and the everyday meaning of the term *theory*.
2. What is meant by descent with modification?
3. Explain the process of natural selection.
4. Explain the process that led to the evolution of the finch species that Darwin observed on the Galápagos Islands.
5. Give two types of evidence other than fossils that support the theory of evolution.

Objectives

After reading this lesson, you should be able to

▶ list characteristics that all primates share.

▶ trace the evolution of hominids, based on fossil evidence.

▶ describe how hominids changed over time.

Hominid
The group that includes humans and humanlike primates.

Homo sapiens
The species to which humans belong.

Primate
The group of mammals that includes humans, apes, monkeys, and similar animals.

Look at the timeline. Which hominid species lived the longest period of time?

Humans belong to a group of mammals called **primates**. Besides humans, primates include monkeys, apes, lemurs, and other similar animals. Primates share several characteristics. They can see color. They have fingers that can move and grasp. They have nails rather than claws.

Hominids

Humans and their humanlike relatives make up a group of primates called **hominids**. The hominid species to which humans belong is ***Homo sapiens***, which means "wise man." *Homo sapiens* is the only living hominid species. All other hominid species are extinct.

Most of what is known about the history of humans is based on fossil evidence. As you can see below, fossils of a number of different hominid species have been found. Hominid species that belong to the genus *Homo* are more similar to humans than are those that belong to the genus *Australopithecus*.

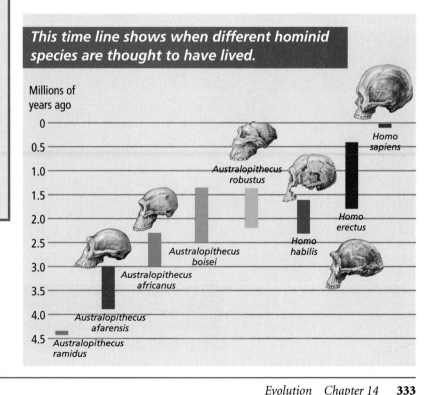

This time line shows when different hominid species are thought to have lived.

Millions of years ago

0
0.5
1.0
1.5
2.0
2.5
3.0
3.5
4.0
4.5

Homo sapiens

Australopithecus robustus

Homo erectus

Homo habilis

Australopithecus boisei

Australopithecus africanus

Australopithecus afarensis

Australopithecus ramidus

Homo sapiens is the only primate living today that walks upright on two legs. All other hominid species walked on two legs as well. Hominids are thought to have started walking on two legs early in their history. One of the earliest fossils of a primate that walked upright is 3.2 million years old. This fossil, which scientists named Lucy, was found in 1974. Lucy's scientific name is *Australopithecus afarensis*. The photo shows parts of Lucy's skeleton.

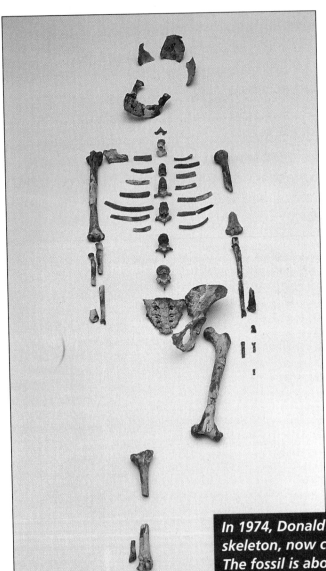

The bottom of Lucy's skull has an opening for the spinal cord. This suggests that Lucy walked upright. Lucy's hip and leg bones show that they could support her body while walking upright on two legs. Scientists estimate that Lucy's brain was only about one-third the size of the brain of a modern human.

Since the 1970s, many hominid fossils have been found. In addition to fossilized bones, fossilized footprints have shown that early hominids walked upright.

In 1974, Donald Johanson found this hominid skeleton, now called Lucy, in eastern Africa. The fossil is about 3.2 million years old.

The Genus *Homo*

In the 1950s, the fossil hunters Mary and Louis Leakey discovered fossils of a hominid species in Africa. They found stone tools near the fossils, suggesting that the hominid used tools. They named the hominid species *Homo habilis*, which means "handy man." You can see a skull of this species on page 333. The *Homo habilis* brain was larger than the brains of species belonging to the genus *Australopithecus*. Fossils of *Homo habilis* are between 1.6 and 2.4 million years old.

Homo erectus is another hominid species belonging to the genus *Homo*. This species lived between about 300,000 and about 1.8 million years ago. *Homo erectus* means "upright man." Compare the skull of *Homo erectus* with the skull of *Homo habilis* on page 333. Notice that the skull of *Homo erectus* could hold a larger brain. *Homo erectus* is thought to be the first group of hominids to leave Africa. Burned bones found near the fossils of *Homo erectus* suggest that this hominid used fire for cooking and staying warm.

Mary and Louis Leakey discovered fossils of the hominid species Homo habilis. *Here, Mary Leaky uncovers another fossil find.*

Cro-Magnons
Homo sapiens *who lived about 35,000 years ago and are direct ancestors of humans living today.*

Neanderthals
Homo sapiens *who lived between about 30,000 and 230,000 years ago but are not thought to be direct ancestors of humans living today.*

Homo sapiens

Most scientists think *Homo erectus* evolved into *Homo sapiens*. **Neanderthals** are *Homo sapiens* who lived between about 30,000 and 230,000 years ago. Neanderthals are thought to have lived in caves and used tools. Some of the tools suggest that Neanderthals wore clothes made from animal hides. The Neanderthal brain was larger than that of modern humans. Although Neanderthals were *Homo sapiens,* some evidence suggests that the Neanderthals are not direct ancestors of humans living today.

Cro-Magnons are *Homo sapiens* who lived about 35,000 years ago in Europe. Scientists think Cro-Magnons were an early form of modern humans. Cro-Magnons made their own shelters. They made beautiful cave drawings and carvings of animals. Their brain was about the same size as that of humans living today. Cro-Magnons are our direct ancestors.

Self-Check

1. List three primate characteristics.
2. What are hominids? Give the species name of one hominid, other than *Homo sapiens.*
3. What evidence suggests that Lucy walked upright?
4. How did the hominid brain change over time?
5. How are *Homo erectus*, Neanderthals, Cro-Magnons, and humans living today related to one another?

- Evolution is change over time. Populations are the smallest units in which evolution occurs. Evolution is the result of changes in the gene pools of populations over long periods of time. Mutations and changes in a population's environment may cause the population's gene pool to change.

- Fossils are the remains or traces of organisms that lived in the past. Fossils are preserved in Earth's rock, in sap, and in other materials.

- The history of life on Earth has been pieced together using the fossil record. The geologic time scale divides Earth's history into time periods. It also shows when certain kinds of organisms first appeared on Earth.

- The geologic time scale is based, in part, on the ages of fossils. Scientists determine the relative ages of fossils by comparing the fossils' locations in rock. Scientists use radioactive minerals to determine the actual ages of fossils.

- A scientific theory is an explanation that has undergone many tests and is supported by different kinds of evidence. Today, Darwin's ideas about evolution are stated as two theories. The first theory is called descent with modification. Darwin's second theory is called natural selection.

- Humans and their humanlike ancestors make up a group of primates called hominids. *Homo sapiens* is the only hominid species living today.

Science Words

adaptive advantage, 331
cast, 317
Cro-Magnons, 336
descent with modification, 329
evolution, 312
extinct, 320
fossil, 317
fossil record, 318

geographic isolation, 315
geologic time scale, 318
half-life, 320
hominid, 333
homologous structures, 332
Homo sapiens, 333
hypothesis, 328
lethal mutation, 314

mass extinction, 320
mold, 317
natural selection, 329
Neanderthals, 336
paleontologist, 318
primate, 333
radioactive mineral, 320
scientific theory, 327
sediment, 317
vestigial structure, 331

Vocabulary Review

Number your paper from 1 to 12. Then choose the word or words from the Word Bank that best complete each sentence. Write the answer on your paper.

1. The changes in a population over time is called _____.

2. _____ result in the death of organisms.

3. The remains or other traces of organisms that lived in the past are _____.

4. The _____ divides Earth's history into time periods.

5. Explanations that are supported by many different kinds of evidence are _____.

6. The _____ is made up of fossils that show the history of life on Earth.

7. A species that is _____ no longer exists.

8. The theory of _____ says that organisms that are best suited to live in a certain environment are more likely to reproduce.

9. Humans and their humanlike ancestors make up a group of primates called _____.

10. Humans belong to the species _____.

11. Scientists who study life in the past are called _____.

12. Scientists use _____ to determine the actual ages of fossils.

Concept Review

Number your paper from 1 to 6. Then choose the answer that best completes each sentence. Write the letter of the answer on your paper.

1. *Homo habilis* was more closely related to _____ than to *Australopithecus afarensis*.

   a. Lucy   **b.** *Homo sapiens*   **c.** monkeys

2. Evolution occurs in the gene pool of a(n) _____.

   a. individual   **b.** population   **c.** cell

3. Suppose a scientist found equal amounts of uranium-238 and lead in a rock. The rock is about _____ years old.

   a. 2.25 billion   **b.** 238 million   **c.** 4.5 billion

4. Natural selection leads to the _____ of new species.

   a. geographic isolation   **b.** evolution   **c.** mass extinction

5. *Homo erectus* mostly likely evolved before _____.

   a. *Homo habilis*   **b.** Lucy   **c.** Neanderthals

6. When an organism that has been trapped in sediment decays, it may leave a fossil called a _____.

   a. mold   **b.** cast   **c.** track

Critical Thinking

Write the answers to each of the following questions.

1. Using radioactive minerals to date fossils was not known during Darwin's times. How was Darwin able to estimate the ages of his fossil finds?

2. Some flies produce up to 100 offspring in two weeks. Why is Earth not covered with flies?

Test Taking Tip | If a word is new to you, try to break it into parts. Then, identify the parts of the word you know to help you understand the word's meaning.

Appendix A: Animal Kingdom

Invertebrates (No backbone)

Group	Description	Examples
Porifera *Phylum*	Body wall of two cell layers; pores and canals; no tissues or organs; no symmetry; live in water; strain food from water	sponge
Cnidarian *Phylum*	Baglike body of two cell layers; one opening leading into a hollow body; tissues; usually mouth surrounded by tentacles; stinging cells; radial symmetry; live in water	jellyfish, coral, hydra
Flatworm *Phylum*	Ribbonlike body; three cell layers; organs; flat, unsegmented body; digestive system with one opening; nervous system; bilateral symmetry; most are parasitic	tapeworm, planarian, fluke
Nematode *Phylum*	Round, slender body; unsegmented body; digestive system with two openings; nervous system; bilateral symmetry; some are parasitic	hookworm, pinworm, vinegar eel
Mollusk *Phylum*	Soft body covered by a fleshy mantle; move with muscular foot; some have shells; all organ systems; bilateral symmetry	
Gastropod *Class*	One shell (slugs have no shell); head, eyes, and tentacles	snail, slug
Bivalve *Class*	Two shells; no head, eyes, or tentacles	clam, oyster, scallop
Cephalopod *Class*	No shell; head; eyes; foot divided into tentacles	squid, octopus, nautilus
Annelid *Phylum*	Round, segmented body; digestive system, nervous system, circulatory system; bilateral symmetry; most are not parasitic	earthworm, leech
Arthropod *Phylum*	Segmented body; jointed legs; most have antennae; all organ systems; external skeleton	
Arachnid *Class*	Two body segments; four pairs of legs; no antennae	spider, scorpion, tick, mite
Crustacean *Class*	Two body segments; usually five pairs of legs; two pairs of antennae; breathe with gills	crayfish, lobster, crab, shrimp, sowbug, barnacle
Chilopod *Class*	usually 15–170 body segments; one pair of legs on each segment; poison claws; flattened body	centipede
Diplopod *Class*	usually 25–100 body segments; two pairs of legs on each segment; body often rounded	millipede
Insect *Class*	Three body segments; three pairs of legs; one pair of antennae; most have two pairs of wings	fly, beetle, grasshopper, earwig, silverfish, water strider, butterfly, bee, ant
Echinoderm *Phylum*	Covered with spines; body has five parts; radial symmetry; live in ocean	sea star, sea urchin, sand dollar

Vertebrates (Backbone)

Group	Description	Examples
Chordate *Phylum*	Internal skeleton of bone or cartilage; skull; sexual reproduction; bilateral symmetry	
Jawless Fish *Class*	Skeleton of cartilage; no scales or jaw; unpaired fins; breathe with gills; live in water; cold blooded	lamprey, hagfish
Cartilage Fish *Class*	Skeleton of cartilage; toothlike scales; jaw; paired fins; breathe with gills; live in water; cold blooded	shark, ray
Bony Fish *Class*	Skeleton of bone; bony scales; jaw; paired fins; breathe with gills; live in water; swim bladder in most; cold blooded	trout, salmon, swordfish, goldfish
Amphibian *Class*	Skeleton of bone; moist, smooth skin; no claws; breathe with lungs as adults or through skin; young live in water, adults live on land; four legs; eggs lack shells; cold blooded	newt, frog, toad
Reptile *Class*	Skeleton of bone; dry, scaly skin; claws; breathe with lungs all stages; four legs except snakes; eggs have shell; cold blooded	turtle, alligator, lizard, snake
Bird *Class*	Skeleton of bone; feathers; wings; beaks; claws; breathe with lungs all stages; eggs have shell; warm blooded	hawk, goose, quail, robin, penguin
Mammal *Class*	Skeleton of bone; hair; mammary glands; breathe with lungs all stages; young develop within mother; warm blooded	bat, kangaroo, mouse, dog, whale, seal, human

Appendix B: Plant Kingdom

Spore Plants

Group	Description	Examples
Bryophyte *Division**	Nonvascular (no tubes for carrying materials in plant); live in moist places	liverwort, hornwort, moss
Club Moss *Division*	Spores in cones at end of stems; simple leaves	club moss
Horsetail *Division*	Spores in cones at end of stems; hollow, jointed stem	horsetail
Fern *Division*	Spores in sori; fronds	fern

Seed Plants

Group	Description	Examples
Palmlike *Division*	Naked seeds in cones; gymnosperm (nonflowering seed plant); male and female cones on different trees; palm-shaped leaves	cycad, sago palm
Ginkgo *Division*	Naked seeds in conelike structures; gymnosperm; male and female cones on different trees; fan-shaped leaves; only one known species	ginkgo
Conifer *Division*	Naked seeds in cones; gymnosperm; male and female cones; most are evergreen; needlelike or scalelike leaves	pine, fir, spruce, yew
Angiosperm *Division*	Produce flowers; seeds protected by ovary that ripens into a fruit; organs of both sexes often in same flower	
Monocot *Class*	One seed leaf; parallel veins; flower parts in multiples of three	grass, palm, corn, lily,
Dicot *Class*	Two seed leaves; crisscross veins; flower parts in multiples of four or five	cactus, maple, rose, daisy

* For plants, biologists use *Division* instead of *Phylum*.

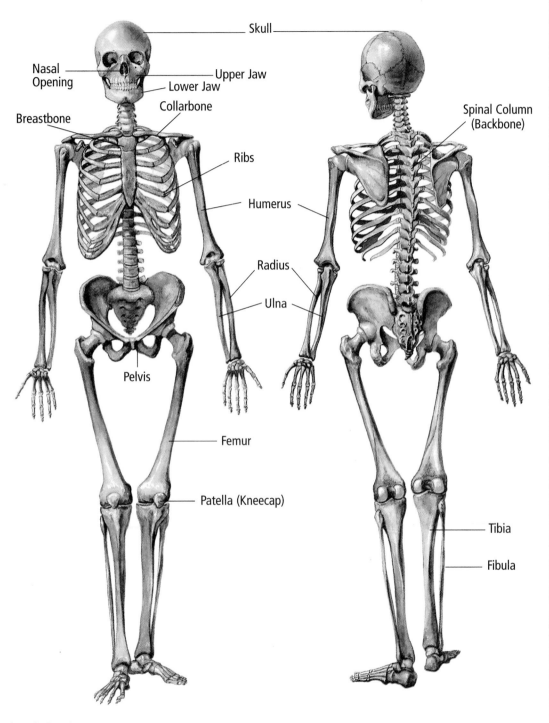

The skeletal system

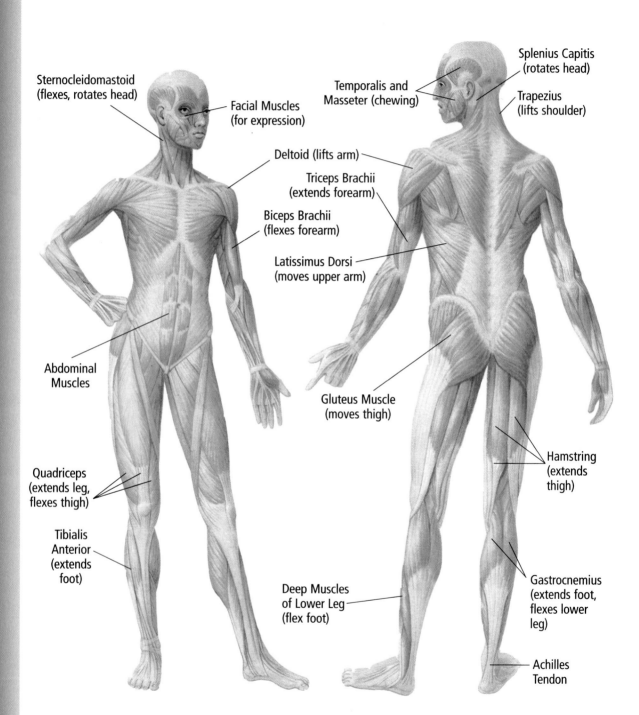

Sternocleidomastoid
(flexes, rotates head)

Facial Muscles
(for expression)

Deltoid (lifts arm)

Triceps Brachii
(extends forearm)

Biceps Brachii
(flexes forearm)

Latissimus Dorsi
(moves upper arm)

Abdominal
Muscles

Quadriceps
(extends leg,
flexes thigh)

Tibialis
Anterior
(extends
foot)

Deep Muscles
of Lower Leg
(flex foot)

Splenius Capitis
(rotates head)

Temporalis and
Masseter (chewing)

Trapezius
(lifts shoulder)

Gluteus Muscle
(moves thigh)

Hamstring
(extends
thigh)

Gastrocnemius
(extends foot,
flexes lower
leg)

Achilles
Tendon

The muscular system. Left: Female front view. Right: Male back view

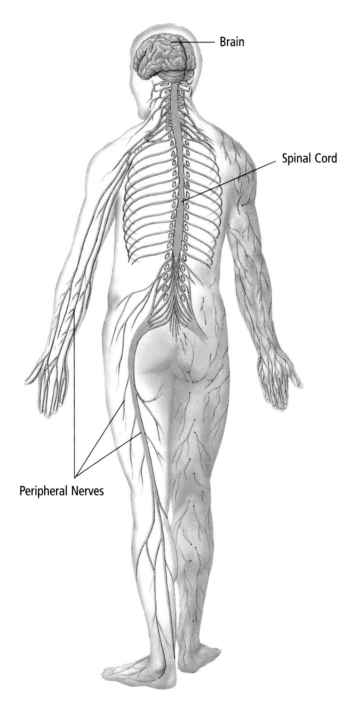

Brain

Spinal Cord

Peripheral Nerves

The nervous system

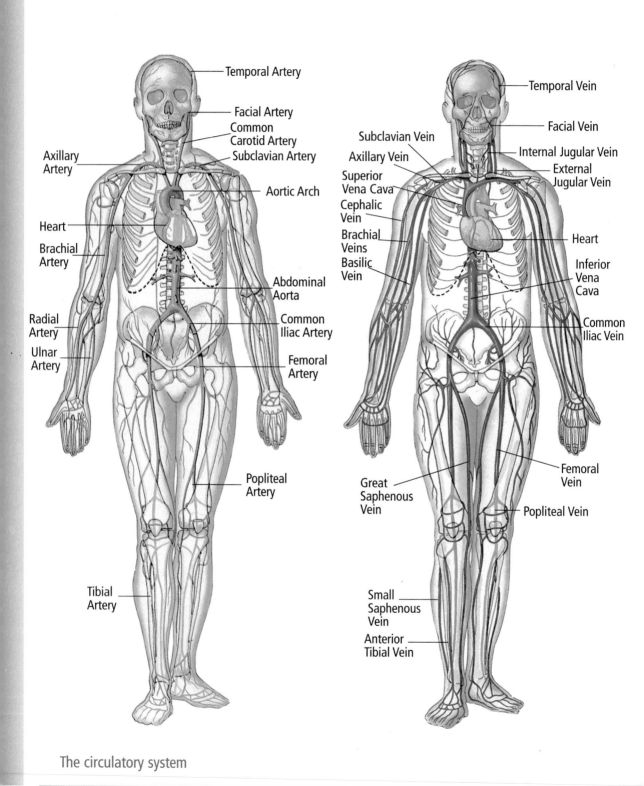

Temporal Artery

Facial Artery

Common
Carotid Artery

Subclavian Artery

Axillary
Artery

Aortic Arch

Heart

Brachial
Artery

Abdominal
Aorta

Radial
Artery

Common
Iliac Artery

Ulnar
Artery

Femoral
Artery

Popliteal
Artery

Tibial
Artery

Temporal Vein

Facial Vein

Subclavian Vein

Internal Jugular Vein

Axillary Vein

External
Jugular Vein

Superior
Vena Cava

Cephalic
Vein

Brachial
Veins

Heart

Basilic
Vein

Inferior
Vena
Cava

Common
Iliac Vein

Great
Saphenous
Vein

Femoral
Vein

Popliteal Vein

Small
Saphenous
Vein

Anterior
Tibial Vein

The circulatory system

Glossary

Glossary

A

Acid rain—rain that is caused by pollution and is harmful to organisms because it is acidic (p. 265)

Adaptive advantage—the greater likelihood that an organism will survive, due to an adaptation it has (p. 331)

Adolescence—the teenage years of a human (p. 209)

Aflatoxin—a chemical that causes liver cancer and is produced by molds growing on stored crops (p. 99)

Algae—protists that make their own food and usually live in water (p. 37)

Alveolus—a tiny air sac where respiration happens; Plural is alveoli (p. 166)

Ameba—a protozoan that moves by pushing out parts of its cell (p. 90)

Amphibian—a vertebrate that lives at first in water and then on land (p. 54)

Anal pore—the opening through which undigested food leaves a paramecium (p. 92)

Angiosperm—a flowering plant (p. 70)

Annual growth rings—rings in a tree trunk formed by the growth of wood in layers (p. 135)

Antibody—a protein in plasma that fights disease (p. 161)

Anus—the opening through which material that is not digested leaves the digestive tract (p. 113)

Applied genetics—the process of using knowledge of genetics to affect heredity (p. 254)

Arachnid—a class of arthropods that includes spiders, scorpions, mites, and ticks (p. 61)

Arthropod—a member of the largest group of invertebrates, which includes insects (p. 59)

Asexual reproduction—reproduction that involves one parent and no egg or sperm (p. 143)

Atrium—a heart chamber that receives blood returning to the heart; Plural is atria (p. 119)

Auditory nerve—a bundle of nerves that carry impulses from the ear to the brain (p. 176)

B

Base—a molecule found in DNA that is used to store information (p. 248)

Behavior—the way an organism acts (p. 290)

Bilateral symmetry—a body plan that consists of left and right halves that are the same (p. 58)

Bile—a substance made in the liver that breaks down fats (p. 156)

Binary fission—reproduction in which a bacterial cell divides into two cells that look the same as the original (p. 85)

Biology—the study of living things (p. 36)

Biome—an ecosystem found over a large geographic area (p. 266)

Biosphere—the part of Earth where living things can exist (p. 267)

Blood pressure—the force of blood against the walls of blood vessels (p. 161)

Bronchiole—a tube that branches off the bronchus (p. 166)

Bronchus—a tube that connects the trachea and lungs; Plural is bronchi (p. 166)

Budding—reproduction in which part of an organism pinches off to form a new organism (p. 103)

C

Carbohydrate—a sugar or starch, which living things use for energy (p. 21)

Cardiac—relating to the heart (p. 158)

Carnivore—an animal that eats other animals (p. 111)

Carrier—an organism that carries a gene but does not show the effects of the gene (p. 245)

Cartilage—a soft material found in vertebrate skeletons (p. 53)

Cast—a type of fossil that is formed when a mold in rock is filled with minerals that harden (p. 317)

Cell—the basic unit of life (p. 16)

Cell differentiation—the process of cells taking on different jobs in the body (p. 198)

Cell membrane—a thin layer that surrounds and holds a cell together (p. 93)

Cellular respiration—the process in which cells break down food to release energy (p. 140)

Central nervous system—the brain and spinal cord (p. 127)

Cerebrum—the largest part of the brain that controls thought, memory, learning, feeling, and body movement (p. 128)

Channel—a way of communicating (p. 302)

Chlorophyll—the green pigment in plants that captures light energy for photosynthesis (p. 138)

Chloroplast—a structure that captures the light energy from the sun to make food (p. 88)

Chromosome—a rod-shaped structure that contains DNA and is found in the nucleus of a cell (p. 194)

Chyme—liquid food in the digestive tract that is partly digested (p. 155)

Cilia—hair-like structures that help some one-celled organisms move (p. 38)

Circulatory—flowing in a circle (p. 118)

Classify—to group things based on the features they share (p. 46)

Climax community—a community that changes little over time (p. 265)

Closed circulatory system—a system in which blood stays inside vessels at all times (p. 118)

Cnidarian—an invertebrate animal group that includes jellyfish, sea anemones, corals, and hydras (p. 57)

Cochlea—the organ in the ear that sends impulses to the auditory nerve (p. 176)

Communication—sending and receiving information (p. 302)

Community—a group of different populations that live in the same area (p. 263)

Condense—to change from a gas to a liquid (p. 280)

Conditioning—learning in which an animal connects one stimulus with another stimulus (p. 298)

Conifer—a cone-bearing gymnosperm (p. 72)

Consumer—an organism that feeds on other organisms (p. 270)

Contractile vacuole—a structure in a protist that removes water that is not needed (p. 93)

Coordinate—work together (p. 124)

Cornea—a clear layer of the eye that light passes through (p. 174)

Courtship behavior—behavior that helps attract and get a mate (p. 291)

Cro-Magnons—*Homo sapiens* who lived about 35,000 years ago and are direct ancestors of humans living today (p. 336)

Crop—the part of the digestive tract of some animals where food is stored (p. 113)

Cross-pollination—the movement of pollen from the male sex organs to the female sex organs of flowers on different plants (p. 235)

Crustacean—a class of arthropods that includes crabs, lobsters, crayfish, and sow bugs (p. 61)

Cyclosporine—a drug that is produced from mold and that helps prevent the rejection of transplanting organs (p. 98)

D

Decompose—to break down or decay matter into simpler substances (p. 38)

Descent with modification—the theory that more recent species of organisms are changed descendants of earlier species. (p. 329)

Development—the changes that occur as a living thing grows (p. 24)

Diabetes—a genetic disease in which a person has too much sugar in the blood (p. 249)

Diatom—microscopic alga that has a hard shell (p. 89)

Dicot—an angiosperm that has two seed leaves (p. 71)

Diffusion—the movement of materials from an area of high concentration to an area of low concentration (p. 116)

Digestion—the process by which living things break down food (p. 23)

Digestive enzyme—a chemical that helps break down food (p. 102)

Digestive tract—a tubelike digestive space with an opening at each end (p. 113)

Diversity—the range of differences among the individuals in a population (p. 192)

DNA—the chemical inside cells that stores information about an organism (p. 191)

Dominant gene—a gene that shows up in an organism (p. 236)

E

Eardrum—a thin tissue in the middle ear that vibrates when sound waves strike it (p. 176)

Ecology—the study of the interactions among living things and the nonliving things in their environment (p. 262)

Ecosystem—the interactions among the populations of a community and the nonliving things in their environment (p. 263)

Electron microscope—an instrument that uses a beam of tiny particles called electrons to magnify things (p. 17)

Embryo—a beginning plant (p. 70); an early stage in the development of an organism (p. 198)

Energy pyramid—a diagram that compares the amounts of energy available to the populations at different levels of a food chain (p. 277)

Environment—an organism's surroundings (p. 247)

Evaporate—to change from a liquid to a gas (p. 280)

Evolution—the changes in a population over time (p. 312)

Excrete—get rid of wastes or substances that are not needed (p. 120)

Excretion—the process by which living things get rid of wastes (p. 23)

Excretory system—a series of organs that gets rid of cell wastes in the form of urine (p. 170)

External fertilization—the type of fertilization that occurs outside the female's body (p. 197)

Extinct—no longer existing on Earth (p. 320)

Eyespot—a structure on many protists that senses changes in the brightness of light (p. 94)

F

F$_1$ generation—the plants that resulted when Mendel cross-pollinated two different kinds of pure plants (p. 235)

F$_2$ generation—the plants that resulted when Mendel self-pollinated plants from the F$_1$ generation (p. 237)

Factors—the name that Mendel gave to information about traits that parents pass to offspring (p. 238)

Fallopian tube—a tube through which eggs pass from an ovary to the uterus (p. 205)

Fat—a chemical that stores large amounts of energy (p. 21)

Feces—solid waste material remaining in the large intestine after digestion (p. 157)

Fern—a seedless vascular plant (p. 76)

Fertilization—the joining of an egg cell and a sperm cell (p. 197)

Fetus—an embryo after eight weeks of development in the uterus (p. 207)

Filter feeding—getting food by straining it out of the water (p. 110)

Flagella—whip-like tails that help some one-celled organisms move (p. 38)

Flame cell—a cell that collects excess water in a flatworm (p. 121)

Flatworm—a simple worm that is flat and thin (p. 58)

Food chain—the feeding order of organisms in a community (p. 270)

Food Guide Pyramid—a guide for good nutrition (p. 224)

Food vacuole—a bubblelike structure where food is digested inside a protozoan (p. 92)

Food web—all the food chains in a community that are linked to each other (p. 272)

Fossil—the remains or traces of an organism that lived in the past (p. 317)

Fossil record—the history of life on Earth, based on fossils that have been discovered (p. 318)

Fraternal twins—twins that do not have identical genes (p. 246)

Frond—a large feathery leaf of a fern (p. 76)

Fungus—an organism that usually has many cells and decomposes its food (p. 38)

G

Gallbladder—the digestive organ attached to the liver that stores bile (p. 156)

Gamete—a sex cell, such as sperm or egg (p. 195)

Gastrovascular cavity—a digestive space with a single opening (p. 112)

Gene—the information about a trait that a parent passes to its offspring (p. 236)

Gene pool—the genes found within a population (p. 250)

Genetic disease—a disease that is caused by a mutated gene (p. 249)

Genetic engineering—the process of transferring genes from one organism to another (p. 256)

Genetics—the study of heredity (p. 234)

Genotype—an organism's combination of genes for a trait (p. 237)

Genus—a group of living things that includes separate species (p. 68)

Geographic isolation—the separation of a population into two populations that have no contact with each other, caused by a change in the environment (p. 315)

Geologic time scale—a chart that divides Earth's history into time periods (p. 318)

Germinate—to start to grow into a new plant; sprout (p. 145)

Gestation time—the period of development of a mammal, from fertilization until birth (p. 202)

Gill—a structure used by some animals to breathe in water (p. 54)

Gizzard—the part of the digestive tract of some animals that grinds food (p. 113)

Gravitropism—the response of a plant to gravity (p. 294)

Groundwater—the water under the Earth's surface (p. 279)

Guard cell—a cell that opens and closes stomata (p. 142)

Gullet—the opening through which a paramecium takes in food (p. 92)

Gymnosperm—a nonflowering seed plant (p. 72)

H

Habitat—the place where an organism lives (p. 263)

Half-life—the amount of time required for one-half of a sample of radioactive mineral to change into another substance (p. 320)

Hemoglobin—a substance in red blood cells that carries oxygen (p. 162)

Hemophilia—a genetic disease in which a person's blood fails to clot (p. 251)

Herbivore—an animal that eats plants (p. 111)

Heredity—the passing of traits from parents to offspring (p. 234)

Hominid—the group that includes humans and humanlike primates (p. 333)

Homologous structures—body parts that are similar in related organisms (p. 332)

Homo sapiens—the species to which humans belong (p. 333)

Hormone—a chemical signal that glands produce (p. 124)

Humus—decayed plant and animal matter that is part of the topsoil (p. 78)

Hypha—a thin, tubelike thread that is produced by a fungus; Plural is hyphae (p. 95)

Hypothesis—a testable explanation of a question or problem (p. 328)

I

Identical twins—twins that have identical genes (p. 246)

Immune system—the body's most important defense against infectious diseases (p. 217)

Immunity—the ability of the body to fight off a specific pathogen (p. 218)

Imprinting—learning in which an animal bonds with the first object it sees (p. 296)

Impulse—a message that a nerve cell carries (p. 125)

Inbreeding—sexual reproduction between organisms within a small gene pool (p. 250)

Infectious disease—an illness that can pass from person to person (p. 216)

Innate behavior—a behavior that is present at birth (p. 290)

Insight—the ability to solve a new problem based on experience (p. 298)

Instinct—a pattern of innate behaviors (p. 290)

Interact—to act upon or influence something (p. 262)

Internal fertilization—the type of fertilization that occurs inside the female's body (p. 197)

Invertebrate—an animal that does not have a backbone (p. 57)

Involuntary muscle—a muscle that a person cannot control (p. 184)

Iris—the part of the eye that controls the amount of light that enters (p. 174)

K

Kidney—an organ of excretion found in vertebrates (p. 121); the organ in the excretory system where urine forms (p. 170)

Kingdom—one of the five groups into which living things are classified (p. 36)

L

Learned behavior—behavior that results from experience (p. 296)

Lethal mutation—a mutation that results in the death of an organism (p. 314)

Lichen—an organism that is made up of a fungus and an alga or a bacterium (p. 104)

Ligament—a tissue that connects bone to bone (p. 181)

Lymphocyte—a white blood cell that produces antibodies (p. 218)

M

Mammary gland—a milk-producing structure on the chest or abdomen of a mammal (p. 56)

Marsupial—a mammal that gives birth to young that are very undeveloped (p. 200)

Mass extinction—the dying out of large numbers of species within a short period of time (p. 320)

Meiosis—the process that results in sex cells (p. 196)

Menstruation—the process during which an unfertilized egg, blood, and pieces of the lining of the uterus exit the female body (p. 206)

Metamorphosis—a major change in form that occurs as some animals develop into adults (p. 54)

Microorganism—an organism that is too small to be seen without a microscope (p. 37)

Microscope—an instrument used to magnify things (p. 16)

Mineral—a chemical found in foods that is needed by living things in small amounts (p. 22)

Mitosis—the process that results in two cells identical to the parent cell (p. 194)

Mold—a type of fossil that is formed when a dead organism decays and leaves an empty space in rock (p. 317)

Molting—the process by which an arthropod sheds its external skeleton (p. 60)

Moneran—an organism that is one-celled and does not have organelles (p. 39)

Monocot—an angiosperm that has one seed leaf (p. 71)

Mutation—a change in a gene (p. 247)

Mutualism—a closeness in which two organisms live together and help each other (p. 86)

Moss—a nonvascular plant that has simple parts (p. 77)

Mycelium—a mass of hyphae; Plural is mycelia (p. 95)

Mycorrhiza—a mutualism between a fungus and the roots of a plant; Plural is mycorrhizae (p. 103)

N

Natural selection—the process by which organisms best suited to the environment survive, reproduce, and pass their genes to the next generation (p. 329)

Neanderthals—*Homo sapiens* who lived between about 30,000 and 230,000 years ago but are not thought to be direct ancestors of humans living today (p. 336)

Nectar—a sweet liquid that many kinds of flowers produce (p. 144)

Nerve net—a bunch of nerve cells that are loosely connected (p. 126)

Neuron—a nerve cell (p. 173)

Neurotransmitter—a chemical signal that a nerve cell releases (p. 125)

Nitrogen fixation—the process by which certain bacteria change nitrogen gas from the air into ammonia (p. 282)

Nonvascular plant—a plant that does not have tubelike cells (p. 69)

Nutrient—any chemical found in foods that is needed by living things (p. 22)

Nutrition—the types and amounts of foods a person eats (p. 221)

Nymph—a young insect that resembles the adult (p. 199)

O

Observational learning—learning by watching or listening to the behavior of others (p. 297)

Omnivore—a consumer that eats both plants and animals (p. 271)

Open circulatory system—a system in which blood makes direct contact with cells (p. 118)

Optic nerve—a bundle of nerves that carry impulses from the eye to the brain (p. 175)

Organ—a group of different tissues that work together (p. 18)

Organelle—a tiny structure inside a cell (p. 17)

Organism—a living thing that can carry out all the basic life activities (p. 33)

Osmosis—the movement of water through a cell membrane (p. 93)

Osteoporosis—a disease in which bones become lighter and break easily (p. 181)

Ovary—the female sex organ that produces egg cells (p. 144)

Ovulation—the process of releasing an egg from an ovary (p. 205)

P

Paleontologist—a scientist who studies life in the past (p. 318)

P generation—the pure plants that Mendel produced by self-pollination (p. 234)

Paramecium—a protozoan that moves by using its hairlike cilia; Plural is paramecia (p. 90)

Parasite—an organism that absorbs food from a living organism and harms it (p. 38)

Pathogen—a germ (p. 217)

Penis—the male organ that delivers sperm to the female body (p. 204)

Peripheral nervous system—the nerves that send messages between the central nervous system and other body parts (p. 127)

Peristalsis—the movement of digestive organs that pushes food through the digestive tract (p. 155)

Perspiration—liquid waste made of heat, water, and salt released through the skin (p. 169)

Petiole—the stalk that attaches a leaf to a stem (p. 136)

Phagocyte—a white blood cell that surrounds and destroys pathogens (p. 217)

Phenotype—an organism's appearance as a result of its combination of genes (p. 237)

Phloem—the vascular tissue in plants that carries food from leaves to other parts of the plant (p. 135)

Photosynthesis—the process in which a plant makes food (p. 137)

Phototropism—the response of a plant to light (p. 293)

Phylum—subdivision of a kingdom (p. 48)

Pigment—a chemical that absorbs certain types of light (p. 138)

Pistil—the female part of a flower (p. 144)

Placenta—a tissue that provides the embryo with food and oxygen from its mother's body (p. 201)

Plague—an infectious disease that spreads quickly and kills many people (p. 216)

Plasma—the liquid part of blood (p. 161)

Platelet—a tiny piece of cell that helps form clots (p. 163)

Pollen—the tiny structures of seed plants that contain sperm (p. 144)

Pollination—the process by which pollen is transferred from the stamen to the pistil (p. 144)

Pollution—anything added to the environment that is harmful to living things (p. 265)

Population—a group of organisms of the same species that live in the same area (p. 263)

Pregnancy—the development of a fertilized egg into a baby inside a female's body (p. 206)

Primate—the group of mammals that includes humans, apes, monkeys, and similar animals (p. 333)

Producer—an organism that makes its own food (p. 270)

Property—a quality that describes an object (p. 32)

Prostate gland—the gland that produces the fluid found in semen (p. 205)

Protein—a chemical used by living things to build and repair body parts and regulate body activities (p. 22)

Protist—an organism that usually is one-celled and has plant-like or animal-like properties (p. 37)

Protozoan—a protist that has animal-like qualities (p. 37)

Pseudopod—a part of some one-celled organisms that sticks out like a foot to move the cell along (p. 38)

Puberty—the period of rapid growth and physical changes that occurs in males and females during early adolescence (p. 209)

Punnett square—a model used to represent crosses between organisms (p. 236)

Pupa—a stage in the development of some insects that leads to the adult stage (p. 62)

Pyramid of numbers—a diagram that compares the sizes of populations at different levels of a food chain (p. 271)

R

Radial symmetry—an arrangement of body parts that resembles the arrangement of spokes on a wheel (p. 57)

Radioactive mineral—a mineral that gives off energy as it changes to another substance over time (p. 320)

Receptor cell—a cell that receives information about the environment and starts nerve impulses to send that information to the brain (p. 174)

Recessive gene—a gene that is hidden by a dominant gene (p. 236)

Rectum—the lower part of the large intestine where feces are stored (p. 157)

Red marrow—the spongy material in bones that makes blood cells (p. 180)

Replicate—to make a copy of itself (p. 249)

Reproduction—the process by which living things produce offspring (p. 24)

Reptile—an egg-laying vertebrate that breathes with lungs (p. 55)

Resource—a thing that an organism uses to live (p. 267)

Respiration—the process by which living things release energy from food (p. 23)

Respire—take in oxygen and give off carbon dioxide (p. 116)

Rhizoid—a tiny root-like thread of a moss plant (p. 77)

Roundworm—a worm with a smooth, round body and pointed ends (p. 58)

S

Sanitation—the practice of keeping things clean to prevent infectious diseases (p. 220)

Saprophyte—an organism that decomposes dead organisms or waste matter (p. 85)

Scientific name—the name given to each species, consisting of its genus and its species label (p. 50)

Scientific theory—a generally accepted and well-tested scientific explanation (p. 327)

Scrotum—the sac that holds the testes (p. 204)

Secrete—form and release, or give off (p. 112)

Sediment—the bits of rock and mud that settle to the bottom of a body of water (p. 317)

Seed—a plant part that contains a beginning plant and stored food (p. 70)

Segmented worm—a worm whose body is divided into sections, such as earthworms or leeches (p. 58)

Selective breeding—the process of breeding plants and animals so that certain traits repeatedly show up in future generations (p. 254)

Self-pollination—the movement of pollen from the male sex organs to the female sex organs of flowers on the same plant (p. 234)

Semen—a mixture of fluid and sperm cells (p. 205)

Sex chromosome—a chromosome that determines the sex of an organism (p. 243)

Sex-linked trait—a trait that is determined by an organism's sex chromosomes (p. 244)

Sexual reproduction—reproduction that involves two parents, and egg, and sperm (p. 143)

Sickle-cell anemia—a genetic disease in which a person's red blood cells have a sickle shape (p. 250)

Skeletal system—the network of bones in the body (p. 180)

Solution—a mixture in which the particles are evenly mixed (p. 20)

Sori—clusters of reproductive cells on the underside of a frond (p. 76)

Species—a group of organisms that can breed with each other to produce offspring like themselves (p. 49)

Spontaneous generation—the idea that living things can come from nonliving things (p. 190)

Spore—the reproductive cell of some organisms (p. 76)

Sporozoan—a protozoan that is a parasite, which lives in blood and causes malaria (p. 91)

Stamen—the male part of a flower (p. 144)

Stimulus—anything to which an organism reacts (p. 290)

Stoma—a small opening in a leaf that allows gases to enter and leave; Plural is stomata (p. 136)

Succession—the process by which a community changes over time (p. 264)

Swim bladder—a gas-filled organ that allows a bony fish to move up and down in the water (p. 54)

Synapse—a tiny gap between neurons (p. 173)

T

Taxonomy—the science of classifying organisms based on the features they share (p. 47)

Tentacle—an armlike body part in invertebrates that is used for capturing prey (p. 57)

Territorial behavior—behavior that defends an area (p. 292)

Testis—the male sex organ that produces sperm cells; Plural is testes (p. 195)

Tissue—a group of cells that are similar and work together (p. 17)

Toxin—a poison produced by bacteria or other organisms (p. 87)

Trachea—the tube that carries air to the bronchi (p. 166)

Trait—a characteristic of an organism (p. 191)

Trial-and-error learning—learning in which an animal connects a behavior with a reward or a punishment (p. 297)

Trypanosoma—a protozoan that is a parasite, which lives in blood and causes sleeping sickness (p. 91)

Tube foot—a small structure used by echinoderms for movement (p. 60)

U

Umbilical cord—the cord that connects an embryo with the placenta (p. 206)

Ureter—a tube that carries urine from the kidney to the urinary bladder (p. 170)

Urethra—the tube that carries urine out of the body (p. 170)

Urine—liquid waste formed in the kidneys (p. 170)

Uterus—an organ in most female mammals that holds and protects an embryo (p. 201)

V

Vaccine—a material that causes the body to make antibodies against a specific pathogen before that pathogen enters the body (p. 218)

Vagina—the tubelike canal in the female body through which sperm enter the body (p. 204)

Vascular plant—a plant that has tubelike cells (p. 68)

Vascular tissue—a group of plant cells that form tubes through which food and water move (p. 68)

Ventricle—a heart chamber that pumps blood out of the heart (p. 119)

Vertebra—one of the bones or blocks of cartilage that make up a backbone (p. 53)

Vertebrate—an animal with a backbone (p. 53)

Vestigial structure—a body part that appears to be useless to an organism but was probably useful to the organism's ancestors (p. 331)

Villi—finger-shaped structures in the small intestine through which food molecules enter the blood (p. 156)

Virus—a type of germ that is not living (p. 217)

Vitamin—a chemical found in foods that is needed by living things in small amounts (p. 22)

Voluntary muscle—a muscle that a person can control (p. 184)

X

Xylem—the vascular tissue in plants that carries water and minerals from roots to stems and leaves (p. 135)

Z

Zygote—a fertilized cell (p. 143)

Index

Index

Flowering plants, 70–71
Fluids, as animal food, 110
Flu shots, 218
Flying behavior, 291
F$_1$ generation, 235
Food
  algae as, 37
  animals getting, 36, 110–113
  energy in, 263
  fungi feeding methods, 102
  getting, as life activity, 23
  human cells getting energy from, 154–157
  invertebrates obtaining, 57–61
  mammary glands producing, 56
  plants making, 36, 137–139
  protist feeding methods, 92
Food chains
  flow of energy through, 276–277
  overview of, 270–271
Food Guide Pyramid, 224–225
Food vacuole, 92
Food webs, 272
Fossil record, 318–319
Fossils
  dating of, 320
  definition of, 317
  and extinction, 320
  humanlike, 333–336
  hunting for, 323
  and living organisms, 322
  types of, 317
Fraternal twins, 246
Fronds, 76
F$_2$ generation, 237
Fungi
  club, 96
  helpful versus harmful, 98–99
  kingdom overview, 38–39
  molds, 97

properties of, 95
rusts and smuts, 96
survival techniques, 102–104
yeasts, 97
Fungi kingdom, 38–39

G

Galápagos Islands, 330
Gallbladder, 156
Gametes, 195, 241
Gas exchange, 116–117
Gastrovascular cavities, 112
Gene pool, 250
Genes
  definition of, 236
  and evolution, 313–314
  pool of, 250
  purpose of, 238
Genetic diseases, 249–250, 252–253
Genetic engineering, 256
Genetics
  applied, 254–256
  and chromosomes, 240–245
  definition of, 234
  heredity overview, 234–238
  human heredity study, 246–251
Genotype, 237, 239
Genus
  grouping animals into, 48
  grouping plants into, 68
Genus *Australopithecus*, 333, 334
Genus *Homo*, 333, 335–336
Geographic isolation, 315–316
Geologic time scale, 318–319
Gestation times, 202
Giardia, causing disease, 37
Gills
  definition of, 54
  gas exchange through, 117
Gizzard, in animals' digestion, 113

Glucose
  as energy source, 140
  plants producing, 138, 139
Gonorrhea, 87
Gravitropism, 294
Groundwater, 279
Growth
  of animals, 198–202
  of humans, 204–209
  as life activity, 24
Guard cells, 142
Gullet, 92
Gymnosperms
  features of, 72–73
  investigation in identifying, 74–75
  sexual reproduction in, 145

H

Habitat, 263, 290
Half-life, 320
Health
  fighting disease, 216–220
  and good nutrition, 221–225
Hearing
  sense of, 176
  and sound signals, 305
Heart, 119, 158–159
Hemoglobin, 162
Hemophilia, 251
Hepatitis B vaccine, 99
Herbivores, 111, 271
Heredity
  definition of, 234
  and DNA, 247–249
  and environment, 247
  F$_1$ generation in, 235
  F$_2$ generation in, 237
  and genetic diseases, 249–250
  genotypes and phenotypes, 237
  and inbreeding, 250–251
  Mendel's studies in, 234–238
  and mutations, 247, 249, 254, 313–314
  and Punnett squares, 236

and sex-linked traits, 244–245, 251
  study of twins, 246
Hominids, 333
Homologous structures, 332
Homo sapiens, 333, 334, 336
Hormones
  endocrine system secreting, 124–125
  overview of, 178–179
Horses
  evolution of, 321
  in geologic time scale, 319
Humans
  adolescent, 209
  birth of babies, 208
  caring for babies, 208
  embryos becoming babies, 206–208
  female reproductive system, 205–206
  fossils of, 333–336
  in geologic time scale, 319
  language of, 305
  male reproductive system, 204–205
  pregnancy of, 206–207, 210
Human body systems
  circulatory, 158–163
  digestive, 154–157
  endocrine, 178–179
  excretory, 170
  muscular, 182–184
  nervous, 171–177
  perspiration, 169
  reproductive, 204–209
  respiratory, 166–168
  skeletal, 180–182
Humus, 78
Hyphae, 95, 102
Hypothesis, 328

I

Identical twins, 246
Immune system, 217
Immunity, 218
Imprinting, 296
Impulses, 125, 173
Inbreeding, 250–251